Jackson School Publications in International Studies

Jackson School Publications in International Studies

Senator Henry M. Jackson was convinced that the study of the history, cultures, political systems, and languages of the world's major regions was an essential prerequisite for wise decision-making in international relations. In recognition of his deep commitment to higher education and advanced scholarship, this series of publications has been established through the generous support of the Henry M. Jackson Foundation, in cooperation with the Henry M. Jackson School of International Studies and the University of Washington Press.

CAN EUROPE WORK?

Germany and the Reconstruction of Postcommunist Societies

Edited by **Stephen E. Hanson** and **Willfried Spohn**

University of Washington Press

Seattle & London

Library of Congress Cataloging-in-Publication Data

Can Europe work? : Germany and the reconstruction of postcommunist
societies / edited by Stephen Hanson and Willfried Spohn.
　　p.　　cm. — (Jackson School publications in international studies)
Includes index.
ISBN 0-295-97460-5 (cloth : alk. paper). — ISBN 0-295-97461-3
(paper : alk. paper)
1. Europe—Politics and government—1989–　　2. Post-communism—
Europe.　3. Nationalism—Europe.　4. Germany—Politics and
government—1991–　. 5. Europe—Economic conditions—1945–
I. Hanson, Stephen, 1963–　　. II. Spohn, Willfried, 1944–　　. III. Series.
D2009.C36　1995　　　　　　　　　　　　95-19960
320-940—dc20　　　　　　　　　　　　　CIP

Contents

III

Reform in Postcommunist Societies: Transition or Regression?

Can
Europe
Work
?

Introduction

Daniel Chirot

When the Henry M. Jackson School of International Studies and the Deutsche Akademische Austausch-dienst (German Academic Exchange Service) set out to organize a conference on the problems raised by German reunification and the collapse of communism, most of us were optimistic about Europe's future. The events of 1989, followed by the failed Moscow coup of 1991 and the rapid disintegration of the Soviet Union, suggested a pleasing historical symmetry. As the twentieth century was drawing to a close, so it seemed was the cycle of bloody wars and totalitarian nightmares that had arisen from the contradictions within the European world order at the start of the century. Now the happy resolution of those problems would allow the progressive promises of the European Enlightenment and of capitalist industrialization to be fulfilled, but in a more peaceful, benign, and egalitarian way than before World War I.

The twentieth century, as many historians would agree, really began in 1914 with the near collapse of the capitalist, bourgeois, and until then increasingly democratic, liberal West European order. The almost fatal flaw in that order was that by 1914 the intense nationalism that was part of the original European liberal world view had become drastically antiliberal. This provoked an accelerating race for new territories, which could only become more desperate as the potential colonies of the world were absorbed in one or another of the empires spreading around the globe. It meant a fierce armaments race between the great and small European powers. It also caused increasing intolerance of anything considered foreign within the national body, and impatience with the inability of parliamentary procedures to resolve such issues quickly.

By the first decade of the twentieth century almost all Europeans who thought about such matters were convinced that it was each nation's duty to seize as large an area as possible to ensure its safety and economic well-being. The alternative seemed to be an economic, physical, and moral stagnation and decline that would lead to the nation's death. Social Darwinists, the major capitalist firms, statesmen, and high military officers throughout Europe, from liberal England to tsarist Russia, and much of informed public opinion in Europe, in the United States, and in Japan, as well as among the newly emergent, partially westernized intelligentsias in the less developed parts of the world shared this view. Marxists and other socialists actually agreed with this analysis, except that they said they would welcome the demise of the capitalist world order.

There was a sense that violent competition between nations was as inevitable as the biological struggle for survival, and along with it came a belief that races were also distinct species, with the superior ones ultimately overcoming their inferiors. It is unimportant that Marxists who believed capitalists were obliged to struggle to the death over control of empires were just as mistaken theoretically as social Darwinists who believed that biological rather than economic imperatives were fundamental. Struggle was everything, and the admirers of Nietzsche, Marx, Gobineau, Prussian militarism, or pan-Slavism could all agree that the future belonged to those who were bolder, purer, and stronger than the dreary, miserly, corrupt parliamentarians, speculators, and dull bourgeois who had risen to such high positions in the late nineteenth century.

The disaster of World War I, with its more than ten million dead, strengthened the very forces that despised the liberal capitalist order. Fascism and communism emerged from the wreckage of that war. The first made its bid to create an entirely new European and world order based on biology and the right of some nations to rule or exterminate others. That ended in 1945 with over fifty million more dead to add to the carnage of the earlier war.

What remained, then, was the communist challenge to the same liberal world order. For a time the communists created an alternative modern civilization that came to rule one-third of the world. In place of a biologically based system, the Marxists substituted one in which certain classes, represented by a self-selected elite, were superior to others, and therefore entitled to rule over and exterminate history's losers. Eventually, however, the Marxist view became an intensely nationalist one as well, in which whole nations—the Russians or the Chinese or, on a smaller but equally intense scale, the Khmer, Albanians, Vietnamese, or Cubans—embodied superior class virtues. This legitimized the killing or enslaving of those who resisted the "inevitable" march of history as the communists prepared for the eventual Armageddon, which would end with their victory over the corrupt and failing bourgeois nations led by America.

Seen in this way, the events from 1989 to 1991 spelled the end of the second great twentieth-century war fought over the issue of whether or not liberal, democratic capitalism would survive. First fascism, and now communism had fallen. Somewhat against the logic of many of the major trends in European history from the middle of the nineteenth century until the middle of the twentieth, societies that were run according to relatively free market principles, governed by relatively democratic parliamentary institutions, and with some measure of continuing faith in the ideals of the eighteenth-century English and French Enlightenments grew stronger. Meanwhile, the newer, bolder utopian totalitarianisms that had seemed to be ascendant foundered because their goals were based on flawed social theories that could not effectively compete.

So, by 1991, European history was coming full circle. The pessimism of a Karl Polanyi or a Joseph Schumpeter, eloquently expressed in the 1940s when democratic capitalism seemed to be an impossible contradiction doomed to failure, had shown itself to be wrong. Europe could now, once again, become great and powerful, united by a triumphant and humane vision that it could export to the rest of the world.

But by mid-1993, when our conference took place, the mood was changing. The midcentury pessimists could be used once more to point out that the victory of classical liberalism was far from assured, and may actually be fatally compromised by the forces of nationalism and intellectual as well as populist reactions against the vagaries of the market. It is in this gloomier context—after the seeming failure of Russian economic reform to take root quickly, during some of the bloodiest fighting in former Yugoslavia, at a time when European unification was stalled in petty bickering and a general loss of momentum, as German neo-Nazis were growing stronger, and with xenophobic forces on the rise throughout Europe—that the papers in this volume were presented. Whether or not the optimism of a few years ago can ever be recaptured is a question only time will answer. But for now, perhaps, the gloom of the mid-1990s can serve to remind us of real problems and the need to solve them before we can claim that peaceful democracy and free markets are so secure that we never again need to worry.

The first two essays in this volume deal with the broad issues of nationalism, classical liberalism, and the historical differences that have marked "Western" from "Eastern" nationalism—that is, chiefly English and French from Central and East European nationalism. As Liah Greenfeld shows, the fact that English and to some extent French forms of nationalism were conceived in countries that considered themselves superior and secure meant that they were less bitter than the resentful and angry reactive nationalisms that followed. As they developed in societies with relatively advanced economies and long philosophical traditions of individualism, their nationalisms were "civic," while those that followed to the east were based on a more collectivistic vision of the nation. The "Eastern" forms were also based on notions of inherited traits, of "blood," making it much more difficult for minorities or immigrants to convert and be accepted as equals. That the two greatest powers of Central and Eastern Europe—Germany and Russia—happened to develop nationalisms based on *ressentiment* and on collectivistic and blood-based solidarity made them particularly dangerous and irreconcilable enemies.

From 1939 to 1989, the attendant wars and the attempts by both Germans and Russians to build satellite zones of influence caused five decades of terrible suffering in the little countries squeezed between those two giants. With the temporary eclipse of Russia, no one in Central or Eastern Europe can help but wonder whether the same pattern will reassert itself, this time with Germany on the ascendant, as it was before 1943.

Arista Cirtautas explains the intellectual origins of East European nationalism, and shows why it has been antiliberal and often antidemocratic. Certainly, old habits do not necessarily reassert themselves, but even today the definition of "democracy" in much of Eastern Europe, including Russia, tends to emphasize the collective will of the nation, as interpreted by the intellectual elite. When the English or Americans speak of democracy, they mean an open and messy competition of ideas and interest groups in which the winners tolerate the continued existence of their enemies because they know that the tables will soon be turned in yet another election. But this is an unusual political philosophy that has spread only slowly and with the greatest of difficulty to other societies. Its acceptance in Eastern Europe and Russia is far from certain.

Finally, in concluding the first section of the book devoted to the return of old problems to Eastern Europe, Ewa Morawska carefully describes the changing role of the Polish Catholic Church. Here again, a force that was once thought to be largely hostile to modern capitalist, liberal democracy showed the world during the communist period that it could be a staunch defender of these "Western" ideals. But with the struggle won, in some ways the Polish Church has reverted to an older pattern, and it is no longer clear to what extent its views are consistent with liberalism. In this instance, as in so many, it now begins to seem that the defeat of the late twentieth century's greatest danger, communism, has served to unearth even older problems that had been buried during the long struggle against totalitarianism.

The second part of the volume is about the past and future major political issue in Europe: Germany. Ever since it became the most dynamic economy in Europe early in the second half of the nineteenth century, and then united to become the most populous nation-state in Europe after 1871—except for backward Russia—Germany has been viewed as a problem by the rest of Europe. The French resented the rise of its great military and industrial power, the Russians believed it blocked their own ambitions to dominate the Slavic and Christian Orthodox parts of Eastern Europe and to keep control over the Baltic, the English were threatened by the dynamism of its export industries and its potential naval power, and the weaker countries in Central Europe feared that they might be swallowed up, purely and simply, by the German colossus. For forty-four years after 1945, this problem was solved by keeping Germany divided and each of its halves firmly under the control of either the Soviets or the Americans. But in 1989 the old quandary unexpectedly came back. What shall we do about Germany, and what are the Germans going to do to the rest of Europe?

Has Germany changed, and are the old fears silly historical memories? Willfried Spohn demonstrates in considerable detail that Germany has indeed changed, and much for the better. Its economy is so firmly anchored in European and world trade that it ought never again try to go it alone with a bunch of East European satellites, as it did in the 1930s. Its institutions have been liberal and democratic for two generations now, and in contrast to post-World War I conditions, its elites are in no way nostalgic about their lost empire and former military predominance.

And yet, the sudden loss of momentum in the process of European unification that manifested itself with the 1992 crisis over the Maastricht Treaty and a common European currency raises the problem of what Germany might do if it did follow a more selfish policy. After all, no matter how different Germany is today, no matter how well it has resolved the old inner conflicts between militarism and liberalism, it is a troubled nation. Germany is beset by growing chauvinism. Its people and political elites are increasingly impatient with their French partners. The French have proved thoroughly unable to provide even a spark of idealism to push forward with the European project, and in recent years they have treated Europe more or less as a cash machine to subsidize their farmers and as an institutional base for sniping at the Americans. This has meant that as the United States begins to pull out of Europe and NATO slowly drifts into irrelevance, the Germans are left to decide their military policies and international positions on their own.

Neither Ivan Berend nor Aleksa Djilas, whose chapters follow Spohn's, make any claim that the bad old Germany has come back to life, but they do point out that some of the structural and ideological circumstances that once made Germany so terrifying are still present. Berend, Central Europe's most distinguished economic historian, looks back at the causes and consequences of Germany's economic domination of its East European hinterland. He finds that it was Germany's enormous dynamism as an industrial engine that caused such a lop-sided relationship to develop, in which the much poorer and less developed economies to the east became subordinated to the requirements of the Germans. Even without ideological or military aggression, Eastern Europe was bound to become dependent on German economic power. Now a somewhat similar relationship is emerging. It may prove to have more benign consequences than in the 1930s because the ideological atmosphere is different. But as far as sheer economic facts are concerned, Germany has reclaimed the position it had sixty years ago, and for decades before then. Should the project of a united Europe fail to advance, Germany will build its own economic sphere of influence throughout Central and Eastern Europe, as it did in the past.

Aleksa Djilas, writing on the German response to the collapse of Yugoslavia, has contributed what is in many ways the most somber paper in the collection. But instead of going over lists of massacres and historical excuses to justify what is going on in his land, he focuses on Germany's contribution to the catastrophe. This time the Germans did not invade Yugoslavia, as in 1941, to let loose a sea of blood. Nor did they intend the consequences that followed from their forceful diplomatic maneuvering in the period just before the outbreak of the new Yugoslav war. Nevertheless, by reverting to old prejudices, namely the easy assumption that the Catholic Croats and Slovenes were more deserving of West European help than the Orthodox Serbs, they hastened the breakup of Yugoslavia, pushed their NATO allies into recognition of the split, and gave the Croat nationalists reason to believe that they could expect substantial NATO aid in case of war. In fact, such aid did not materialize, and we know now that there was never much chance that it would. But with Yugoslavia broken, and open war beginning between Serbs and Croats, the Bosnian Muslims felt they had no choice but to declare independence, too. It seemed that if the West was going to help the Croats, no doubt they would help an independent Bosnia. Indeed, this appeared to be confirmed by the haste with which Bosnian independence was recognized by the West. But that decision turned out to be the biggest mistake of all. Having been the leading contributor to this false sense that Western Europe and the United States were going to keep the peace after Yugoslavia broke up, the Germans have gone back to worrying more about their own problems and leaving the South Slavs to kill each other.

This has not been a promising start to the postcommunist era, and as Djilas shows, we should all worry about why, in a crisis, Germans reverted to some of their old ideological reflexes about the hierarchy of virtue among nations. Does this augur well for the future? And now that Europe as a whole has proved utterly incapable of solving this crisis, what conclusions will the Germans draw when they next involve themselves with one or another of the inevitable conflicts that will arise in Eastern Europe?

The final section of the book tries to explain why economic reconstruction has been so slow in Eastern Europe and Russia. Kazimierz Poznanski details the problems of "shock therapy," and shows that some economic decline was inevitable after communism. Unlike political change, economic transformations simply cannot take place quickly, and the speed with which communist regimes disintegrated from 1989 to 1991 gave rise to unrealistic expectations. Yet, Poznanski argues, the situation is far from hopeless. What is required most of all is the establishment of clear property rights, and time to let suitable economic institutions evolve. There are signs that this has begun to happen in some of the former countries, though not yet in all of them. But there is little recognition, either by the foreign advisers to the new governments or by the people in these societies, that institutional evolution takes place over decades, not months.

Stephen Hanson concludes the volume with an analysis of Russia's economic problems. He provides a sobering long-term perspective by drawing parallels between postcommunist economies today and Western Europe at the start of the industrial era. He uses Karl Polanyi's theories about the rise of capitalism to emphasize the similarities. Polanyi, one of the few economic analysts whose critique of conventional economics has stood the test of time, emphasized that despite the great material success of market-driven economies, human societies would rebel against laissez-faire principles. He stressed that even in England, from the start of the Industrial Revolution, society fought against the commoditization of labor and land. Though markets are very old institutions, Polanyi believed that it had been the goal of almost all governing political and social institutions in precapitalist societies to buffer people from the vagaries of market forces and competition, and from the perceived unfairness of letting pure economic efficiency govern distribution of goods and services. Though this resistance to markets greatly slowed economic growth, it was widely accepted and enshrined in public morality. Somehow this old pattern was broken, after much turmoil, in Great Britain. The phenomenal success of the British economy then forced similar changes in other societies, but always at the cost of revolutionary upheavals and continuing moral revulsion against unchained capitalism.

Socialism, whether in its Marxist form or other versions, always presented itself as more modern and progressive than capitalism. But it was part of the resistance against market forces, and in many ways the goal of socialism has always been to recapture the supposed solidarity and rootedness of precapitalist social structures. In its Stalinist-Soviet form, it was surprisingly successful, though only at very great cost. To shield Soviet society from the market forces operating in the West, Stalin had to prohibit intercourse with the outside world. To make sure that capitalist forces did not arise spontaneously, as they had in Western Europe, the Soviet leadership had to exterminate whole classes of potentially entrepreneurial peasants and bourgeois, and enslave others. To guarantee that there would be no unemployment or considerations of market efficiency to mar socialism, gross inefficiency and distribution by political influence had to be tolerated. The results, later imposed on Eastern Europe as well, were the distorted, corrupt societies that collapsed from 1989 to 1991. But despite all its sins, the Soviet system did shield its people from the market and put off the day when adaptation would be necessary.

It is not surprising, writes Hanson, that people in the former Soviet Union have almost no idea of what markets really mean, or how to go about creating the institutions that make it possible to operate a capitalist society. What took centuries to construct in England and the rest of the West, and still continued to meet resistance throughout the nineteenth and twentieth centuries, was only very partially in place in Russia in 1914. Since then, though it built factories and other modern structures, Russia and the various parts of its former empire have actually regressed even more. Institutionally, if not materially, the gap between Russia and the West is much greater than in 1914. To believe that such a disparity will be overcome in less than a couple of generations is wishful thinking.

So, if Europe is to work, if Eastern Europe and Russia are to be brought into the modern world of the twenty-first century, and if Germany is to remain integrated as a peaceful and harmonious part of Europe, then something more than the mere repetition of a few stock phrases—privatization, democratization, let markets work, abandon inefficient industries—will be required. What will be needed, as Vaclav Havel wrote recently, is faith in the morality of the original Western liberal ideal. Belief in the goodness of liberal values will have to be accompanied by a determination to sacrifice in order to ensure the triumph of this vision. Making Europe work is not primarily a matter of ironing out technical details, but of loyalty to something much grander.[1]

After World War II, it was the determined vision of the United States that gave the West Europeans the confidence and security needed to rebuild their societies. It was the willingness of the United States to spend vast sums to aid the economies ruined by war, and even greater amounts to defend them, that allowed this to take place. At the same time, the Americans agreed for over two decades to absorb imports on favorable terms from Europe and Japan to stabilize and expand the world trading network. This is what ultimately made the somber mid-century predictions about the decline of capitalism and democracy turn out to be wrong. All of this benefited the United States as much as anyone, of course, but it still took faith and vision to make it happen.

Now, who will provide the moral energy to do the same thing for Eastern Europe and the former Russian empire? The United States is unwilling, and psychologically incapable, of performing the same role it did after 1945. It is virtually paralyzed by self-doubt, and its elites no longer have the moral confidence to press forward with their ideal. And Western Europe, which is certainly materially able to take over the role of savior, is locked into petty squabbles and protectionist meanness. The West Germans have provided what is needed for East Germany, but alone they are unable to carry the rest of the postcommunist world. If Western Europe as a whole does not join in a great and self-confident effort to ensure the triumph of liberal values and policies, then Europe will not work. And if Europe fails, the most dire fears about revived German nationalism, about endless ethnic wars in Eastern Europe, and about eventual Russian revanchism may come back to trouble us in the next century.

NOTES

1. Vaclav Havel, "How Europe Could Fail," *New York Review of Books,* November 18, 1993, p. 3.

I

The Past and Future
of Nationalism
and National Identity

Nationalism in Western and Eastern Europe Compared

Liah Greenfeld

An assumption that the nationalisms of Eastern Europe are different in kind from those of Western Europe—which is necessary in making a meaningful comparison between them (and therefore in believing that such a comparison is possible)—is based on a presupposition that a cultural, "civilizational" divide[1] corresponds to the geographical borderline, wherever it may lie, between the Eastern and Western parts of the continent, or, in other words, on investing geography with cultural significance. In order to draw this comparison, therefore, I must begin by examining the assumption behind it.

"Europe" in general is a value-laden concept. Only among other things is it the name of a continent, though it was first imagined as such a geographical entity by the people who lived on the outskirts of it, the Greeks. Its name "Europa" meant "mainland," and referred to the northern and western lands, with a distinctive climate and topography, different from Asia, northern Africa, and the Mediterranean region.[2] From a very early time this geographical image had a cultural dimension. To begin with, Europe was not considered a part of the Greek world, and was therefore culturally "barbarian." But when the Roman Empire drew most of this geographical entity into its sphere of influence, the image of Europe changed, and it was defined as a superior cultural entity. It is possible that already by then its geographical image was eclipsed by a cultural one. In the eighteenth century, Vico regarded the Roman legacy of Europe as central to its definition. "Europe [was] integral only in so far as it recapitulated *Romanitas*."[3]

Christianity, which became the European religion, greatly reinforced this image of cultural unity, adding to it a moral dimension. Europe became coterminus with *respublica Christiana*. Moreover, it came to be imaged specifically as Western Christianity, and then as "the West," although geographically Eastern Europe was as much Europe as Western Europe.

It is to this West, which he called Europe, that the great Russian poet Alexander Blok contrasted Russia in his stunning poem "Scythians." The opening lines of the poem are: "Yes, we are Scythians, yes, Asians we are." But geographically Scythians were a European people. Clearly, Blok accepts the definition of Europe arrived at by the eighteenth-century West Europeans, what Nancy Struever calls the "powerful and seductive definition of Europe as civil/moral identity."[4]

This Western Europe, or "the West," indeed became a moral ideal, a standard by which one was measured. Another extraordinary Russian, Peter Chaadaev, characterized this moral ideal thus:

The sphere in which the Europeans live is the only one in which humanity can achieve its final destiny; despite all that is incomplete, vicious, evil, in European society as it stands today . . . it is nonetheless true that God's reign has been realized there in some way, because it contains the principle of indefinite progress and possesses germinally and elementarily all that is needed for God's reign to become established definitely upon earth one day.

Russia, thought Chaadaev, was not a part of Europe, but he wished it to strive to become one. In his mind, there could be no other ideal: he dismissed the rest of the world. "Do you believe," he asked, "that Abyssinian Christianity or Japanese civilization will produce the world order . . . which is the ultimate destiny of mankind? Do you believe that these absurd aberrations of divine and human truths will cause heaven to descend upon earth?"[5]

Chaadaev, on his own testimony, was not a European, he just wished he were. German Romantic thinkers, smack in the middle of Europe, could not deny their European identity, and yet they were not secure in it either. The definition of Europe and Germany's place in it preoccupied them constantly. For these thinkers Europe was West European civilization, the only civilization worthy of the name, and—however meaningless the proposition was geographically—they insisted that Germany was the most European country of all. Adam Müller, the political philosopher of Romanticism, declared: "the great confederation of European nations will . . . wear German colors; for everything great, through and lasting in all European institutions is German."[6] Unfortunately, the other Europeans (the French foremost among them) betrayed the noble principles of their identity, for which reason Germany had to step in and put things right. "Should the German not assume world government through philosophy," warned Fichte, "the Turks, the Negroes, the North American tribes, will finally take it over and put an end to the present civilization."[7]

Because Western Europe—or Europe for short—was defined as a moral ideal, as a superior cultural community, (West) European identity was considered to be very dignified, enhancing the dignity of national identities within those nations that could lay claim to it. Those nations that could not lay claim to the (West) European identity had to live with the indignity of being left out of it. This explains, for example, the insistent declarations of Russia's rulers, from Catherine the Great to Mikhail Gorbachev, that Russia is a European nation. The reason for their insistence is that this is debatable. Part of Russia is obviously in Europe, and it occupies a very large chunk of Europe, but does this make Russia a European society? Part of Russia is, evidently, in Asia, but is geography everything? In fact, Russia's claim to European identity only veils its desire to be considered part of the "West." In Germany, whose geographical location is unequivocally European, the very same question, whether or not Germany is a part of Europe, is phrased in terms of Germany and the West to begin with.

The concept of "Eastern Europe" did not become morally and culturally significant until the eighteenth century. Then, however, the image of "Eastern Europe," which, as Larry Wolff tells us, for the French at least "ever since the Enlightenment . . . has been *l'orient de l'Europe* . . . or even *l'Orient européen*,"[8] became the moral opposite of the image of the West, and as a result was frequently excluded by Westerners from Europe altogether. "Eastern Europe," Wolff writes, "like the Orient, may best belong between quotation marks, [for] it was invented by travelers and philosophers in the Age of Enlightenment, as a politically charged, cultural construction . . . an ideological convenience." We may owe the idea of "Eastern Europe" as a civilizational unity to Voltaire, who did not base his conclusions on field research in the area, and therefore was more likely to leave us a brilliant misconception than a faithful depiction of the actual state of affairs.[9]

I begin with this somewhat lengthy preamble in order to make the point that nationalisms—or any other cultural complexes—of Eastern and Western Europe cannot be meaningfully compared, because the geographical divide between the eastern and western parts of the continent does not correspond to the civilizational differences denoted by the concepts East and West. These concepts, and to a significant extent even the concept of "Europe," hardly have a geographical application any longer; they signify moral and cultural ideals (or anti-ideals) rather than parts of the world. And if we assigned individual societies to any of these originally geographical categories on the basis of civilizational characteristics, we might have to characterize many West European societies as "Eastern Europe," while most of the "West" or "Europe," paradoxically, would move to another continent. A recent interview on the subject of Russian national identity in the wake of *perestroika* provided me with a fine example of such geographical "liberation" of "Europe." A Russian scholar confessed that his dream was for Russia to become a European society. I asked him what his definition of Europe was. Did it, for example, include Poland? He answered: it included Poland perhaps, but, more important, it included the United States.

The only meaningful comparison when it comes to nationalism is the one between different types of nationalism. The type of nationalism—the essential character of the particular national identity and consciousness—provides the framework for a society's culture broadly defined and thus is the basis for placing it within one or another "civilization." The concept of "the West" goes back to the Roman Empire and then Western Christianity, but it is further delineated and redefined with and because of the birth of nationalism. For reasons of historical accident, nationalism is an originally Western phenomenon: it is born in a part of (the geographical) Western Europe—England. As a result, the English type of nationalism has become perhaps the central characteristic of a Western society, while the English nation—the quintessential example, the paradigm of "the West."

I shall very briefly recapitulate certain parts of the argument I made in *Nationalism: Five Roads to Modernity*.[10] The inventors of nationalism were members of the new Tudor aristocracy in England in the sixteenth century. Upwardly mobile commoners who reached the top of the social ladder, they found unacceptable the traditional image of society in which social mobility was an anomaly and substituted a new image for it, that of a *nation* as it came to be understood in modern times. Before this happened, the word "nation" meant something entirely different; it referred to a political and cultural elite, rather than to a society as a whole. Tudor aristocrats, however, made the "nation" synonymous with the English "people," a concept which previously—in English as in other languages—referred specifically to the lower orders of society, the commons (or worse: the rabble or plebs), as members of which so many of the new aristocrats were born. As a result of this redefinition, every member of the people was elevated to the dignity of the elite— becoming, in principle, equal to any other member, as well as free, invested with the right of self-government, or, in other words, sovereignty, and the people or the nation collectively was, in turn, defined as sovereign.

It is important to recognize that the sovereignty of the nation was, in this case, derived from the assumed sovereignties of each member in the national collectivity. The nation was defined as a composite entity existing only insofar as its members kept the social compact and had neither interests nor will separate from the individual interests and wills of these members. This original nationalism, therefore, was essentially individualistic (which, it should be noted, in no way prevented it from serving as a very firm foundation for social solidarity). It was also civic in the sense that national identity—nationality—was in effect identical with citizenship, and since the nation existed only insofar as its members kept the social compact, could be in principle acquired or abandoned of one's free will.

The principles of this original individualistic and civic nationalism, the location of sovereignty within a people defined as a social compact of free and equal individuals, are the fundamental tenets of liberal democracy, which is considered the essential characteristic of a Western society. This type of nationalism, however, though historically first, is the rarest type of all. Much more often a nation is defined not as a composite entity but as a collective individual, endowed with a will and interest of its own, which are independent of and take priority over the wills and interests of human individuals within the nation. Such a definition of the nation results in collectivistic nationalism. Collectivistic nationalisms tend to be authoritarian and imply a fundamental inequality between a small group of self-appointed interpreters of the will of the nation—the leaders—and the masses, who have to adapt to the elite's interpretations. Collectivistic nationalisms thus favor the political culture of populist democracy or socialism, and as such furnish the ideological bases of modern tyrannies.[11]

Collective nationalisms can be civic. French nationalism is a nationalism of a collectivistic and civic type, which was historically the second type of nationalism to evolve. The civic criteria of national membership acknowledge the freedom of the individual members, which the collectivistic definition of the nation denies. Collectivistic and civic nationalism is therefore an ambivalent, problematic type, necessarily plagued by internal contradictions. The turbulent political history of the French nation is eloquent testimony to these contradictions. Few would doubt the West European and simply Western identity of France, and yet it is interesting that French nationalism began as an anti-English—and by derivation anti-Western—sentiment. France, therefore, at least in the days of its national infancy, could be seen as the first anti-Western nation.

The purely anti-Western (and thus Eastern?) type of nationalism, however, was historically the third and the latest type to appear. It developed first in Russia and very soon after that in Germany. It also became the most common type of nationalism, today characteristic of all East European nations (with the possible exception of the Czech Republic) and, no doubt, of some West European nations as well. This type combines the collectivistic definition of the nation with ethnic criteria of nationality. Ethnic nationalism sees nationality as determined genetically, entirely independent of the individual volition, and thus inherent. It can be neither acquired, if one is not born with it, nor lost, if one is. The freedom of the individual in this type of nationalism is denied consistently, or rather it is redefined as inner freedom or as recognized necessity. This denial and redefinition are predicated on the rejection of the individual as a rational being and an autonomous actor. Individuality itself is equated with the true human nature, which expresses itself in self-abnegation and submersion or dissolution in the collectivity.

In *Nationalism: Five Roads to Modernity*, I analyzed how the three types of nationalism developed and how they acquired their specific forms in England and the United States (which represent the first type of the individualistic and civic nationalism), in France (the model of the second type of collectivistic and civic nationalism), and in Russia and

Germany (which represent the third, the collectivistic and ethnic type). Here I shall only note some general tendencies.

The initial definition of the nation in every case (whether it is defined as a composite entity or in unitary terms) depends on the nature of the groups actively involved in the articulation of the new ideology, and the situations they face. The individualistic type of nationalism is likely to develop if during its formative period nationalism appeals to and serves the interests of wide sectors of the population (e.g., the English squires and newly literate urban masses, the American colonists, the French bourgeoisie, etc.), and new, open, upwardly mobile influential groups. (Examples in this case are the sixteenth-century English aristocracy and squirearchy. The German *Bildungsbürger* as a group were new, fairly open, and upwardly mobile, but before the intellectuals were incorporated into the traditional elite, they had no influence.) The collectivistic type is to be expected if originally the social basis of nationalism is limited: that is, if nationalism is adopted by and serves the interests of a narrow traditional elite intent on preserving its status (such as the French or the Russian nobility), or a new group trying to attain status within the traditional social framework (German *Bildungsbürgertum*), which then transmits it to the masses by indoctrination. A significant change in the situation of the relevant participants may result in a change in the definition of the nation (the American South provides an example of this). But such changes are extremely rare. It must be noted that geography plays no part in this process and, what is perhaps more important, neither does the date of the emergence of a particular nationalism relative to other nationalisms: a society which is among the first to define itself as a nation may develop a collectivistic nationalism, and a recent nation may have an individualistic nationalism.

What does play a part, and especially in determining whether a particular nationalism will be defined as civic or as ethnic, is the perception of a nation's status relative to other nations, or its symbolic place—specifically, whether it is perceived as a part of the West or not. To a certain extent, such perception is dependent on the traditional, prenational beliefs in the society in question, which in all cases exert a significant formative influence on the nature of the developing national identity. Sometimes, as in Russia, the central factor in the development of ethnic nationalisms has been *ressentiment,* a sustained sentiment of existential envy and resentment based on a sense of one's inferiority vis-à-vis the societies from which the ideas of nationalism were imported, and which therefore were originally seen as models. Historically, the sources of importation were to the west of the importers and, more important, were invariably defined as parts of the symbolic West. In consequence, ethnic nationalisms developed as variants of an explicitly anti-Western ideology. Societies which imported national ideas from elsewhere—whether they defined themselves as nations early or late—but which did not at the moment of the adoption of national identity believe themselves to be inferior to their models, tended to define themselves in civic terms. In such cases, the record of their achievement provided them with sufficient reasons for national pride, and they had no need to resort to the claim that their superiority was inherent (in their blood, soul, soil, unadulterated language, or whatnot).

It is therefore possible to distinguish between Western, less Western, and anti-Western nationalisms in Europe and elsewhere. But the geographical location of a nation does not tell us which type of nationalism is characteristic of it. On the contrary, the type of nationalism characteristic of a given society allows one to locate it on the symbolic map as we have charted it, and define it as a part of the West or of the East, and of Western or Eastern Europe.

For the purposes of this volume it is, of course, important to compare Eastern and Western Europe. And the crucial question to ask is whether it is likely that East European societies, recently liberated from the Soviet yoke, will go the way of the West and, like the core West European societies, develop into liberal democracies. Since this is directly related to the kind of nationalism in these societies, the question may be reformulated to inquire about the likelihood that East European nations will exchange their ethnic nationalisms for nationalisms characteristic of *some* West European nations, for example the individualistic and civic nationalism of the English, or the collectivistic but civic nationalism of the French.

It must be understood that what this implies is nothing less than a transformation of the identities of these nations. Such transformations, while possible, do not seem likely in most of the East European societies and former Soviet republics today. They are unlikely, first of all, because the respective social elites of these societies, namely their intelligent-sias, have a vested interest in ethnic nationalism (to which they owe their position as social elites). By the same token, they have absolutely no interest, whatever they may say, in democratization, which implies equality and therefore leveling of their group status with that of the rest of the population. Of course, an identity may also be transformed under pressure from outside. Germany, which was the quintessential example of ethnic nationalism, may be the model of a successful transformation of identity under pressure from without. But as Germany proves, a transformation of identity from without requires a very heavy pressure indeed—as heavy as a long-term occupation or partition. The sad experience of Bosnia-Herzegovina teaches us that the international community is not ready for such measures even under the worst of circumstances.

NOTES

1. A divide of the kind, though not necessarily of the specific nature, delineated by Samuel Huntington in his provocative piece in the *New York Times,* "The Coming Clash of Civilizations, Or, the West Against the Rest," June 6, 1993.

2. See "Europe," *Encyclopaedia Britannica,* 18:648, 680–817.

3. Nancy Struever, "Vichian Inquiry and the Issue of European Identity," presentation at the research conference "European Identity and Its Intellectual Roots," Harvard University, May 6–9, 1993.

4. Ibid.

5. Peter Chaadaev, excerpts from "The First Philosophical Letter," in R. T. McNally, ed. and trans., *The Major Works of Peter Chaadaev* (Notre Dame: Notre Dame University Press, 1969), pp. 32–44.

6. Hans Kohn, "Romanticism and German Nationalism," *Review of Politics* 12 (1950): 471.

7. Hans Kohn, "The Paradox of Fichte's Nationalism," *Journal of the History of Ideas* 10:3 (June 1949): 327.

8. Larry Wolff, "Teaching 'Eastern Europe' Without the Iron Curtain," *Perspectives* 31:1 (January 1993): 10.

9. Ibid., p. 8. See also Wolff's "Voltaire's Eastern Europe: The Mapping of Civilization on the Itinerary of Charles XII," *Harvard Ukrainian Studies* 14:3/4 (December 1990): 623–47. The construction of "Eastern Europe" is the focus of Wolff's *Inventing Eastern Europe: The Map of Civilization on the Mind of the Enlightenment* (Stanford: Stanford University Press, 1994).

10. Liah Greenfeld, *Nationalism: Five Roads to Modernity* (Cambridge: Harvard University Press, 1992). See especially the Introduction.

11. The links between collectivistic nationalisms and modern tyrannies are discussed in Daniel Chirot's *Modern Tyrants: The Power and Prevalence of Evil in Our Age* (New York: Free Press, 1994).

The Role of Nationalism in East European Latecomers to Democracy

Arista Maria Cirtautas

Louis Hartz in *The Liberal Tradition in America* stated that "nationalism is not an argument but an emotion: one of the most powerful social emotions of modern times."[1] This statement seems to be fairly representative of the way nationalism has been understood in the post–World War II era. Nationalism has been seen as powerful, almost primal, and therefore not readily comprehensible through logical analysis. Furthermore, while Hartz himself recognized that liberalism and nationalism can be complementary social action orientations, there has been a general tendency in the social sciences to oppose liberalism and nationalism to one another as representing widely divergent modes of thought and action. Whereas liberalism is based on individual rights and the securing of individual freedoms, nationalism is based on the duties and obligations owed to the community by each member, and the securing of collective freedom. How then could these "isms" have anything to say to one another?

Yet, when one carefully examines the historical evolution of these two ideologies, it becomes clear that nationalism emerged in conjunction with the liberal revolutions of the eighteenth century. The language of rights with which the American and French revolutionaries legitimated their opposition to monarchical authority encompassed both the rights of man and the rights of nations. As the old hierarchies of privilege, status, and order collapsed both domestically and internationally, they were replaced by institutions that stressed the rights of formal equality and sovereignty for both individuals and nations. There is therefore a direct, albeit complicated, relationship between liberalism and nationalism that needs to be addressed in order to attain a more nuanced appreciation of the role of nationalism in East European late-comers to liberal democracy.[2]

This essay will examine how the common origins of liberalism and nationalism led to the creation of an international community that, while dominated by liberal countries, has consistently provided favorable conditions for the emergence of nationalist regimes on its periphery. Seen from this perspective, nationalism is not an irrational product of immature societies but a rational response to two factors: the socioeconomic and cultural features of latecomer societies, and the structure of the liberal international community. Specifically, three central issues will be addressed. First, the process whereby nationalism and liberalism originally evolved as complementary components of the eighteenth-century revolutionary agenda will be illuminated. Second, the nature of the international community that emerged from this revolutionary era will be examined carefully, since this community provided the context within which latecomers must operate. Third, the interwar struggles of East European latecomers will be analyzed in regard to the way these polities reacted to the constraints and conditions they faced domestically and within the international context. Such a historical overview will facilitate a concluding analysis of the current role of nationalism in Eastern Europe. The extent to which similar constraints and conditions are prevalent today is the extent to which one can, unfortunately, expect similar outcomes.

Origins of Liberalism and Nationalism

Given the general bias against analyzing nationalism and liberalism as interrelated phenomena, few scholars have attempted to explore the nature of the relationship between these two ways of organizing political life.[3] But analysis from a historical perspective reveals that nationalism was first given form and substance under liberal auspices. By articulating the rights of nations in universalized form, liberals created the fundamental legitimating principle underlying nationalism. Subsequently, the rights of nations became the guiding norm of an international community dominated by core liberal countries, namely England and the United States. The pursuit of national interest was thereby originally legitimated by the same language of rights that validated liberalism itself. In other words, nationalism was based on rational arguments as well as on irrational emotion. Clearly, the civically based national identity that evolved in the liberal democratic core countries has since come into conflict with the ethnically or racially based nationalisms of latecomer societies. Yet these conflicts should not obscure the fact that without the liberal articulation of national rights, nationalism itself was unlikely to have developed—at least not in the way we have experienced it. The fundamental consequence of this liberal articulation has been the creation of a tension-filled world in which the norms of an international community based on the rights of nations often come into conflict with the norms of national communities based on the rights of man.

What we now understand as the rights of nations—essentially the rights of national self-determination and national sovereignty or self-rule—took shape in two historical contexts: the American Revolution and the French Revolution. During this revolutionary era, the rights-bearing individual was first created and then transformed into the rights-bearing nation. As we shall see, in the liberal core countries the nation never replaced or supplanted the individual—although liberal countries have developed and maintained different accommodations between individual and collective rights—while latecomer societies found it easier to accept national rights without accepting individual rights.

In justifying their struggle for independence from Great Britain, the American colonists created the rights-bearing individual citizen as the fundamental category of political membership. The religiously derived right of freedom of individual conscience was restated in secular form as the right of every individual citizen freely and independently to exercise his conscience in political matters. In other words, the people, as citizens, had a legitimate right to determine the policies and to participate in the governing of their community. This revolutionary concept of the people as the constituent power or authority delegitimated the sovereign monarchy in favor of a civic and individualistic concept of popular sovereignty. However, since not all citizens could participate directly in the governing of the political community, their authority had to be delegated to democratically chosen representatives, who were then bound by the mandate granted to them by their constituents.

What is significant about the American Revolution in this context is that rights were not defined particularistically as the rights of Englishmen or the rights of Americans; they were defined in universal terms as the natural rights of all men:

We hold these truths to be self-evident, that all men are created equal, that they are endowed by their creator with certain unalienable rights; that among these are life, liberty and the pursuit of happiness; that to secure these rights governments are instituted among men, deriving their just powers from the consent of the governed; that whenever any form of government becomes destructive of these ends, it is the right of the people to alter or to abolish it, and to institute new government, laying its foundation on such principles and organizing its powers in such form, as to them shall seem most likely to effect their safety and happiness.[4]

This passage from the Declaration of Independence clearly presents the American cause within the framework of a universally conceived right of people everywhere, as sovereign rights-bearing individuals, to choose their form of government and to create a revolution if they are dissatisfied with existing circumstances. However, no specific national connotation or context for these rights is indicated.

The development of a nationally expressed consciousness of rights occurred during the French Revolution. While the French revolutionaries also legitimated their cause with reference to the natural rights of individuals, they believed that individuals as citizens naturally and inevitably belonged to a national community. This state of belonging bound the individual in service to the greater good of the community. Whereas in the American Revolution government belonged to the people, in the French Revolution citizens belonged to the nation. Since the task faced by the French revolutionaries was to unite the disparate social and regional elements of the revolutionary effort into a concerted whole, it is not surprising that the collective right of membership in a greater body was stressed over the right of individuals to be represented in the governing of their community. In this process, the nation itself was transformed and reified into a rights-bearing individual standing above the rights of the individuals comprising it.

Two quotations, the first from the Abbé Sieyès and the second from Robespierre, illustrate this transformation:

The nation is like the individual in the state of nature who can without difficulty do everything for himself. The individual like the nation requires direction: in order to accomplish this nature has given the individuals a will . . .

[T]he nation, in contrast, as an artificially constituted body, achieves a general will . . . through its members.[5]

The Abbé goes on to say that the nation is "everything for itself alone" just like the individual in the state of nature, and therefore possesses "the entire range of all powers and rights."[6] As different as the Abbé and Robespierre were in revolutionary style and temperament, they clearly shared a similar view of the nation, as indicated in this statement made by Robespierre:

Every man has by nature the ability to govern himself by virtue of his will; it follows that the people unified as a political body, or nation, has the same right. The ability of the general will, or the legislative power, comprised as it is of the abilities of particular wills, is inalienable, sovereign and independent of society, just as every man is independent of every other man.[7]

In short, whereas the American Revolution universalized the concept of individual rights and the collective right of a people to revolt, the French Revolution generalized the concept of the nation as a rights-bearing individual. In both contexts, liberalism and nationalism were complementary components of the same revolutionary agenda. Democratic revolutionaries, whether in the American colonies or in France, believed that by fulfilling the rights of man they would simultaneously be fulfilling their collective or national rights. This conflation of one's individual rights and freedoms with the freedoms and rights of all of one's fellow citizens created a powerful and novel sense of shared destiny. In place of the segmented, hierarchical relationships of the *ancien régime,* diffuse and associational relationships evolved that created linkages between people of radically different backgrounds. Such linkages were established on the basis of a common membership in the nation. Status differences were thereby minimized as both advantaged and disadvantaged citizens acknowledged one another as equal members of the same community.

This formal equality of membership was ultimately replicated in the new international community established under liberal auspices. Ironically, an emphasis on the formal equality and sovereignty of all members of the international community facilitated an eventual parting of the ways between liberalism and nationalism. That the struggle for national rights in latecomer societies could legitimately be separated from the struggle for the rights of man is due, in part, to the nature of the international community that emerged in the wake of the eighteenth-century revolutions.

The Liberal International Community

The liberal articulation of national rights reoriented the relationships of nations to one another, just as the liberal articulation of individual rights reoriented the relationships both among citizens and between citizens and their governments. During the course of the eighteenth century, the old concept of a common Christian community composed of subordinate nations was decisively delegitimated in favor of a community of sovereign, separate nations ruling themselves independently of papal interference. While the influence of the papacy had long since been undermined, the question of how nations were to relate to one another was still dominated by Christian notions of a common community transcending territorial borders. It was not until Vattel published *Le droit des gens, ou Principes de la loi naturelle, appliqués à la conduite et aux affaires des nations et des souverains* in 1758 that a new basis was established for the conduct of sovereign nations. Significantly, Vattel legitimated his vision of a community of sovereign nations by applying the logic of the rights of man to the rights of nations.[8]

Within such a community, the European nations no longer formed a single Christian "societas," just as individuals were no longer embedded in corporate entities. Instead, nations were to be seen as independent polities whose relations with one another were based on mutually recognized rights, contingent consent, and common interest, rather than on conceptions of organic harmony. In essence, Vattel proposed something of a social contract between free and equal nations to complement the contract between free and equal individuals within nations. This complementarity assured *Le droit des gens* a prominent and influential position both in England and in the newly born United States, where Daniel Webster considered Vattel's work to be the guide "to all those principles, laws and usages which have obtained currency among civilized nations."[9]

In the wake of the liberal revolutions, the personalized dynastic connections between the Christian monarchies in Europe were eroded, while impersonal, formal modes of interaction between separate, sovereign nations were able to evolve and become institutionalized in the newly forming international community. For example, from the 1820s on, Great Britain and eventually France resisted the efforts of Austria, Russia, and Prussia to establish an international consortium of Christian nations that would intervene in the domestic affairs of neighboring states to prevent democratic revolutionaries from coming to power. After the collapse of this consortium in 1822, George Canning, the British foreign minister, declared with relish: "Things are getting back to a wholesome state again. Every nation for itself and God for us all!"[10]

These tendencies toward recognizing the sovereignty of all states and the concomitant principle of nonintervention were strengthened in the Western Hemisphere by the Monroe Doctrine. This Doctrine, announced in 1823, stated that the United States would safeguard the new revolutions in Latin America from interference by European powers.[11] Together, then, the liberal core nations—Britain, the United States, and France—were beginning to establish a new international community based on different norms and principles.

In the wake of World War I, the collapse of Europe's autocratic powers—Prussia, Russia, and Austria—removed the last impediment to the firm entrenchment of an international community dominated by the liberal nations. In 1918, therefore, Woodrow Wilson was able to concretize the liberal understanding of rights that underlay the creation of this new community by proclaiming the universal right of "freedom of self-determination of the nation" as one of his Fourteen Points. He thereby articulated an enduring international standard or norm for the rights of nations. International law, and the institutions of the international community that subsequently developed under the auspices of the liberal core, have all been founded on the recognition that nations constitute separate and sovereign entities, and are at least formally equal in standing, with legitimate rights and interests no matter what their size and substance.

Just as business corporations are considered juridical individuals under liberal capitalism, so too are nations. Nations, just as individuals, are sovereign entities possessing the rights of self-determination and self-rule. Just as individuals are free to pursue their happiness as they see fit, so too are nations—hence the reluctance of liberal democracies to interfere in the internal affairs of other countries. Indeed, the rights of national self-determination and self-rule, combined with strict prohibitions against intervention, have been firmly anchored in all multinational declarations, treaties, and covenants, especially since World War II.[12] Accordingly, only when the pursuit of national interests crosses established borders—that is, infringes upon rights of other nations—is outside interference warranted.

Having established the rights of formal equality, sovereignty, and self-determination as the guiding premises of the new international community, the liberal core provided the language with which all subsequent national struggles for independence from foreign domination—or, in the case of Germany and Japan, struggles for national supremacy—were legitimated. Seen from this perspective, nationalism as the pursuit of national rights is indeed the child of liberalism. But it is a child that soon went its own way. While the original liberal understanding of the natural rights of man as a universal construct valid independently of time, space, and culture was weakened and undermined in the early nineteenth century by competing philosophical trends that embraced cultural relativism, the original liberal understanding of the rights of nations was accepted, and if anything strengthened, by belief systems such as Romanticism and Realism. In this context, popular sovereignty was increasingly equated with the collective rights of a nation to determine its own destiny, rather than with the rights of individuals to "form a more perfect union."[13]

Paradoxically, the disintegration of the original revolutionary synthesis between liberalism and nationalism was furthered by the international community created by the liberal nations themselves. Given the nature of this community, the language of national rights alone, without concern for the rights of man, generated a powerful and compelling claim on the liberal countries to accept and formally recognize all nations seeking to enter into the community, no matter how these new nations were internally constituted—as long as they accepted the concept of formal equality that bound the community of sovereign nations together. No international sanctions or prohibitions were placed on nationalist regimes that were manifestly illiberal in their domestic arrangements. Furthermore, the embedded principle of nonintervention guaranteed the international security of these regimes. Only nations seeking to reorganize the international community along different principles—such as Nazi Germany, with its ideal of a substantively determined hierarchy of better and lesser nations—were ultimately rejected.

Interwar Eastern Europe

In the nineteenth and early twentieth centuries, therefore, political elites in latecomer societies such as the East European nations found themselves facing a choice between pursuing the natural rights of man and pursuing national rights. The two revolutionary causes were no longer seen as synonymous, as they were in the American and French revolutions. The tolerance of the international community for manifestations of nationalism is a critical component of the constellation of factors that led to the almost universal pursuit of national rights over the rights of man in Eastern Europe. This international context, operating in conjunction with domestic conditions, generated a powerful impetus for the emergence of nationalist regimes throughout the region.

Domestically, the new East European states were characterized, at least initially, by political battles between liberal and nationalist politicians competing for a stable basis of social support in the interwar period. In this competition, nationalist forces proved more adept at gaining and retaining the support of critical social groups such as the nobility.[14] The fact that liberalism itself was transformed and weakened when it came into contact with the Central and East European societies, including Germany, inhibited the ability of East European liberals to create strong links with their populations. Having taken on a rather elitist cast, East European liberalism was unable to appeal to a broad social audience.

Without the basis in religion provided by the dissenting Protestant sects, the core concept of liberalism—the freedom of conscience of the individual—lost its divinely sanctioned authority. The ability of every individual to reason, determine, and pursue his interests was therefore never fully accepted by East European liberals. Autonomous individuality and the universal ability to reason were not simply held to be inherent in human nature, as they were in the Anglo-American and French traditions. Reason and rationality had to be demonstrated by attaining the requisite degree of *Bildung,* or by manifesting a sovereign disregard for material interests. In other words, citizenship rights were no longer automatically derived from the natural rights of man. Instead, those who would claim civic rights had to demonstrate their merit, and the burden of proof would be on them. This elitist interpretation of liberalism was strengthened by the fact that most East European and German liberals were drawn from the ranks of the intelligentsia. Since their rise and standing in the social hierarchy had been determined by the acquisition of knowledge and *Bildung*, they saw nothing wrong or inappropriate in generalizing their experience as the only proper way to become a citizen and attain citizenship rights.

The fatal flaw of this casting of liberalism is that it replicated the paternalistic attitudes of the monarchical regimes without offering the people even a false sense of participation in the greater community. The aristocracy of birth was simply to be replaced by an aristocracy of *Bildung* that would continue to keep the common people in their place. Unfortunately, neither the existing aristocracy nor the common people were inspired by this vision of a tutelary democracy wherein liberal intellectuals would teach the population how to become true and virtuous citizens. Consequently, liberals found themselves isolated, marginalized, and increasingly oriented toward the sophisticated and cultured West, where liberalism was already firmly established. With this added taint of "cosmopolitanism" and its implied dislike and distaste for native culture, East European liberals were unable to withstand the superior attractions offered by their intellectual peers who were presenting a nationalist vision of the political community.

Undoubtedly, the weakness of liberalism created opportunities for nationalist politicians, but the fact that nationalism itself provided a compelling ideological agenda cannot be overlooked. Although national identities were also developed and promulgated by members of the intelligentsia, their views appealed to a much broader social audience. The Romantic values such as honor, pride, virtue, purity, and blood that lie at the heart of most nationalist ideologies have a clear affinity with the values and self-image of the traditional aristocracy, which was therefore very receptive to nationalistic imagery. Moreover, the common people were also accorded a place in the nationalist vision. Simply by virtue of one's birth, one could be a participant in the glory and pageantry of the nation. Unlike elitist liberals who required evidence of people's ability to reason, nationalists were ready, symbolically at least, to admit everyone of the right birth to the national community. Clearly, this all-inclusive vision of collective popular sovereignty was better able to mobilize support from a wide range of social groups, and was therefore better able to overcome the disparate social and regional divisions that riddled these societies.

But we would minimize, and therefore misunderstand, the appeal of nationalist visions if we simply dismissed them as instrumental and opportune ideological vehicles for political success. Nationalism and the sense of community it projects was and is a way of overcoming what Louis Hartz has called the bleakness of everyday existence: "There is a feudal bleakness about man which sees him fit only for external domination, and there is a liberal bleakness about man which sees him working autonomously on the basis of his own self-interest."[15] The intellectuals of the East European societies, Germans in particular, were well aware of these forms of bleakness. Nationalism provided a way of transcending them both.

In short, a sense of shared destiny as members of a permanent community evolved under nationalist auspices in the countries of Eastern Europe. As the natural rights doctrine lost its appeal in the early nineteenth century, politics based on collectivities, whether ethnic groups, societies, nations, or classes, became the order of the day. In Western Europe these collectivities became reconciled to one another on the basis of the formal equality fostered by the liberal institutions already established. As we have seen, there is a tendency in liberalism to reify collectivities as rights-bearing individuals. Formalized equality subsequently becomes the procedural basis upon which these "individuals" are to relate to one another, just as real individual citizens are formally equal under the law.

In Eastern Europe, however, collectivities were not understood as rights-bearing individuals, since individualism had lost its compelling revolutionary quality. Rather, collectivities were defined and felt as sacred entities or unities that embodied a general will to survive. A unity defined as sacred cannot be reconciled to formal equality with other unities, since it is held to be substantively superior to all others. Thus we get the virulent forms of nationalism characteristic of Eastern Europe in the interwar years. The irony is that as long as the subsequent struggles for substantive superiority between ethnic groups did not challenge the principles of the international community established by the core, the core liberal countries did very little to intervene or to support institutional outcomes more to their liking.

Apart, then, from nationalism's intrinsic appeal to diverse social audiences, its political success was also facilitated by the norms of the international community that accepted the pursuit of national rights as valid in principle—although particular expressions of national rights might be deplored. Indeed, the nations of Eastern Europe were created as formal entities by the victorious Allies after World War I under the influence of Wilson's belief in the validity of national self-determination. The international acceptance of nationalist regimes was further facilitated by the presence of the facade liberal institutions that prevailed throughout the region during much of the interwar period.[16] Even Hitler's extreme nationalism was tolerated by the international community until Germany violated the border with Poland. Prior to that event, the British and French efforts at appeasement derived much of their strength from the widespread conviction that Germany had been unjustly denied the principle of national self-determination after World War I. In this context, even the dismemberment of Czechoslovakia could be accepted as an expression of the desire of that state's minorities to join their appropriate national communities, namely Germany, Poland, and Hungary.

Clearly, the liberal international community had been unaware of the consequences of imposing national borders in the wake of World War I and granting sovereignty to the nations thus formed. Sovereignty acquired by such means was unlikely to be accepted domestically or respected by neighboring states with irredentist claims. Consequently, nonliberal Russian and German influences loomed large in the region as they exploited the tensions caused by such claims. These nations, unlike the liberal core, were not averse to interfering on a massive scale in the domestic arrangements of fellow European nations. Ultimately, after World War II, Eastern Europe fell under the sole influence of the Soviet Union and was forced to replicate the political, social, and economic institutions established by the Community Party of the Soviet Union.

By ensuring that the rights of nations would be respected as an overarching principle, liberal countries tolerated the separation of national rights from the rights of man. As the original complementarity between liberalism and nationalism proved untenable in latecomer societies, nationalism as an independent force was subsequently able to derive its strength from international as well as from domestic sources. In other words, the strength of nationalism in latecomer societies is not simply a result of their general backwardness, it is also a consequence of the system of international relations established by the first liberal nations. Within this system, the pursuit of national rights is considered legitimate whether or not a nation espouses the liberal rights of man. Furthermore, all nations are considered equal and sovereign without regard for their substantive internal differences and domestic political arrangements. Nations are expected to win or lose on a supposedly level playing field largely on the basis of their indigenous resources and capacities. To recall the words of George Canning: "Every nation for itself and God for us all." The liberal world system does not, therefore, have a neutral effect on latecomers.

Supporting the principle of national self-determination without a concomitant support for liberal outcomes has historically created a favorable international environment for the development of nationalist regimes. As the fate of the interwar East European states demonstrates, not even new nations attempting to replicate the liberal democratic institutions of the West, such as Czechoslovakia, could count on the active support or assistance of Western countries. As nationalist parties proved to be successful in mobilizing domestic resources to create stable regimes, they were just as readily accepted into the international community.

At first glance, then, it would appear that the substantial engagement of the international community in Eastern Europe today on behalf of liberal outcomes represents a positive new effort to create a favorable environment for the consolidation of liberal regimes. When viewed in historical perspective, however, it becomes clear that the current engagement is an anomaly unlikely to be sustained, and likely to have counterproductive effects as well.

Eastern Europe Today

In the aftermath of 1989, the countries of Eastern Europe again have an opportunity freely to construct institutions in keeping with their needs and aspirations. The context in which these institutions will evolve is strikingly similar to the interwar period. Communist party rule has left highly divided societies and economic chaos in its wake, just as the withdrawal of the German, Russian, Austro-Hungarian, and Ottoman empires from the region did after World War I. Again, the critical question is which political orientation will determine the direction of institutional change. Will liberals or nationalists succeed in providing a more compelling sense of community and of national identity around which political actors and social groups can coalesce and organize? Moreover, how is the current role of the international community to be assessed?

While it is often supposed that the strength of liberalism today should outweigh the strength of nationalism, unfolding tendencies indicate that history might repeat itself. The social constituency for nationalist political groupings again appears to be stronger than the social support garnered by the liberal parties that are emerging from the former opposition. Today's liberally oriented political elites in Eastern Europe manifest many of the same elitist tendencies as their liberal forefathers, and are therefore finding it difficult to retain the euphoric social support of the immediate post-1989 period. Nationalist political groups have been quick to take advantage of the resulting gap between liberally oriented politicians and the populations they are attempting to serve and represent. With varying degrees of success, nationalist leaders throughout Eastern Europe have been able to capitalize politically on a growing sense of social alienation and frustration.

The bias toward elitism among East European liberals is again emerging as a major factor in the current processes of political transformation. To date, this has manifested itself primarily in three ways. First, as former leaders of the opposition drawn mainly from the intelligentsia, liberal politicians and political groupings are largely untrained and inexperienced in democratic pluralist politics.[17] Moreover, these politicians have also demonstrated a conscious unwillingness to adapt to the more routinized tasks of democratic political life. The moral purity, heroism, and intimacy of their former lives changed overnight when they entered the more mundane world of messy political compromise, and circumscribed—yet glaringly public—roles and procedures. In this new world, more often than not, former "heroes" find themselves vilified by their opponents and distrusted by the population at large. This political culture shock has resulted in a preference for small groups and parliamentary activity as, respectively, the primary organizational basis for the formation of political parties and the primary forum for political life. In the effort to limit their exposure to this new and often hostile world, liberally oriented politicians have failed to develop strong bases of support within the population. The effort to maintain grass-roots connections has essentially been given up even by former popular movements such as Poland's Solidarity and Hungary's Fidesz.

While a distaste for developing social constituencies under the mobilizing auspices of a mass party is understandable given the experience with Leninist parties, this has proved to be a debilitating development in the post-Leninist context, leaving populations uninformed and frustrated by their lack of interaction with public figures. Even the former "people's tribune," Lech Wałęsa, no longer communicates directly with the voters who elected him president in 1990. By and large, a sense of being responsible primarily to one's constituency is absent among East European liberal politicians, who choose either to focus on the more nebulous national interest or to represent the "theoretical interests" of social groups, such as an active bourgeoisie, that do not yet exist.[18]

This tendency to ascribe less weight to the actual interests of existing social groups than to the theoretical interests of the social groups deemed necessary for liberal capitalist development represents a second form of liberal elitism. In Poland, for example, it is evident that all liberal post-1989 governments have followed this logic. Since communist rule did not result in a middle class supportive of liberal capitalism, it was, and is, believed that this class must be created by administrative fiat. The emphasis placed on the creation of a new class through guided reform from above has resulted in the neglect of real groups, such as workers and peasant farmers.[19] While it is clear that these groups must bear the brunt of a transformed market economy, it is less clear why they should become second-class citizens politically simply because they do not conform to an image of the model liberal capitalist citizen. In other words, Polish liberals tend to assume that these groups are hostile to reform because of their socioeconomic standing, and that they are generally unfit for participation in democratic politics because of their lack of education. Therefore, no consistent effort is made to engage these citizens in a dialogue about the pace and direction of change.

Clearly, the belief in the benefits of a tutelary democracy run by a virtuous elite on behalf of a passive citizenry is still present in Poland. This was evident in the commentary surrounding the 1990 presidential candidacy of Stan Tyminski, a rather shady émigré entrepreneur who proclaimed himself to be the savior of Poland. When it became clear that every fourth adult Pole had voted for Tyminski against Wałęsa, the overwhelming consensus among even the liberal intellectual-political elite was that the Polish population had yet again proved itself to be irrational and unprepared for the exercise of civic responsibility. Instead of analyzing the negative impact of Mazowiecki's aloof and exclusionary style of leadership in conjunction with the hardship of shock therapy and the breakup of Solidarity, preeminent figures such as Father Józef Tischner preferred to deplore the pernicious influence of the "Homo sovieticus" syndrome embedded in the population.[20] Undoubtedly, the years of communist rule have had an impact on the way people think, but to define this impact in terms of irrationality goes against classic liberal theory that ascribes the ability to reason to every individual, regardless of experience or circumstances.

Perhaps to counteract the supposed irrationality and the lack of civic virtue in the population at large, liberal political elites throughout Eastern Europe have set a very high standard of rationality and virtuous political conduct for themselves. The resulting preoccupation with the rule of law, as the only correct and rational guide to political conduct, represents the third form that elitist liberalism has taken. A rigid adherence to legal formalism, without communicating the substantive benefits of a liberal rule of law to populations accustomed to the systematic abuse of legality under communist rule, has weakened liberal governments and violated people's sense of justice. In Poland, for example, Mazowiecki's government was ultimately undermined by its strict legalistic observance of the Roundtable Accords, even beyond the point at which Solidarity's original negotiating partner, the Polish Communist Party, had ceased to exist as a viable organization.

Furthermore, throughout the region, the ability of former communist bosses to hide behind the rule of law has led to considerable disenchantment with the formal legalism of liberalism. This disenchantment is perhaps most extreme in East Germany, where the general inability to prosecute the glaring human rights offenders of the former regime on procedural grounds has preoccupied public debate since reunification. Providing exemplary rational and virtuous leadership based on the rule of law, while dismissing or suppressing the legitimate claims people have for some kind of substantive justice, can be self-defeating. Since the rule of law so avidly proclaimed by the new liberal elites is apparently protecting the old elites, the population at large can readily assume that nothing much has changed on the political level. For example, equating Solidarity's liberal elites with the old communist elites is already rather firmly entrenched in Polish public opinion.

These elitist tendencies among liberally oriented politicians in Eastern Europe have had critical consequences for the overall strength of liberalism in the region. Essentially, the weak organizational base of liberal parties has been reinforced by a general disinclination among liberal elites to view existing social groups as potential constituencies. In the absence of a middle class, the effort to maintain social support has been sacrificed in favor of parliamentary activity designed to create that class by political design. While this class is in the making, the liberal West has become something of an alternative constituency from which East European liberals expect both support and guidance. Clearly, the West, especially the European Community, does have a great deal to offer, and this must be taken into consideration in the policy-making process. Ultimately, however, the political fate of these politicians will be decided in their own domestic arenas, not in Brussels or Berlin.

Unfortunately, the East European publics that will judge the performance of their elected officials have begun to lose faith in the efficacy of political leadership in general, and in liberal leadership in particular. Rising levels of apathy and frustration with the existing state of political affairs have been documented in opinion polls throughout the region. Paradoxically, the gap between liberal politicians and the societies they represent has served only to reinforce a sense of elitist isolationism among East European liberals. As we have seen, the tendency has been to dismiss voter displeasure as a manifestation of irrationality, rather than as the logical outcome of policies pursued by liberal politicians. Inevitably, the fragility of this type of liberalism has left the door open for other political parties to cultivate increasingly disaffected social audiences.

Predominant among these political parties have been those espousing explicitly nationalist agendas. Unlike liberal parties that are struggling to create a new social constituency, nationalist parties have begun to champion the interests of existing social groups. Workers and peasants who find themselves locked into the partially reformed structures of the old economic system, for example, are particularly vulnerable to nationalist economic programs that promise a slower and protected pace of reform. Given the weakness of liberal parties and this affinity between the interests of major social groups and nationalist platforms, the question arises why nationalist parties have not been more successful in acquiring political power and influence. The answer lies in the divided state of nationalism itself.

Nationalist political groups are currently split over how to define membership in the political community. Two central groupings, historically based nationalists and morally based nationalists, have emerged in almost all of the East European countries. For the former, membership in the nation should be determined on the basis of ethnic origins and cultural heritage. For the latter, legitimate membership in the community should be restricted even more, to include only those who are free of "contamination" from the past regime. In Poland, for example, this division between nationalist parties is clearly evident. On the one hand, the KPN (Confederation for an Independent Poland) presents a traditional nationalist platform based on the historical and cultural values of the Polish people. On the other hand, members of the Catholic parties and the new right-wing political groups (such as the one founded by former Prime Minister Olszewski after his ouster) claim, as their raison d'être, the task of purifying Poland from the pernicious influence of the communists and their agents, among whom they number Lech Wałęsa and Leszek Moczulski, the leader of the KPN. Given the tense and paranoid world view of these political actors, cooperation even with the KPN would appear unlikely.

The competing nationalisms in Poland and elsewhere are further divided by their attitudes toward the West and toward economic reform and development. Whereas traditional, ethnically based nationalism has historically not been hostile to liberal capitalism, and even allowed forms of liberal government to be established before World War II, the position of today's morally oriented nationalists toward Western institutions is decidedly more hostile. A "plague on both your houses" mentality seems to be developing in which communism and liberalism are jointly condemned as products of a foreign, un-Christian culture. Former Slovak Prime Minister Carnogursky exemplifies this tendency to attack liberalism as "another deviant philosophy":

Liberalism threatens the necessary balance between different groups in society . . . , promotes a culture of artificial consumption . . . , promotes an environment which divorces the individual from values of morality and the articles of the true faith . . . , [and] allows the individual to do everything, but forgets that the devil is present in the human soul.

He adds that while the struggle against liberalism might seem different from the fight against socialism, "I can see a time when this conflict will emerge and new methods will have to be used in order to defeat liberalism."[21]

The presence of left-wing, postcommunist successor parties has further complicated the struggle for the hearts and minds of disaffected voters. Generally, all of these competing political groups, nationalist and postcommunist, have split their common constituency to such an extent that no one group has been able to gain political preeminence. In those cases, however, where a nationalist political agenda has been successfully fused with a socialist economic program, thereby uniting the nationalist and postcommunist successor parties, both morally based nationalists and liberal political actors have been marginalized. To date, the nationalist-postcommunist hybrid regimes in Slovakia, Lithuania, and Romania would all appear to be following this model.[22]

Despite the initial, post-1989 rejections of a "third way" throughout Eastern Europe, these regimes are apparently attempting to reject the extremes of both liberal capitalist and Leninist socialist development. While critics can warn that this is likely to result in no development whatsoever, such a path undoubtedly resonates with the interests of significant social audiences, ranging from workers, to peasants, to bureaucrats. For the time being, the political success of this "third way" seems limited to the three cases mentioned above. Overall, however, it does represent a powerful alternative to the liberal program of political and economic reform, and under continuing unfavorable socioeconomic conditions may well prove to be the model of the future.

Elsewhere in Eastern Europe something like a stalemate among liberal, nationalist, and postcommunist political groups and orientations seems to have developed. This stalemate is characterized most vividly by political battles over the appropriate spheres of authority between governing institutions, such as the presidency and the parliament. In the absence of an accepted balancing of powers, attempts to expand one sphere of authority at the expense of another are common occurrences. Even forceful and popular presidents like Havel and Wałęsa have been unable to convert their personal authority into a stable from of institutionalized authority. The resulting institutional instability has weakened political and economic reform efforts throughout the region. Politicians who are more concerned with the internal distribution of power and influence do not have much attention left for the difficult task of extricating their countries from the legacy of communist rule.

On a different, less public level, battles are being fought in the realms of culture and education. Conservative political groups, most notably in Poland where the Catholic Church is forcefully attempting to implement its agenda, have set their sights on influencing both the present population and future generations by exposing them only to the customs, values, and mores they deem appropriate. The immediate objective of these groups would appear to be control over the media and public education. Decisive victories by either liberal or conservative forces have yet to occur, but it is clear that these battles have sapped resources and energies that would have been better directed toward improving the funding for public education, health, and culture.

At this point, two scenarios seem likely for future developments in Eastern Europe. On the one hand, hybrid regimes consisting of nationalist-postcommunist alliances may continue to take shape and gain influence in other countries of the former Soviet bloc. As we have seen, such regimes do reflect the interests of many social groups struggling to survive within the confines of inherited socioeconomic structures. On the other hand, continued political and institutional stalemate is likely in those countries where liberal groups are strong enough to present a viable political alternative (mainly in Poland, the Czech Republic, and Hungary) but are too weak to achieve the decisive monopoly of political power needed to continue implementing wide-reaching liberal capitalist reforms.

In this context, the influence of the liberal international community can clearly have a major impact in strengthening the hand of liberal forces in the region in order to either overcome an existing stalemate or break an emerging alliance between left and right. This is certainly the stated intention of international actors as they develop their relations with postcommunist countries. Currently, in sharp contrast to the interwar period, the international community appears to have relaxed its prohibitions against intervening in the domestic affairs of sovereign nations. As is well known, in the economic realm, the International Monetary Fund and the World Bank have directly imposed a set of strict conditions for international aid. In the political realm, this new interventionism has mainly consisted of efforts to impose a rigid standard of formal proceduralism on the conduct of political affairs. For example, the liberal international community has consistently monitored the formal correctness according to which political processes, such as elections, take place.[23]

Upon closer examination, however, this type of intervention does not represent a complete departure from the established principles of sovereignty and nonintervention. Efforts to structure the political processes in Eastern Europe along procedural lines have been accompanied by a policy of noninterference with the substantive outcomes of these processes. In other words, an attempt is being made simultaneously to remain true to the principles of self-determination and nonintervention while trying not to repeat the perceived mistakes of the interwar era when complete Western noninvolvement led to disastrous consequences.

Unfortunately, the current policy of attempting to square the circle by becoming involved in Eastern Europe without directly intervening on behalf of desired outcomes is inherently inconsistent, and therefore vulnerable to criticism. On the one hand, this policy will not satisfy those political actors, in both Eastern Europe and the West, who hope for more substantive engagement on behalf of liberal outcomes. On the other hand, even a limited Western engagement involving only a limited expenditure of resources will be resented by those in the West who believe that domestic priorities should come first. Since this latter position is consistent with the established logic of the international community, it will tend to carry greater weight, especially as problems mount in the region. Overall, then, it is highly likely that the tensions and conflicts generated by current policy inconsistencies will be resolved by an eventual return to strict nonintervention.

Apart from being unsustainable over the long run, the involvement of the international community is proving to be counterproductive. Unfortunately, even the imposition of formal proceduralism has not been neutral in its impact. For example, the Western engagement in Eastern Europe since 1989 has been critical in undermining the linkages democratically oriented political actors had created between themselves and their populations. During the period of communist party rule, the democratic opposition in Eastern Europe, especially in Poland

and Hungary, had managed to establish social bases of support within their own populations. In the process of establishing such bases, the aforementioned elitist tendencies of East European liberalism were overcome. These tendencies have, however, reemerged as post-1989 Western involvement provided East European liberals with an additional incentive to replace their domestic constituencies with the surrogate constituency represented by the West.

After East European liberals abandoned their grass-roots connections, and increasingly oriented themselves toward the West, nationalist political groups stepped into the vacuum. In this context, Western engagement has simply reinforced the arguments of nationalist politicians, who represent themselves as the sole force capable of protecting the nation from undesirable and pernicious Western involvement. As we have seen, the international community has historically been receptive to nationalist demands that the principles of self-determination and nonintervention be upheld. Consequently, if liberally oriented politicians continue to lose ground with their own populations, there is little reason to assume that the current situation will ultimately result in anything but a repetition of the interwar period, when the international community left Eastern Europe to go its own way under nationalist auspices.

NOTES

This article owes a great deal to the invaluable criticism offered by my colleagues Stephen Hanson and Kenneth Jowitt. Financial support for research and writing was provided by a grant from the American Council of Learned Societies. Responsibility for the contents, however, rests solely with the author.

1. Louis Hartz, *The Liberal Tradition in America* (New York: Harcourt, Brace and World, 1955), p. 207.
2. For the purposes of this article, "latecomers to democracy" can be defined as those countries attempting to establish liberal democratic institutions after the original wave of liberal revolutions had already taken place in England, the United States, and France.
3. A notable exception is the recent work by Liah Greenfeld, *Nationalism: Five Roads to Modernity* (Cambridge: Harvard University Press, 1992).
4. Quoted in Carl Becker, *The Declaration of Independence* (New York: Vintage Books, 1958), p. 8.
5. Quoted in Marcel Gauchet, *Die Erklärung der Menschenrechte* (Hamburg: Rowohlt Taschenbuch Verlag, 1991), p. 99.
6. Ibid.

7. Ibid., p. 26.

8. The following analysis relies heavily on F. H. Hinsley, *Sovereignty* (New York: Basic Books, 1966), pp. 158–213.

9. Ibid., pp. 200–201.

10. Quoted in R. R. Palmer and Joel Colton, *A History of the Modern World* (New York: McGraw-Hill, 1992), p. 483.

11. While the Monroe Doctrine would later be used to justify American intervention in Latin America, its original intention was precisely the opposite. Ibid., pp. 482–83.

12. On the extent to which these rights are anchored in international treaties see, for example, the United Nations Declaration on the Granting of Independence to Colonial Countries and Peoples, adopted in 1960, and other UN documents contained in Ian Brownlie, ed., *Basic Documents on Human Rights* (Oxford: Clarendon Press, 1971). According to such international covenants, the only time a nation's rights, such as sovereignty, can be breached legitimately is when that nation has been defeated in war. At that point, the international community can impose policies on the loser and set aside the principle of nonintervention. Most recently, Iraq provides an example of this abridged sovereignty, as does Germany after both world wars, and Japan after World War II.

13. This phrase is taken from the preamble to the United States Constitution.

14. On the history of the interwar period see Joseph Rothschild, *East Central Europe Between the Two World Wars* (Seattle: University of Washington Press, 1974).

15. Hartz, *Liberal Tradition*, p. 80.

16. On the "facade" character of these regimes see Andrew Janos, *The Politics of Backwardness in Hungary, 1825–1945* (Princeton: Princeton University Press, 1982).

17. For an examination of the new political elites in Eastern Europe see Valerie Bunce and Maria Csanadi, "Uncertainty in the Transition: Post-Communism in Hungary," *East European Politics and Societies* 7:2 (Spring 1993): 240–76.

18. On the tendency to represent "theoretical interests" see Jadwiga Staniszkis, *Ontologia socjalizmu* (Warsaw: In Plus, 1989).

19. On the interest of "real" social groups in the period of transition see Edmund Mokrzycki, "The Legacy of Real Socialism, Group Interests, and the Search for a New Utopia," in Walter D. Connor and Piotr Ploszajski, eds., *Escape from Socialism: The Polish Route* (Warsaw: IFiS Publishers, 1992), pp. 269–83.

20. See Józef Tischner, *Etyka Solidarności oraz Homo sovieticus* (Warsaw: Wydawnictwo Znak, 1992). For a sober and highly analytical account of the 1990 elections see Krzysztof Jasiewicz, "From Solidarity to Fragmentation," *Journal of Democracy* 3:2 (April 1992): 55–70.

21. Quoted in the *East European Newsletter*, February 3, 1992, p. 8.

22. More recently, Poland and Hungary have seen the return of former communists at the helm of government.

23. On a more dramatic level, the international community was also involved in supervising the formal procedures whereby Czechoslovakia was divided into two states.

The Polish Roman Catholic Church Unbound: Change of Face or Change of Context?

Ewa Morawska

During the forty-five years of communist rule in Poland, the Polish Roman Catholic Church remained an integral component of sociocultural life and an important partner in politics, ostensibly weak but actually powerful because of the sustained support of the majority of Poles. Since the collapse of the communist regime in 1989, the Polish Catholic Church seems to have reversed sides, as it were: it has gained significant power in the public forum, but its popular support appears to have decreased considerably. In the fall of 1993, victory in the parliamentary election by a populist coalition of postcommunist social democrats and the largest peasant party was primarily a result of the discontent of a large part of Polish society with the detrimental effects of radical economic reforms moving toward laissez-faire capitalism.[1] However, in no little measure this electoral result also reflected popular protest against the expansionism of the politically empowered Catholic Church.

It is reasonable to assume that regardless of the direction of Polish politics in the near future, the Catholic Church will remain an important political player. How significant it will be (Poland's new constitution is still in preparation), and how effective its political initiatives, will depend on a configuration of factors among which popular expectations and views regarding the church and its public role will be influential. It is therefore of interest to look at the main issues of concern to the Polish Catholic Church as well as the popular perceptions thereof by Poles during the postwar era.

In the view of many disappointed Poles, the position of the Polish Roman Catholic Church has changed rapidly since the fall of communism in 1989. Instead of being seen as a staunch defender of the freedom of the Polish nation and the social and political rights of its members, it now seems to many to be an unwelcome "meddler" in the affairs of the nation-state, infringing on the group and individual civil liberties of its citizens. This perception of the Catholic Church's chameleonlike behavior after shaking off communist control has also been common among Western commentators on Polish affairs. Both in Poland and in the West, discussion of the role of the Catholic Church in the public forum usually focuses on the whys and hows of this transformation.

I propose a different and, I believe, better interpretation. It shifts the main focus of analytic attention from the represented—that is, the Polish Catholic Church—to those forming representations, in this case Polish public opinion. It also assumes that the changing political contexts of the relations between the state, the church, and the society in Poland's postwar history have played an important role in coloring (not determining) the church's public pronouncements. Finally—and this is of central significance—my interpretation sees these changing political contexts as having been the crucial factor in shaping the perceptions of the church's position by Polish society.

Specifically, I argue that although the church's agenda during the four and a half decades of communist rule did indeed include appeals for national freedom and civil liberties, it also, and with much greater emphasis and consistency, reiterated the same desiderata regarding "Christianization" of the public and private spheres that the majority of Polish society perceives today as detrimental to the satisfactory functioning of the democratic nation-state and to the well-being of its citizens. Put differently—and this is my main thesis—it is not the church's position that has changed; allowing for conditional shifts of emphasis, this position has remained much the same during the last half-century (and actually much longer than that). Rather, the political context in which the church functions has been significantly altered. With this transformation the primary concerns of the Polish people changed as well, and in consequence so did social perceptions of the views and initiatives of the church. I also argue that the change in political circumstances, combined with the altered popular perceptions of the church's public role, has heightened the impact of other factors contributing to negative attitudes toward the church's post-1989 public behavior. The latter include—to mention only those largest in social scale and probably of greatest consequence—the accumulated effects of several decades of enforced secularization that are coming to the fore now that the traditional public, ceremonial type of "national religiosity" has largely lost its meaning and appeal in sovereign Poland, as well as the increasing privatization or "denationalization" of religion among Poles who remain within the Catholic fold.

As sources of information and data for this paper, I have used the available church documents published in separate volumes or individually in the Polish press from 1945 to the present: pastoral letters, sermons, and other public statements by Polish primates and bishops; recently published transcripts of closed-door talks of the so-called Joint Commission made up of representatives of the Polish episcopate and the Central Committee of the Polish Communist Party between 1980 and 1989; interpretative accounts of postwar church history written primarily by Catholic clergymen and laypersons, and also by political scientists in the communist establishment; records of public statements and parliamentary initiatives of the programmatically Catholic political parties and their leaders for the period 1990 to the present; public opinion surveys and sociological analyses of the religious beliefs and practices of Poles as well as their attitudes toward the church, its teachings, and public behavior during the postwar period up to the present; and material from the post-1989 Polish press related to the issues described above.[2]

I will first identify the fundamental concerns of the Polish Catholic Church as the church defines them, present on the church's agenda throughout the postwar era regardless of current political circumstances and the resulting particular emphases or messages. I will then briefly discuss the entanglement of Catholicism with problems of Polish national identity and survival, due to the peculiarity of Poland's history of the last two hundred years. (This relationship is presumably familiar to my readers, but because it is central for the main arguments of this chapter, its brief reiteration is necessary.) Next, within the double framework of church-state and state-society relations, I will illustrate the church's pronouncements and the perceptions thereof by Polish public opinion with concrete examples: first, at different moments of Poland's "communist" history from 1945 to 1989, and, second, during the four years since Poland regained national independence and established a democratic government. In conclusion, I will consider possible developments—such as appear most likely in the wake of the electoral victory in September 1993 of the coalition of postcommunist and peasant parties—in the triaxial relations between the church, the state, and the society in present-day Poland.

Under Communist Rule: 1945 to 1989

Inspection of church documents issued between 1945 and 1993 reveals one major and several derivative fundamental concerns of the Roman Catholic Church. The former is grounded in the axiomatic belief that, as the future Cardinal Primate Stefan Wyszyński put it in an open letter to the clergy and parishioners at the occasion of his ingress to the Lublin diocese in the spring of 1946: "In the long march of peoples through the earth, we have always been, and will ever remain, first and foremost the people of God."[3] From this assumption there naturally follows the underlying, or perhaps better, overarching, concern that men and women, created by God to serve His purposes, carry on their mundane existence in a way that will earn salvation of their souls and eternal life.

The recognition of the ultimate purpose and obligation of human life in all its expressions as striving toward the *sacrum* imposes the duty on the church—the earthly representative of the divine, and the teacher and guardian of the people—to persevere in efforts to make this purpose supreme in all areas of human affairs: in micro (interpersonal) situations of everyday life as well as macro (institutional, public) social and cultural activities. From this general assumption derive the church's more specific concerns. Those reiterated most often and with greatest emphasis in Polish Roman Catholic Church pronouncements over the last half-century—sometimes accompanied by expressions of concern about political repression and limitations of civil liberties, or the exploitation of human labor and undignified living conditions—have been the following: (1) concern for the Christian family, that it perform its duties of permanence, faithfulness, and procreation; (2) concern for the religious education of children and youth, that it be regularly and intensively provided at home and in the schools; (3) concern for the legal rights of the church and its practical opportunities to conduct its religious missions; and (4) concern for the presence of and respect for Christian values in public life and institutions.[4]

Concern with these matters is of course not an idiosyncratic interest of the Polish Church, but is shared by the Roman Catholic Church in general. What has been distinctive, however, is the long-standing conflation of the ideas, institutions, and, so to speak, behavioral displays of religion with nationality in Polish history. Since the seventeenth century, in connection with the Counter Reformation and prolonged wars with Protestant Sweden, and particularly since the loss of state sovereignty in 1795 for nearly two hundred years (including the forty-five years following the communist takeover in 1945), the Polish Roman Catholic Church has provided the means for the emergence and then preservation of a modern national consciousness among the Poles. Participation in Catholic ceremonies and institutions has also served as an important mechanism, symbolic as well as practical, of nationwide social integration.

The communist rule installed at the conclusion of World War II was perceived by the majority of Poles as an alien imposition, and thus a replay of Poland's unhappy history of subjugation to foreign state interests and foreign ideologies. The programmatic atheism of the despised Marxist-Leninist regime, combined with its centralized control of information and of social and cultural activities, could only sustain, or even strengthen, the traditional association of nationality and religion in the consciousness of most Poles.

In this situation, the Polish Catholic Church, through its religious rituals, weekly sermons in the local parishes (the only uncensored means of mass communication), and seasonal episcopal proclamations to the nation, continued to function as the traditional carrier of Polish national identity and defender of national survival. Nationwide sociological studies of Polish historical consciousness conducted in the mid-1960s, and repeated in the same form in the mid-1970s and mid-1980s, found that respondents consistently associated the value concepts of "religion" and "nationality."[5] And equally consistently, national opinion surveys conducted in the same period showed the church, and, after his election in 1978, Pope John Paul II, ranking first as "the best representative of the interests of the Polish nation."[6]

Although modern Polish nationalism absorbed large portions of Catholic identity and rituals in the early phase of its development and maintained them because of particular historical circumstances, the conflation of religion and nationalism also "worked," as it were, in the opposite direction—a phenomenon which, by the way, is seldom considered in Western discussions of the "Polish national question." Features typical of Polish nationalism—such as primary concern with the collective and public realm and neglect of the individual and private realm, and emphasis on group-integrative ritual ceremonies rather than subjective individual responsibilities—have also shaped the character of popular Polish Catholicism.[7]

One important consequence of the entanglement of religion and nationalism in Polish history during the communist era has been a peculiar, enduring "misunderstanding" between the Polish Catholic Church (or its spokesmen, rather) and the majority of the Polish people who listened to church pronouncements. The church, whether it engaged in political negotiations with the ruling communist party or addressed the Catholic masses directly, had consistently followed the principle of *lud polski ludem bożym,* the Polish nation *as* the nation of God, implicitly subsuming the former under the latter. It prioritized Christian fundamentals—that is, its values and prescriptions regarding the conduct of private and public affairs—over all other matters. Meanwhile, the recipients of church messages, or Polish popular opinion, usually prioritized in a reverse manner, centering primarily (although, it should perhaps be emphasized, not exclusively) on the *lud polski,* or the national civil-political and social concerns perceived to be violated by communist usurpers.

The association of the Catholic religion experienced primarily as a public-national creed (rather than as derived from the Christian practical ethos for individual and group conduct), the undifferentiated and deindividualized idea of nationhood, and the popular recognition of the Catholic Church as the legitimate representative and moral defender of Polish national interests against foreign and predatory communism made possible a mass misperception—selective perception is probably a better term—of the nature and meaning of the church's public statements. Focusing primarily on the national collective dimension of church "double-talk," this selective social perception contributed, like collective religious-national rituals, to the sustained integration of Poles around the "imagined community" of a Polish nation. I should note here my disagreement with a thesis propounded by some specialists on contemporary Poland, claiming that the church has considered national/civil-political concerns as irrelevant and merely instrumentally "played" this theme both in negotiations with the Polish Communist Party and in communications to Polish society.[8] Without denying the political-instrumental treatment of this issue by the church, I nevertheless consider most of its higher- and lower-level functionaries to be committed "religious nationalists."

The following are some fairly typical illustrations of this mutual misunderstanding, and specifically of the selective perception of the church's position by Polish popular opinion, drawn from the "settled" as well as "unsettled" periods in Poland's postwar history from 1945 to 1989. The presentation is chronological because it brings out the enduring pattern of misperceptions in the relationship between the speaker and the listeners or readers.

In 1946, when, shortly after it was installed in power by the Soviet Army, the Polish Communist Party organized the first so-called election so as to give legitimacy to its rule, the Polish episcopate in a well-known address to the nation openly criticized "Modern states [that] want absolute power . . . and some of them [that] move as far as to deny any other influence besides their own, any other power."[9] Although no state was mentioned by name, it was obvious which one was meant. As contemporary and historical accounts note, the church's statement was widely interpreted as a voice of strong protest against the trampling of political freedom and civil liberties of the Polish nation and its members. What largely escaped public attention at that time (and, for that matter, in the subsequent four decades of state socialism in Poland, as later citations of that famous denouncement of 1946 indicate) was the perspective from which the episcopate criticized the absolutist tendencies of the communist state. In the proclamation, the passage that immediately followed the quoted statement specified the kind of political order the church had in mind: "Certain states deny any power besides their own . . . even the power of God. . . . [They] wish to remove religion from the influence on public life, aiming at the division between religion and human existence, the Church and the State, trying to enclose the Church within the four walls of the temples."

In 1950, after a period of sharp propaganda attacks and repression by the communist state apparat against members and institutions of the Catholic Church, an agreement was signed between the Polish episcopate and the government. The latter hoped thereby to gain the support of the church in maintaining "peace" in the country, that is, eliminating or at least quieting political resistance to the new regime, and obtaining international recognition of Poland's westward-expanded borders. The communist authorities agreed to permit the resumption of traditional church activities, such as public religious celebrations, voluntary religious classes in public schools, and unobstructed functioning of Catholic associations. In return, the church agreed to "respect the law and state authority," to contribute to the rebuilding of the country destroyed by Nazi occupation, and "not to use religious gatherings for anti-state purposes."[10]

Significantly, however, the communiqué about the signed agreement, issued by the Polish episcopate in a pastoral letter delivered from church pulpits across the country (with its preamble reading, "The Catholic church, united through several centuries with the Nation by bonds of coexistence, religious-moral work, and cultural and historical contributions, will not let anyone cut it off from this Nation and their common fate"), explained in detail concessions to religious practices offered by the communist state, but did not mention the reciprocal guarantees provided by the church.[11] The most likely explanation of this omission seems to be the unwillingness of the episcopate to alienate and thus lose control over large segments of Polish society. The bishops were well aware of anticommunist sentiments and the image of the church as a staunch opponent of the new regime and defender of the Polish nation. They probably also believed that alienating the Catholic masses would in turn weaken the church's negotiating position vis-à-vis the communist rulers.

Soon after the agreement was signed, however, it became obvious that the communist establishment was not about to comply with its declarations, and the church replied with a series of protests and declamations. Some were delivered directly to the party's Central Committee, and some took the form of pastoral letters to Polish Catholics at large. In the latter, transparent metaphors were common: "today, when treacherous paganism penetrates into human souls even by force, we must stand with all our powers of conviction by the Divine Victor over death, hell, and satan." To gain strength for resistance against treacherous paganism (read: the atheist communist state), Polish bishops "consecrated the Nation to the Divine Heart of Jesus," calling on Poles to "feel, each and every one of you, not as an individual anymore, but as if united with the Nation, embracing in your hearts its past, present, and future . . . and offering this entire Nation to Jesus."[12] The church's protests concerning repression of religious practices aimed at breaking the link between *lud polski* and *lud boży,* and its efforts to reassert this equation, were perceived by the populace primarily as an expression of the independence of the "Polish national spirit" and as support for the resilience of the Polish nation against "satan"—that is, the familiar Russian oppressor in the new disguise of Marxist-Leninist internationalism.

The death of Stalin in 1953, followed by Khrushchev's famous speech at the Twentieth Party Congress denouncing communist "errors," brought about a general thaw in the Soviet bloc. In Poland, political relaxation included the improvement of church-state relations, and specifically the reinstitution, and even expansion, of all the religious activities guaranteed in the 1950 agreement. Again, however, relief was short-lived. By the late 1950s, party control had tightened in all areas of sociocultural life, including those of primary concern for the church. Religious classes were removed from public schools, permission for the construction of new churches withdrawn, paper allocations for the Catholic press severely limited, and censorship of the existing press intensified.

As before, the episcopate replied with a series of publicly read or otherwise circulated pastoral letters and religious-national rituals symbolizing collective resistance. From the perspective of the speakers and managers of these events (i.e., church officials), this resistance was directed primarily against what one of the letters referred to as "the encroachment of government onto the altars."[13] But the listeners and participants once again perceived church resistance mainly as an expression of protest against renewed encroachments by the despised regime on the political freedom of the Polish nation. Mixing proclamations of liturgical and political language in church—probably deliberately, to sustain the "religious nationalism" of the Poles—facilitated such selective perception. An episcopal letter in 1963 stated:

On every possible occasion the idea of tolerance and respect for citizens' personal convictions is proclaimed [by official propaganda]. A beautiful idea, but what was behind it? All citizens know about the formal and unequivocal prohibitions and threats of disciplinary action directed against certain state employees [e.g., members of the police and the army] forbidding them to marry in the Church, baptize their children, or attend church and religious ceremonies. . . . These facts are commonly known and very numerous—but who [read: who but the church] will dare talk about them, who will dare point them out as signs of obvious intolerance and discrimination?[14]

Another episcopal letter, addressed to the clergy, but circulated as well among lay Catholics, criticized the same constraints, but phrased the critique in general terms that could be (and were) understood as the church's support for political resistance:

These incidents are clear indications of the duplicity and insincerity characterizing the authorities' attitude toward our society. . . . We consider these lies to society as a great harm done to our Nation. It is not surprising that people in Poland perceive this harm and, in self-defense, begin increasingly to resist. There comes to the fore in our Nation a healthy criticism of the official action of lying.[15]

Three years later, the celebration, with the weary acquiescence of the communist authorities, of the one thousandth anniversary of Poland's Christianization in 966 C.E. provided an unprecedented occasion for a spectacular religious-national festival with all the traditional themes on display. In his widely publicized sermons, Cardinal Wyszyński, recalling the "unbreakable bond" between Polish national history and the Catholic religion, repeatedly criticized the separation of church and state.[16] This issue, today the centerpiece of contestation in Polish political life and the main source of popular annoyance with the Catholic Church, in 1966 passed virtually unnoticed by most Poles, perhaps because it appeared to them utterly irrelevant to the status quo; but it did not appear so to the Communist Party.[17] Most Poles just enjoyed the opportunity to sing collectively the nineteenth-century religious-patriotic hymn, symbol of national resistance to the partitioners, whose most important verse concludes, "Return to us, Lord, our Free Fatherland."

In 1968, in several Polish cities, the police dealt brutally with student demonstrators demanding recognition of national traditions in cultural life and the removal of communist censorship thereof. In the aftermath, the Polish bishops protested, in a famous proclamation read from church pulpits across the country, against "the use of state power to impose upon the citizens [particular] views and beliefs. . . ."[18] Again, what the Polish public heard, or heard primarily—and in this case, I myself was among the listeners (at seventeen, I had just been expelled from Warsaw University for participating in these student demonstra-tions)—was a protest, in the name of the Polish nation, against the po-litically oppressive regime that denied its citizens freedom of opinion. What remained unnoticed, or, as in the previously cited cases, appeared practically irrelevant in the contemporary political context, was that the imposed "views and beliefs" the episcopate protested against were specifically materialist views, and that the "freedom" the Catholic Church demanded was "the true freedom to carry on the mission of Christ."

During the 1970s, the enunciations of the church and their popular perceptions by and large conformed to the established pattern, but as the decade progressed, the balance of political power increasingly shifted from the ruling Communist Party to the church. With this shift, popular nationalist emotions intensified as well. The progressive dete-rioration of the economic situation after the short-lived "bonanza" un-der the leadership of Edward Gierek (installed after workers' strikes in 1970) and fed by large Western credits, increased popular discontent. Weakened by the dependence on Western credits and by popular dis-satisfaction in the economic sphere, and, in matters of political free-dom, subject to the political pressure of international opinion after the Helsinki Conference, the ruling Communist Party looked toward the Catholic Church as a potential partner in maintaining "social stability." The episcopate, for its part, played a double game: it assured the authori-ties, as Cardinal Wyszyński declared in a memorial to the Central Com-mittee in 1971, that it "[did] not want to turn the church into a political opposition, [did] not want to be a political leader, and [was] not mobi-lizing social forces to overturn the regime."[19] At the same time the epis-copate continued to send messages to the Polish people intended to in-vigorate their religious nationalism.

The election of Cardinal Wojtyła as pope in 1978, and his visit to Poland the following year, probably had the most electrifying effect on popular sentiments of national pride and a sense of social unity since the installation of the communist regime. Although the papal sermons dwelled, basically, on the same religious-national themes and expressed the same concerns as those cited in the previous illustrations, the over-whelming feeling among the millions who listened was national exhila-ration and collective defiance. (Again, I was there among the listeners, soon to leave for the United States. Although I never liked, or shared, such frenzied nationalistic sentiments, this one time I felt, not without some embarrassment, swept away by the shared experience in the enormous crowd.)

In the unanimous opinion of commentators on Polish and Soviet-bloc affairs as well as Poles themselves, the visit of Pope John Paul II to Poland in 1979 was the spark that flamed into mass strikes and the birth of the Solidarity movement the following year. This sixteen-month national "liberation movement" expressed, in my view, the quintessence of the popular understanding—an *experience,* lived and felt rather than intellectualized—of the conflation of religion and nationalism. This natural association expressed itself in the ever-present crucifix at Solidarity meetings and the religious ceremonies that frequently accompanied public gatherings; in the incorporation into Solidarity's basic twenty-one demands, formulated as the union's program in the Gdansk shipyard in August 1980, of a demand for complete freedom of religious beliefs and activities in both private and public spheres; and in seeking the mediation of the Polish episcopate in negotiations with the communist authorities.

The Solidarity program demanded freedom of religious convictions and practices, but it did not question the separation of church and state, and certainly did not call for subordinating all areas of life to the requirements of Catholic doctrine. Meanwhile, the public pronouncements of church representatives, as well as information leaked from their talks with communist authorities, clearly indicated that these two purposes, as before, remained the fundamental concern of the church. Church representatives actually voiced their demands more loudly as their position seemed to grow more powerful vis-à-vis the besieged rulers. But despite this discrepancy, in the Solidarity period no significant popular discontent with the church's position surfaced. The most likely reason for this apparent acquiescence was the public's preoccupation with the communist "enemy" still solidly in power, whereas the church was perceived—by tradition, and also because of the usual mixed religious-national messages it sent from the pulpit—as an ally in the political confrontation. (Recently published records of church-state negotiations behind closed doors during 1980–81 revealed—to this reader anyway—uncanny portraits of the two parties involved. By the standards of Western liberal democracy, the communists appear the more tolerant and pluralistic of the two sides!)[20]

During the "Jaruzelski war," as the period following imposition of martial law in December 1981 and the outlawing of Solidarity has commonly been called by Poles, popular attitudes toward the Catholic Church came to approximate the "classical" pattern found in nineteenth-century Polish history textbooks. Churches were, again, the natural place of public gatherings to express solidarity with those assembled, imprisoned Solidarity activists, and the underground opposition; religious ceremonies were occasions for singing old songs of national resistance together and praying for a "free Fatherland." Pope John Paul II's two visits to Poland, in 1983 and 1987, allowed by the authorities in the hope of "national reconciliation," had the opposite effect, further deepening the perceived gap between *us* (Polish society) and *them* (the communist rulers).

Well aware of this popular sentiment, the communist authorities sought, as on many earlier occasions, collaboration with the Polish episcopate for "normalization" and "rebuilding social confidence." As before, church officials played a double game, aiming to gain as many political concessions as possible on matters of major concern to them by declaring their support for social peace, and, on the other hand, seeking within the limits of political prudence to satisfy the Polish "national aspirations" entrusted, as it were, to church hands. (It should be noted, however, that political divisions within the church, probably always present but hidden from the public, became visible, or audible, during the "Jaruzelski war": some bishops as well as a considerable number of younger clergy were evidently more radical and outspoken in their criticism of the regime than was the official line of the episcopate.)

And so, alongside memoranda to the authorities and pastoral letters to the Catholic public protesting "what in popular perception appears as the government's war on the church and religious practices after the disbanding of 'Solidarity,'"[21] clergy expressed the spirit of national resistance and sustained it by so doing. Here is an excerpt from "radical" Bishop Gulbinowicz's sermon delivered in 1982 to women pilgrims to the sacred icon of Saint Mary of Częstochowa at the Jasna Gora monastery, and circulated around the country in *samizdat* copies reproduced by the underground opposition. He thundered against the repression of Solidarity members by the Communist Party apparat, using thinly veiled metaphors and invoking the familiar code-image of the oppressed nation:

The tears of those to whom harm has been done burden the harm-doers more than the greatest violation. . . . No one will wash the fraternal blood off the hands of the murderer. To put chains on a guiltless brother is a crime that will cry out for vengeance to the heavens. [Let us then] offer today to St. Mary of Czestochowa all that is dearest to Poles, and bring before her a supplication that all injustice, falsity, and wrong-doing end on our Polish land.[22]

In a more typical (i.e., less fiery) sermon during a Sunday mass in a Gniezno parish in 1983, a local priest intoned prayers, "for the day [December 13, 1981] when the authorities broke contact with the nation" and "for those imprisoned for their convictions," intended to sustain collective endurance and hope.[23]

Party-controlled media and government representatives to the Joint Commission, which continued to meet regularly throughout the 1980s, repeatedly attacked the church for letting religious ceremonies be used for political demonstrations, and generally for having assumed, from the time the communists came to power, "a role of the defender of national interests and the spokesman for the discontented working masses."[24] To these charges the Polish episcopate replied in Joint Commission meetings that the church and public religious rituals "[had] always, for years, been associated with national ceremonies"; that defending the imprisoned and the politically persecuted and demanding the lifting of "the state of war" in Poland were the church's evangelical duty; and that bishops also were attempting "to appease the society," though the government did not seem to notice.[25] Indeed, the episcopate and especially the new Polish primate, Cardinal Józef Glemp, did make such attempts. For these efforts church officials, specifically its top hierarchy, were even accused of "collaboration" by some members of the Solidarity underground and by émigré Poles in the West.

Any criticisms of the Catholic Church's position that *were* expressed by the public during this period, however, claimed that the church's demands were not strong *enough* in the political sphere, especially regarding group and individual civil liberties violated by the "Jaruzelski war." Preoccupied with confronting the communist oppressor, the Polish people (except for the church's communist partners in Joint Commission negotiations) did not seem to notice the episcopate's persistent calls to purge Polish culture of "immoral contents" and social life of "sins," or the visiting pope's linking demands for individual and collective rights and freedom with condemnation of the separation of church and state, and of atheism as "the evil of democracy and moral pruri-ence" [*sic*].[26]

In Free Poland: 1989 to the Present

When it became evident at the beginning of 1989 that "normalization from above" was not going to bring the desired effects, and Communist Party leaders decided to reopen talks with Solidarity, it was of course only natural that the Polish Catholic Church, consistently ranking in public opinion polls as "the best representative of the interests of the Polish nation" (on a par with Pope John Paul II), was invited as a "mod-erator and guarantor of the talks, and then of the agreement." Nor was it a surprise when the first postcommunist, Solidarity-based gov-ernment formed in September 1989 wholeheartedly supported the church.[27] National opinion polls conducted shortly after the collapse of the old regime showed over 90 percent of the respondents, virtually re-gardless of socioeconomic status, age, and urban or rural place of resi-dence, declaring support for the Catholic Church and appreciation for its contributions to Poland's "national liberation."

Almost immediately after the establishment of a new democratic government, high ranking and rank-and-file church officials, assisted vigorously by members of Christian-national political parties and me-dia that had sprung up after the fall of the communist regime, initiated a systematic campaign for the subjection of the public and private life of Poles to the fundamental principle *lud polski ludem bożym*. They made the traditional claims that Polish national existence, even sur-vival, depended on this subordination. The primary concerns of the church have remained the same as in the communist period: guarantees of unimpeded procreation in the family, provision of religious educa-tion in schools, and, more generally, respect for Christian values in pub-lic life. But since the newly established democratic political order has not only lifted all previous constraints on church activities but actually welcomed the church's participation in public affairs, the political power of the church—that is, its ability to turn its desiderata into prac-tice prescribed by the law—has very significantly increased. Besides national-religious parties and their press, church political intervention could count at the beginning of the postcommunist era, and can still count at present, on the support, or at least silent acquiescence, of a majority of the largest peasant party, of a considerable number of Catholic liberal democrats tied to the church by loyalty resulting from long-standing relations or by various interests, and, out of conformism and fear of losing their positions, of several politicians, journalists, and intellectuals who were members of the Communist Party *nomenklatura*.

For example, regarding religious education in public schools—one of the Catholic Church's major concerns today as in the past—the episcopate not only demanded (in 1990) and obtained (in 1992) legal provisions in this regard, but it also felt morally authorized to insult and scold in public those who dared to contest these provisions. Polish school students who organized a demonstration in protest of regulations introducing prayers before and after classes and requiring parents to submit written declarations about their children's participation or lack thereof in religious classes were called by the press spokesman of the episcopate "the sons and daughters of Russian officers." More recently, Cardinal Glemp, annoyed by Professor Tadeusz Zieliński, the Chief Arbiter of Civil Rights who considers these provisions unconstitutional and who turned the matter over to the Constitutional Tribunal, in a nationally televised appearance compared the Tribunal's proceedings to a circus. Catholic bishops then organized a protest campaign of letter-writing. In April 1993 the Tribunal pronounced half of these laws unconstitutional, but the decision will be appealed. Meanwhile, according to Polish press reports, high ranking church representatives, in collaboration with members of ultra-Catholic Christian-national parties who hold political offices in the Ministry of National Education, are working on a project of "sexual education according to Christian teachings" to be introduced in the public schools.[28] Meanwhile, in local communities, priests have been warning parents of children who do not attend religious instruction that such behavior excludes their family from the ranks of good Christians and, by implication, of good Poles.[29]

The church's interventions have been even more forceful, and its messages more dramatic, regarding the notorious issue of abortion. During nearly three years of heated parliamentary and media debate, church officials and their political allies, initiators of the antiabortion project, repeatedly used pressure to force antiabortion legislation. Calling abortion "murder of unborn life" and its prevention the sine qua non of the preservation of the Polish nation, the Bishops' Conference sent an open memorandum to the Parliament encouraging its members' "perseverance and courage in seeking legal measures to secure the life of each conceived child." That similar encouragements apparently worked well on some congressmen and senators is demonstrated by a pilgrimage of a group of them to the Jasna Gora monastery, where they pledged to "fight in defense of every child and every cradle as courageously as our fathers fought for the survival and freedom of the [Polish] nation."[30] A law delegalizing abortion—except in cases of incest or rape, danger to the mother's life, or a serious impairment of the fetus—was passed in 1993 without the national referendum on the issue preferred by the majority of the Polish public. Interviewed on national television after the Parliament's vote was announced, the associate general secretary of the Polish Bishops' Conference stated that the church was "unhappy with the law as passed because the principle 'Thou shalt not kill' does not allow any exceptions,"[31] implying an intention to continue efforts toward full prohibition. (Even before this legislation, by the way, in 1991 the episcopate and its political allies by vote or by silence had already accomplished the imposition of legal constraints on—not yet prohibition of—divorces, also with reference to the principle of *lud polski ludem bożym.*)

A similar campaign regarding "legalizing" conformity to Christian values has been conducted in the Polish mass media, and generally in public life and institutions—another of the traditional desiderata of the Polish Catholic Church. In their public statements, church officials repeatedly made it clear that, as Cardinal Glemp declared in 1992 in his televised Christmas greetings to the nation, "God's law is above human law" (and, of course, all other human inventions and interests), and that, as a priest invited to take part in a recent discussion on Polish television on the principles of the liberal democratic system pointed out, the fundamental value of Christianity is not tolerance and pluralism, but the salvation of Man.[32] As in the case of abortion and religious instruction in schools, church officials have exerted pressure on parliamentary clubs and their individual members. Cardinal Glemp paid a personal visit to the Parliament to lobby, and the Conference of Polish Bishops issued a communiqué refusing the Parliament "the moral right to vote against a law granting respect for Christian values in public life."[33] These political demarches of the church have been accompanied

by continuous public protests and proclamations concerning the supposedly immoral form and content of the Polish press, television, and
radio programs (jointly referred to by the episcopate's secretary of the
media and communications as "a great garbage dump"), and cultural
life in general.[34]

A law requiring respect for Christian values in Poland's public life
was indeed passed early in 1993, and subsequently top church representatives focused on pressuring "uncertain" members of the special commission in the Parliament working on a project of concord between
the Roman Catholic Church and the Republic of Poland. Presented to
the Parliament at large later that year, the project in fact conformed
to the episcopate's wishes: "in a long preamble and in twenty-nine articles [it] declared liberties and privileges of the church, without giving
the civil state any reciprocal rights."[35]

Within a year after the collapse of communism, however, the concord between Polish society and the Roman Catholic Church was replaced by a growing public annoyance. Protests have come from law-
yers concerned about the church's cavalier treatment and occasional
open disregard of the law; from the intelligentsia (including journalists,
actors, and scientists, and former dissidents who a few years earlier had
found support in the church for their anticommunist activities and
who, though nonbelievers, considered the Catholic Church their ally
and protector); from liberal-minded Catholics embarrassed by the
church's arrogance and triumphalism; from women who found their
personal freedom violated, including the small Polish feminist movement which was born during the abortion campaign, partly in defiance
of public prayers by the priests for the "return into God's fold of these
confused and erring women"; and finally from rank-and-file citizens
who write to the newspapers, talk radio and television stations, or otherwise let their opinions be heard. All these voices, in group statements
or individually, express discontent with the church's expansionism and
concern about what Adam Michnik has recently called a danger of in-
tegrism—that is, a collusion of church and state not much different in
its effects from the communist party-state. Reacting to such suggestions,
and to what it perceives as a frontal attack on the Catholic Church and
religion in the national media, the Polish episcopate has recently compared the "destructive consequences" of this aggression to the calami-

ties brought about by nazism and communism.[36] Church officials seem to strike out against present-day liberal politicians and journalists with much sharper language than they used to criticize the communist regime. One reason for this disproportionate ire may be that the bishops perceive the liberal democratic model of society to be a more serious competitor for the minds and hearts of Poles than "real socialism" ever was.

National opinion surveys, too, indicate a considerable diminution in the support for the church on the part of Polish society at large. Between 1989 and 1992, within two and a half years, such support dropped by almost half, from over 90 percent to slightly over 50 percent. Between 1991 and 1992, we may add, the proportion of children attending religious instruction in schools dropped from more than 90 percent to about 80 percent. More recent opinion polls show 75 percent of the Polish population in general, and about 65 percent of self-declared practicing Catholics, as seeing the church as "too involved in public matters"; over 80 percent want separation of church and state, and only about 10 percent think that the episcopate should be consulted about nominations to high level state positions. In more concrete matters, such as divorce, abortion, the use of contraceptives—all of which are unequivocally condemned by the church—a majority (counting "no opinions") of the respondents among self-declared Catholics (over 80 percent of the Polish population), gave a negative answer to a question whether "the church has the right to demand subordination" in each of these three matters.[37] Analysis conducted by the National Opinion Research Center of the returns in the 1993 parliamentary election that brought postcommunist officials to power confirmed these popular sentiments. The Alliance of the Democratic Left (SDL), openly opposed to the enforced Christianization of Polish life and campaigning under the slogan of removing the legislation of "Christian values" in the public sphere, was the most frequent choice of the voters who reported attending religious ceremonies (a large group of conventional Catholics), and a close third choice of those who declared themselves as regular, weekly practitioners. At the other end of the political spectrum—and another measure of popular rejection of the church's vision of Poland—the two Christian-national parties that are the church's closest allies each received less than 5 percent of all votes; as expected, they were the most frequent choice of the small minority of Polish Catholics who reported attending church "several times a week." [38]

The question, then, is what has happened and why? Why is it that Polish public opinion, which a few years ago expected, and appreciated, the church's involvement in public matters, is now overwhelmingly against it? Why are public statements of the representatives of the Polish episcopate deploring "the ongoing erosion of the Nation in our Fatherland" and the atheistic antivalues that "rob the Polish Nation of its Spirit, its Idea, its [inner] Power" [39] perceived today by a large, and increasing, part of Polish society as "meddling in" and "obstructing" the democratic process? As we have seen, similar, sometimes even identically worded, church pronouncements ten, twenty, or thirty years ago were then virtually unanimously received as expressions of courageous opposition to communist oppression and a defense of national freedom and civil liberties.

The arrogance and triumphalism with which many of the top- and lower-level church officials use, and abuse, their recently acquired political power surely contribute to the general change of attitude. And so does the perceived, and resented, material enrichment of the Polish clergy in the "new era." In a recent opinion poll nearly 70 percent of respondents evaluated the material situation of the priests as "very good" or "good," whereas about the same proportion of the Polish population consider their own standard of living as "bad" or "very bad." [40] The church's campaign to regain its extensive property confiscated by the communists in 1945, much of which is now occupied by schools, hospitals, and other public utilities, is also widely resented and well publicized by the media. Poles particularly resent the church's perceived insufficient practical care and assistance for the quickly growing numbers of truly needy.

Behind all these contributing factors, however, I believe there lies a more general "framing cause" of this popular change of mind regarding the church's position. Namely, after the collapse of the communist regime, which was perceived by most Poles as an alien graft onto the national body, and as Poland regained state sovereignty under a government recognized as legitimate by practically all Poles, a shift occurred in the primary civic-political concerns of the majority of the Polish population—a shift from the idea, and the accompanying emotions, of the *nation* to that of the *society*. Put differently, while the primary interest in the undifferentiated and deindividualized national collectivity—Benedict Anderson's "imagined community"[41]—has considerably weakened, the recognition of Poland as a differentiated, plural society composed of a multitude of groups continues to increase.

Even though the Polish episcopate included concepts of legal order and justice, and group and individual freedoms, in its 1993 memorandum on Christian values—apparently unaware of, or unconcerned with, the discrepancy between those ideas and its own autocratic practices[42]—the traditional "national language" has remained much more common in church proclamations. The church not only repeats the previously mentioned warnings of dangers to national survival, but issues dramatic appeals, as in a recent nationally transmitted sermon of one of the Polish bishops, not to fear "the word Nation."[43]

In the context of the sovereign, independent state, however, "nation" denotes an idea whose emotional force is incomparably weaker than in the times of foreign domination and political oppression. A 1992 national opinion survey revealed that the public's evaluation of the role of the Catholic Church is most positive for periods when Poland's existence was threatened or endangered.[44] The nation is also a concept whose generalizing character dims rather than clarifies social complexities inside the modern nation-state. From the perspective of a new political situation, then, the traditional "dedifferentiating" discourse of the church, appealing to a national-Catholic unity of society and using this value concept to justify the subordination of group and individual interests—however meaningful and attractive in times of national trials—is perceived today as threatening the transformation of Poland into a democratic society. Although the September 1993 parliamentary election showed that a significant proportion of Poles are against a Jeffrey Sachs style of economic Westernization of the country (according to national opinion surveys conducted in the last two years, between 75 and 80 percent of the adult Polish population support inclusive welfare-state provisions), democracy as a political system has the support of the solid majority of Poles.

The general weakening of the psychological and social-integrative relevance of "the word Nation" in the perceptions of Poles, as a consequence of the changed political circumstances, diminished in turn the significance of what has traditionally been the characteristic feature of popular Polish Catholicism: its collective-ceremonial emphasis and specifically the fusing therein of religious and national themes in a symbolic representation of Poland as Saint Mary-Mater-Dolorosa. In times of national dependence and oppression this served the purpose of upholding the national "imagined community" through the performance of symbolic rituals and the encompassing social bonding that they generated. In independent Poland today, these religious-national ceremonies, instead of uplifting the spirit, seem increasingly to annoy the mind—especially, as survey reports indicate, of the young generation, who barely remember their country "in chains."

The Catholic Church imposes the practical requirements of Christian conduct wrapped in national imagery. In the changed political situation, when these national messages and invocations do not resonate for large numbers of Poles, the normative prescriptions for everyday life derived from Catholic doctrine stand out in high relief. When Poles confront these naked requirements for a concrete Christian ethos, I argue, the negative perceptions of the church as "meddling" and encroaching upon people's lives are enhanced. The accumulated effects of four and a half decades of secularization under Communist Party rule, which had stayed largely hidden during that period under the umbrella of "national religion," suddenly loom very large.

Conclusion

After this significant rearrangement of the tripartite relations between the Catholic Church, the state, and Polish society since the fall of communism in 1989, how will they develop in the future? I see several possible scenarios.

To look first at the current political situation: a postcommunist-peasant coalition is at the country's helm, and the church continues its aggressive posture on Christian values in public and private spheres, phrasing its philippics in the nationalist discourse. If the Alliance of the Democratic Left manages, as promised, to constrain the church's encroachments on the political process and remove or modify the "Christianizing" laws implemented during 1990–93 while retaining complete freedom of belief and religious practice and other civil liberties, *and* if it is possible to avoid a major economic downturn, the following developments seem likely. The intelligentsia in the media and arts, in professions, and in the political forum will continue to oppose the church's verbal attacks and renewed interference when the opportunity arises and in the larger Polish population there will be a progressive dissociation of believers from the Catholic Church, or, put differently, an increasing privatization of religion. Indicative of the latter development have been the findings of recent national opinion surveys showing a surprisingly high 60 percent among self-declared Catholics responding affirmatively to a proposition that "a good Catholic does not have to be a practicing [church attending] person" (an additional 10 percent were not certain). This proportion was the highest—over 70 percent—in large cities and among young people; but even in the countryside, the traditional bastion of church-going and ceremonial Catholicism, it was a sizable 48 percent.[45]

Two important caveats should be noted. First, it is not at all certain whether the Alliance of the Democratic Left, which although a winner, received only a minority of votes, and, more important, whose anxiety not to be associated with the dethroned Communist Party may turn out to have a paralyzing effect, will be able to carry through with its legislative goal of eliminating the church's involvement in political affairs. Although its main coalition partner, the peasant party (PSL), has declared its support for the separation of church and state and for civil liberties, a large proportion of its members are traditional Catholics. Since the Catholic Church has, of course, significant vested interests in maintaining and expanding its own position and the place of "Christian values" in Polish affairs, it was not surprising that immediately after the election results were announced, the episcopate began courting peasant leaders during secret talks; Andrzej Micewski, the leading PSL intellectual with established top-level church connections, published a long essay on the urgent need for the "Christian left" in Poland.[46] Should this wooing turn out to be effective enough to make impossible the elimination or at least restraint of the church's encroachments on Poland's legislative and administrative authorities, antichurch attitudes and the privatization of religion among Poles are likely to spread at a considerably faster rate than in the first case. The second caveat concerns the Polish economy. It is highly probable that, should the coalition decide to deliver on campaign promises to slow down Poland's economic transformation and reverse some of its harshest effects, the economic situation will dramatically deteriorate. Then the government is likely to fall and a different political configuration will emerge.

In another scenario, the ruling postcommunists, specifically the old-school wing of the Alliance, would manage not only to remove the Catholic Church from politics and get rid of all the legislation won by the episcopate since 1990, but also to constrain religious and other civil liberties. Then large segments of Polish society would be likely to revert to the old pattern of "national religion," and their perceptions of the Catholic Church would improve considerably. This popular support, in turn, especially in the context of the deteriorated economy, would empower the church as the *éminence grise* in Polish politics, and in a replay of history would force postcommunists to seek church collaboration in maintaining social stability.

Yet another scenario would require the Polish Catholic Church, especially its leadership, to change—a trifle!—its fundamental ideological (theological) position, by giving up its present "Thomist" orientation, which assumes that freedom of individuals and the groups they form is limited to the choice of means only, with the goal set in advance and permanently; replacing it would be in "Augustinian" perspective whereby the concept of human freedom, understood as the capacity, and effort, to absorb ideas and make them one's "own," includes the choice of the goal itself.[47] Should such an unlikely transformation take place, the church would be better equipped to learn and practice the rules of political democracy, and its peaceful and effective cooperation with a democratic government would be possible. In such a scenario, the position of the church in popular perceptions could improve significantly, and a progressive "denationalization" of Polish Catholicism would probably take place without many Poles abandoning the association with the church (more precisely: with the numbers dissociating themselves smaller than in the first case considered above). Such a reconfiguration would be more likely, and "denationalization" of Polish Catholicism more thorough, if the transformation "from above" would be accompanied "from below" by the emergence on the Polish political scene of a Catholic moderate left in the tradition of West European Christian social democracies, elaborating, perhaps, some ideas from the recent papal encyclical *Centesimus Annus*.[48]

It may also happen that amid a dramatic economic downturn resulting from attempts to reinstate a welfare state in Poland with "empty" money, the postcommunist-peasant coalition government will fall, and a new election will install a right-wing national-Christian configuration (at present in extraparliamentary opposition). Then the Catholic Church, with its strongly Thomist orientation, would be likely to regain all or part—depending on the parliamentary strength of the ruling coalition—of its earlier legislative victories, and to continue its aggressive public campaign for similar ordinances. Such a development would be likely to evoke public protests from various professional milieux, accelerate the "privatization" of religion among Poles I described earlier, and possibly bring about the formation of a new, center-to-left political party programmatically combating church public encroachments; at present only a few small and dispersed civic associations organized for this purpose exist. At the same time, however—assuming that the democratic political order were maintained—the legislators, pressed by the church, would also have to take into consideration popular sentiments against the enforced Christianization of Polish life, or soon be removed from office.

Finally, there is a scenario in which President Lech Wałęsa dissolves the quarreling parliament, suspends the inept government, and moves himself to the helm in order to "restore order." Wałęsa is a deeply, even ostentatiously, believing and practicing Catholic, and a devout Polish patriot, but at the same time he is a shrewd and pragmatic politician with a distinctly populist bent. Should Wałęsa impose presidential rule, unlike many Polish commentators I would not expect an immediate legislation of wholesale Christianization of Polish life in the name of the traditional "national religion," but rather a zigzag policy, leaning to the church but also constraining its political ambitions and courting the Polish public. The latter, I believe, would be likely to follow the path of privatizing their religiosity, and to maintain their disapproval of the church's political involvement. They might even intensify this resentment if the president and the episcopate were to be perceived as joint rulers.

NOTES

1. Affairs in Eastern Europe are so unsettled still that a chronological note is in order. This paper was written in the spring of 1993, and updated in the

wake of the electoral victory in Poland in September of the same year of the postcommunist-peasant coalition.

2. As the basic sources for the church's position I used *Listy Pasterskie Prymasa Polski, 1946–1974* (Pastoral Letters of the Polish Primate, 1946–1974) (Paris: Éditions du Dialogue, 1975); Stefan Wyszyński, *Kościół w Służbie Narodu.* (Poznań: Pallotinum, 1981); *Listy Pasterskie Episkopatu Polski, 1945–1974* (Pastoral Letters of the Polish Episcopate, 1945–1974) (Paris: Éditions du Dialogue, 1975); *Tajne Dokumenty: Państwo-Kościół, 1980–1990* (Confidential Documents: State-Church, 1980–1990) (London and Warsaw: Aneks, 1993). I also inspected a sample of seasonal and other occasional statements of higher- and lower-level Polish clergy and Catholic laypersons in the leading Catholic press: *Tygodnik Powszechny, Znak,* and *Więź,* 1964 to the present; a sample of various Catholic newspapers established after 1989 (to the present). Readings in postwar church history included Wincenty Chrypiński, *Kościół a Radz i Społeczeństwo w Powojennej Polsce* (London: Odnowa, 1989); Witold Zdaniewicz, *Kościół Katolicki w Polsce, 1945–1982* (Poznań: Pallotinum, 1983); Adam Michnik, *Kościół, Lewica, Dialog* (London: Overseas Publications Interchange, 1980); Jerzy Turowicz, *Kościół Nie Jest Łódźią Podwodną* (Kraków: Znak, 1990); Dominik Morawski, *Kościół w Polsce* (Monachium: Studium Polskiej Myśli Demokratycznej, 1983); Peter Raina, *Kościół Polsce, 1981–1984* (London: Katolicki Ośrodek Wydawniczy "Veritas" 1985); Andrzej Micewski, *Kościół Wobec "Solidarności" i Stanu Wojennego* (Paris: Éditions du Dialogue, 1987). I also inspected data regarding church membership and participation contained in the special volume prepared by the Central Statistical Bureau, *Kościół Katolicki w Polsce, 1918–1990* (Warsaw: Główny Urząd Statystyczny, 1991); church and religion-related results of public opinion surveys published, for the pre-1989 period, in the reports of *OBOP* (National Center for Research on Public Opinion) and analyzed in *Studia Socjologiczne* (occasionally also in a weekly *Polityka*), and, after 1989, in the reports of various opinion poll centers as well as (seasonally), in *Demoskop;* non-Catholic press titles: *Polityka, Wprost,* and *Gazeta Wyborcza,* all of which I also searched for articles devoted to problems of relations between the Polish Catholic Church, politics and society. I also read the available recent, unpublished manuscripts of Polish sociologists dealing with these matters and used pertinent data from other sources quoted therein.

3. *Listy Pasterskie Prymasa Polski,* 1:14.

4. A reference to similar fundamental concerns of the Polish Catholic Church during the 1920s and 1930s can be found in *Listy Pasterskie Episkopatu,* p. 117.

5. Barbara Szacka and Anna Sawisz, *Czas Przeszły i Pamięć Społeczna* (The Past and Social Memory) (Warsaw: Instytut Socjologii Uniwersytetu Warszawskiego, 1990), pp. 52–53 and passim.

6. Ewa Morawska, "Civil Religion v. State Power in Poland," in Thomas Robbins, and Roland Robertson, eds., *Church-State Relations: Tensions and Transitions* (New Brunswick, N.J.: Transaction Books, 1987), p. 228.

7. On the Polish variety of "Christianity," primarily ceremonial and group oriented (a textbook case, it seems, of Durkheim's theory of the social functions

of religion), formed during the nineteenth century, see Ewa Jabłońska-Deptuła, "Religijność i patriotyzm doby powstań" (Religiosity and Patriotism in the Era of National Uprisings); Daniel Olszewski, "Polska religijność na przełomie XIX i XX wieku" (Polish Religiosity at the Turn of the 19th and 20th Centuries); and Bohdan Cywiński, "Uniwersalizm i swojskość w życiu ideowym Polski lat 1880–1914" (Universalism and Particularism in Polish Thought, 1880–1914)—all in Jerzy Kłoczowski, ed., *Uniwersalizm i Swoistość Kultury Polskiej* (Universalism and Particularism of Polish Culture) (Lublin: Redakcja Wydawnictw KUL, 1990), vol. 2, pp. (respectively 85–135, 221–45, 183–201.

8. For a typical illustration of such an argument, see Andrzej Korbonski and Luba Fajfer Wong, "Poland: Church and Solidarity: Myth and Reality," a paper presented at the Annual Meeting of the American Association for the Advancement of Slavic Studies, New York, November 1–4, 1984.

9. *Listy Pasterskie Episkopatu*, p. 43.

10. *Tajne Dokumenty Państwo-Kościół*, pp. ii–iii; *Listy Pasterskie Episkopatu*, pp. 91–92.

11. *Listy Pasterskie Episkopatu*, pp. 96–97. The guarantees made by the church in this agreement were specified, however, in the episcopate's letter to the clergy, who were instructed to follow them carefully (pp. 106–7).

12. Ibid., pp. 108–11.

13. *Tajne Dokumenty Państwo-Kościół*, p. iv.

14. *Listy Pasterskie Episkopatu*, p. 301.

15. Ibid., pp. 303–4.

16. *Listy Pasterskie Prymasa Polski*, pp. 504–13, 523–28.

17. A confidential report on the context and possible consequences of Wyszyński's rejection of the separation of church and state was prepared by the party's Central Committee's Commission on Church and the Clergy (*Tajne Dokumenty Państwo-Kościół*, p. vi).

18. *Listy Pasterskie Episkopatu*, p. 522.

19. Cited from *Tajne Dokumenty Państwo-Kościół*, p. vii.

20. *Tajne Dokumenty Państwo-Kościół*. I was also admittedly somewhat startled reading exchanges such as this one from a meeting in March 1981: "You have tendencies to rule over people," a government member said to church representatives; "You also," replied one of the latter. "Let's then 'rule' together," proposed the vice-secretary of the episcopate Council; "That's better," replied a member of the State Council (p. 30).

21. Ibid., pp. 353–59.

22. Ibid., p. 187n.

23. Ibid., p. 340.

24. Ibid., pp. 183–84, 240–41, 339–43.

25. Ibid., pp. 183–84.

26. Ibid., pp. 272–99, 339–43, 503–9; "Film o Chrystusie: Episkopat zwraca się z uprzejma prośba." *Polityka*, May 1, 1993, p. 9.

27. Grabowska, "The Church in Poland at a Turning Point" (unpublished manuscript), p. 12.

28. "Kronika Niepojętej Agresji," *Neutrum*, February 20, 1993, pp. 2–4;

"Rzecznik o Prymasie," *Gazeta Wyborcza*, April 16, 1993, pp. 1–2; and "Interweniuje w sprawach cesarskich, a nie boskich. Rozmowa z rzecznikiem praw obywatelskich, prof. Tadeuszem Zielińskim," *Gazets Wybotcza*, April 20, 1993, p. 2; *Donosy*, April 21, 1993, p. 3; "Czy teologia jest dobrana wszystko," *Polityka*, September 25, 1993, p. 13.

29. This and similar incidents have been reported in Polish press, such as in *Polityka*, December 5, 1992, p. 3, and May 1, 1993, pp. 1–4; and *Gazeta Wyborcza*, January 14, 1993, p. 11. Catholic education and rituals have also been introduced in the Polish Army, whose soldiers and officers the episcopate wishes to see, in the words of the field bishop, "engaged in devout prayer, and singing religious hymns." Observance of these practices is apparently also expected from soldiers who are not Catholic; for example, a few Protestant musicians in the Concert Orchestra of the Polish Army have recently been punished for refusing to play a Marian hymn (as reported in *Polityka*, May 1, 1993, p. 7, and February 6, 1993, p. 5).

30. *Słowo Biskupow*, November 27, 1992; "Kronika Niepojętej Agresji," p. 3.

31. As reported in the *New York Times*, March 11, 1993, p. A3.

32. "Kronika Niepojętej Agresji," p. 3; "Groźba Tolerancjonizmu," *Neutrum*, November 9, 1992, p. 10—a transcript of a discussion in the television program "Lewiatan" on September 12, 1992.

33. As reported by Roman Graczyk, "Jak bronić neutralności państwa wobec kościoła?" *Gazeta Wyborcza*, December 19–20, 1992, p. 10.

34. As reported by Stanisław Podemski in "Perly na smietniku," *Polityka*, July 31, 1993, p. 23.

35. As reported in *Donosy*, July 29, 1993, p. 2.

36. After *Gazeta Wyborcza*, "Biskupi polscy o wartościach," May 4, 1993, pp. 12–13. The most vicious of the church-run media is probably "Radio Maryja" (Radio Saint Mary) and its leading figure, Father Tadeusz, who regularly thunders against the "anti-Christian minority who controls the country."

37. Data compiled from Irena Borowik, "Religion in Post-Communist Countries," a paper presented at the Annual Convention of the Society for the Scientific Study of Religion, Washington, D.C., November 6–8, 1992, pp. 8–9, 12–14, Appendix; Halina Grzymala-Moszczynska, "Factors Affecting Unconditional Acceptance of the Institution of the Church in Poland," unpublished manuscript, 1993, pp. 1–9; Krzysztof Wolicki, "Przed Egzaminem Dojrzałaści," *Kultura*, Paris, March 1993, p. 71; *Gazeta Wyborcza*, January 18, 1993, p. 7; *Polityka*, December 5, 1992, p. 5, and March 27, 1993, p. 13.

38. As reported in the national opinion survey (N=1,135) conducted September 24–29, 1993 (Centrum Badania Opinii Spolecznej, Warsaw, Zespół Realizacji Badan).

39. Excerpts from a sermon delivered by Field Bishop Slawoj Glodz during Mass celebrated May 3, 1993, transmitted on national radio, as reported in *Polityka*, May 15, 1993, p. 2; and *Donosy*, May 5, 1993, p. 4.

40. As reported in *Polityka*, "Polski Katolicyzm Anno Domini 1992," part 2, December 12, 1992, p. 14.

41. *Benedict Anderson, Imagined Communities: Reflections on the Origin and Spread of Nationalism* (London and New York: Verso, 1991).

42. These values have also been specified in the Memorandum on Christian Values issued by the Polish episcopate during public debate on the project. Contrasting such declarations with the church's authoritarian practices, some commentators have emphasized the ambivalence, or even contradiction, in church views on these matters (see, for example, in *Gazeta Wyborcza*, May 10, 1993, Roman Graczyk's "Przymys czy wojny wybór," p. 2, and Zbigniew Mikolejko's "Słowo i Kamień," p. 6).

43. As reported in *Gazeta Wyborcza*, May 6, 1993, p. 8.

44. Respondents evaluated most highly the role of the Polish Catholic Church during the Nazi occupation, and, more recently, during the "Jaruzelski war"; the church received the lowest scores for the interwar period, and for the present-day postcommunist era—as reported in *Gazeta Wyborcza*, January 18, 1993, n.p.

45. Data cited after "Polski Katolicyzm Anno Domini 1992," parts 1 and 2, *Polityka*, December 5, 1992, p. 14, and December 12, 1992, pp. 14–15. Generally, the survey related "two Polands": one that is more traditionally Catholic (with lower than the national average percentages of affirmative answers to the question) in the eastern and southern parts of the country, and one that is more secular (with higher than the average proportions of affirmative answers) in the western and northern regions.

46. See Krzysztof Teodor Toeplitz, "Wszystko płynie," *Polityka*, October 9, 1993, p. 28; Andrzej Micewski, "Trwałe wartości," *Polityka*, October 2, 1993, p. 3.

47. I found this apt distinction in an essay signed by A. W. and entitled "Czy Kościół się rozbroi?" (Will the Church Disarm?), in *Neutrum*, May 20, 1993, pp. 5–6. The author claims that there exist among the Polish clergy small milieux in which the Augustinian orientation predominates (for example, in part at least, the Akademia Teologii Katolickiej in Warsaw).

48. In the above-mentioned article by Micewski on the Christian Left there are several ideas that could also serve as a basis for the formation of such a popular party (Micewski, "Trawałe wartości").

II
Germany:
New Core or
Old Problem?

United Germany as the Renewed Center in Europe: Continuity and Change in the German Question

Willfried Spohn

The collapse of communism has transformed the political and social order in Eastern Europe and fundamentally changed the physiognomy of the European continent as well.[1] The disintegration of Soviet hegemony over Eastern Europe has renewed, albeit in novel form, the traditional unevenness and dependence between Western and Eastern Europe characteristic of the modern era before the fascist-Stalinist division of Europe. At the same time, the revolution in Europe has enabled the unification of Germany, reconstructing the traditional core position in the middle of Europe it had lost in the postwar European order. Thus the postcommunist revolution has revived the basic structure of the German question: the problem of how the German national state with the largest population, the strongest economy, the greatest political impact, and potentially the strongest military power in Europe may be brought into lasting equilibrium within the architecture of Europe as a whole.[2]

This has understandably stirred up conflicting emotions, attitudes, and views. What role will unified Germany now play in the emerging European order? Will Germany have a benign influence on Europe in contributing to European integration and East European modernization? This is the hope of optimists, including most Western and German politicians, based on their positive experiences with postwar Germany. Or will Germany again pursue the traditional aims of German nationalistic hegemony within Europe? This is the fear of pessimists, including many East European and German left-wing intellectuals, as a result of their traumatic experiences with the German Empire. In short, will we be witnessing a more "Europeanized Germany" or a more "Germanized Europe"? Or is this opposition perhaps only fictitious, since both variants represent different sides of a future German hegemon?[3]

The differences between the first unification of the German nation-state in 1870–71 and the second in 1989–90 seem obvious.[4] Even taking into account the basic formal and material continuities from the German Empire to the new Federal Republic of Germany, German unification has not been forced on its neighbors by war or coercion; it has materialized through mutual consent. Also, unified Germany does not confront the surrounding nation-states as a nationalistic competitor for power, but is institutionally anchored in the West European state framework. In addition, in contrast to its previous status as Europe's strongest military power, Germany today possesses only a middle-sized military. Moreover, Germany is integrated in various ways into Atlantic and European military organizations and security alliances. Finally, the newly united Germany no longer represents a semiconstitutional, authoritarian nation-state, but a relatively solid parliamentary democracy—one that has been, since unification, also imposed on the former GDR. Without these differences, a second unification of Germany would not have taken place.

Despite these apparent discontinuities between the German Empire and the new Germany, the geopolitical, geoeconomic, and geocultural dimensions of the German question, temporarily immobilized by the division of Germany and Europe, have reemerged as central problems of the contemporary sea change.[5] Thus united Germany has undergone a distinct gravitational shift to the East that has been—at least symbolically—articulated by the choice of Berlin, again, as Germany's capital. At the same time, Germany's population has greatly increased; since unification it is twice that of its most populous neighbors. In addition, Germany's already powerful economic position before unification will be strengthened by its strategic advantage in the potentially vast economic markets of Eastern Europe—an advantage that will be even greater after economic reconstruction of East Germany is completed. Germany will also gain more political weight and impact in the region, though West Germany's influence on the European Community had been considerable. Even if Germany's military limitations do not change in the near future, the question remains whether its economic and political power could be transformed into military power in the long run. Finally, despite the present relative stability of Germany's political system, the internal ambivalence about German national identity leaves it uncertain to what degree the symptoms of crisis in the present unification process will lead to internal political power shifts that could seduce the new Germany into aspiring to greater hegemony and a more independent nationalistic course between Western and Eastern Europe.

The crucial problem here is how the discontinuity and continuity of the German question are interrelated. Does unified Germany, in contrast to the German Empire, constitute a nation-state that, despite its increased power potential and its renewed core position in the middle of Europe, is essentially in structural equilibrium with its European neighbors? Or will the basic dimensions of the German question eventually result in renewed European imbalances and conflicts? In this essay, I attempt to answer these questions by sketching a historical-sociological comparison between the first phase of the construction of the German nation-state from 1871 to 1945 and the second phase of its division, reconstruction, and reunification from 1945 to 1992. I base my analysis on the following three methodological and theoretical premises:

1. The German question has internal and external aspects. The internal aspect relates to the problematic experiences of German national identity and is the main focus of the German public debate. The external aspect relates to the imbalances and conflicts of the German nation-state with the surrounding European nation-states and is categorized in the English-speaking world as the "German problem." It is not adequate to analyze the question one-sidedly, either from a solely national perspective or from a solely international one. The first bias has often been characteristic of the dispute about the "German *Sonderweg*," in which the emergence of the national socialist regime was explained by taking the internal political and social structure of the German Reich as the sole reference point for the problem of historical continuity.[6] The second bias, conversely, could be seen in the work of critics of this position who thought that the national socialist dictatorship emerged primarily as the result of European transnational power relationships rather than neglected internal societal conditions of the German Empire.[7] It is important to combine both approaches, taking into account

the inner structure of the German nation-state in its interaction with international constellations.[8]

2. In order to combine both aspects, I attempt to analyze the continuity or discontinuity of the German question from a historical-sociological perspective, focusing on the positional change of the German nation-state within the context of European social geography. For this purpose, I refer to the basic idea of Stein Rokkan's conceptual map of European state formation and nation-building.[9] Instead of taking an isolated perspective on a single national trajectory, this macro model conceptualizes the formation and development of European nation-states within the framework of an interdependent, multipolar, and changing network of center-periphery relationships. This implies a long-range perspective on state formation and nation-building and also an analysis of the three main geographically interdependent components of this changing network: the political, economic, and cultural dimensions.

3. Within this macro framework, the analysis of the German nation-state in the nineteenth and twentieth centuries can be made in more complex ways in terms of Germany's changing geopolitical, geoeconomic, and geocultural position within the European network. Such comparative analyses often fall short by falsely generalizing from partial components and processes, or by imprecisely defining constants and variables within the macrohistorical process of change. As the German sociologist Rainer M. Lepsius has emphasized, it is methodologically necessary to analyze the domestic and international factors influencing Germany's development both synchronically and diachronically.[10]

These theoretical and methodological assumptions ground the two major parts of my analysis. First, I will outline the structure of the German nation-state in terms of its basic political, economic, and cultural components in relation to its international constellations in the era from the foundation of the German Empire up to the national socialist dictatorship. Second, I will analyze how those components have been reconfigured by the division, reconstruction, and unification of Germany from 1945 to 1992. In conclusion, I will summarize the basic geopolitical, geoeconomic, and geocultural continuities and discontinuities of the German nation-state.

The German Nation-State
in the European Context, 1871–1945

Historical Preconditions

When one looks at the formation of nation-states in Europe, Germany is something of a paradox. Despite its relatively developed economic resources for political centralization compared with Western Europe, it achieved national unification relatively late—not before the second half of the nineteenth century. Rokkan has attempted to explain this paradox with reference to two fundamental conditions: Germany's density of urbanization and its geopolitical position within the sphere of influence of the West Roman Empire or, later, the Roman Catholic Church.[11] In this central zone, it was precisely the high relative urban density that contradicted any transregional state centralization, supported more local-regional power concentrations, and consequently resulted in territorial fragmentation and political decentralization. By contrast, the power balance between cities and territorial principalities at the fringes of the West Roman Empire encouraged processes of state centralization and power concentration leading to formation of "empire-nations" or "city-state consociations."[12] But the further decrease of urban density beyond the borders of the West Roman Empire reduced the power base for state formation to such an extent that these regions became peripheries or parts of transnational and multinational empires.

Two epochal economic and cultural-political changes also had a crucial impact on German state formation. First, the discovery of the New World and the development of a world economy shifted the economic center from the middle of the Roman Empire to the Atlantic periphery.[13] This led to a developmental unevenness from western Europe to eastern Europe; at the same time, it weakened the economic resource base for political centralization in the middle of Europe.[14] Second, the relative political power vacuum in the middle of the continent facilitated "double revolution," the division of Europe between Protestantism and Catholicism through the Reformation and Counter Reformation, creating a new geographical focus in the heart of the Roman-German Empire.[15] In these ways, the European geographical center began to lose its economic resources, political power, and cultural coherence, wedged as it was between the emerging nation-states in northwestern and northern Europe and the growing multinational empires in eastern and southeastern Europe.

As a result, the European geopolitical power balance took the form of a weak center with strong fringes. Within this structure, the German-speaking regions in the west developed as modern nation-states (Switzerland, The Netherlands, and France), and those in the east came under the domination of multiethnic absolute empires (Prussia and Austria). Meanwhile, the geographical center fragmented into more than three hundred principalities, forming a network of absolutist and confessionalized ministates mediated by the Reich.[16]

During the nineteenth century, this European power balance with a weak center and strong fringes was transformed by two secular processes spreading from northwestern and western Europe: the Industrial Revolution in England and the democratic national revolution in France.[17] This not only resulted in a growing developmental discrepancy from western to eastern Europe, but influenced the modernization processes that concentrically expanded to the east as well.[18] As a result, the industrial and democratic national revolutions increasingly made themselves felt in the older center of the Roman Empire, and consequently created the conditions for the gradual change of the European power configuration that had been formed since the early modern period.

The French Revolution and the Napoleonic Wars immediately affected the position of central Europe, and particularly the German-speaking regions within the European center-periphery network.[19] Quite in accord with the modernizing interests of the absolutist regimes and the educated middle classes, at least at the beginning, the French intervention decisively centralized the fragmented structure of the German regions. Formally, this resulted in the dissolution of the Holy Roman Empire in 1806 and the founding of the Germanic Confederation in 1815. Compared to the former fragmentation, this confederation was now composed of only a little more than thirty regional, absolutist regimes which were constitutionally softened in the western and southern states. As such, the Germanic Confederation formed a state structure that represented a considerably stronger European center, yet was weak enough to conserve the traditional pattern of weak center with strong fringes.[20]

The Industrial Revolution, too, had a great impact on the continent after 1815, and increasingly brought the German regions under its sway.[21] At the beginning, the gap between the quickly developing northwestern European core regions and the slow-moving, moderately backward German semiperiphery widened. Eventually, however, the competitive pressure on the German protoindustrial regions led to the German industrialization drive, as a result of which Germany gradually began to catch up to the West in the middle of the nineteenth century.[22] Both the expansion of the internal markets and incentives created by western European industrialization played major roles in supporting the growth of the western German industrial regions and, simultaneously, of eastern German agriculture. Thus the Industrial Revolution, expanding in concentric waves from western to eastern Europe, gradually liberated the economic forces that had stagnated in the densely urbanized German regions. Thereby it also created the preconditions for a geopolitical change of the traditional European center-periphery structures that had been institutionalized since the beginning of the modern era.

However, the unification of the German nation-state in 1870–71 depended on two additional factors: the emergence and development of German nationalism and the growing power of the Prussian state. German nationalism, based on the history of the German Reich and the common German language, essentially came into being as a reaction to the French Revolution and the Napoleonic Wars. Whereas French nationalism, emerging in the frame of a previously formed state organization, was primarily politically defined, German nationalism, born within a dispersed political structure, can be characterized as a primarily ethnic-linguistic-cultural nationalism.[23] Its main goal was to unify all German-speaking tribes and regions politically within the borders of the former German Reich as a sovereign nation-state. But German nationalism was also liberal democratic, in that it opposed the dynastic absolutist fragmentation of the federation and pressed for liberal constitutional reforms or revolutions. Without a previously formed state, however, German nationalism was politically ambiguous and also threatened the traditional European power balance because of its pan-

German implications. This became manifest during the Revolution of 1848 and later in the construction of the German Empire in 1870–71.[24]

Finally, Prussia's future role in German national unification was shaped by the European order established in 1815.[25] Within this framework, Prussia was moved more to the west into Germany, and Austria was pushed more to the east out of Germany. With this shift, German economic development strengthened the Prussian absolutist state in particular. Conversely, the Prussian state, pursuing its mercantilist tradition, supported this economic development through a carefully directed arsenal of economic policies.[26] This mutually reinforcing economic dynamic strengthened Prussia's political and military power potential; by comparison, Habsburg Austria, limited to its central and southeastern European markets, was falling behind. Moreover, Prussia, based on its Protestantism, bureaucracy, and liberal reform policy, was also the more modern state in the federation compared to the Catholic, multinational, and patriarchal absolutist Habsburg Empire.[27] Without assuming any historical necessity for the Prussian unification of Germany, the emerging symbiosis between German nationalism and Prussian dynastic power interests was endowed with a certain developmental logic.

German unification in 1870–71, which materialized through three wars fought under Prussian leadership, effectively destroyed the traditional European power balance.[28] Suddenly, a power center in the middle of Europe as strong as the western European great powers had emerged, while the eastern and southeastern European empires suffered a relative decline. But it was not the German geographical center position as such that was responsible for this transformation of the traditional power balance into increasing international imbalances and conflicts. To analyze the problem in this way would be to adhere to a problematic geopolitical determinism.[29] Rather, the geopolitical structure of the German Empire, the geoeconomic form of its industrial growth dynamics, and the geocultural structuring of its national identity were crucial for the general intensification of the nationalistic and imperialistic power competition in the period that followed. Only as a result of the interplay between national and international structures did the transformation of the European power balance, brought about by the growing power position of the German Empire in the European center, lead to the European catastrophes in the first half of the twentieth century.

Geopolitical Structures of the German Empire

The German *Kaiserreich,* formed as "small Germany" under Prussian leadership, was not the only possible German nation-state. Legitimizing the *Kaiserreich's* historical necessity was rather the a posteriori construction of "Borrussian" historiography.[30] However, this type of state formation corresponded closely to the aspirations and imagination of the German national movement. The German Empire brought nation and state into basic, albeit not complete, congruence, and in so doing essentially formed the foundations of the eventful history of the German nation-state during the course of the twentieth century.[31]

The unification of the German Empire made possible for the German nation what the West European nations had achieved long before. But whereas in Western Europe state formation and nation-building went hand in hand, in Germany they developed later, one after the other. German nation-building—as national idea, movement, and community—preceded state formation, and thus had to be adapted to the newly founded nation-state over a longer period. Moreover, the German nation-state created specific internal and external problems in the era from unification to national socialism. On the one hand, it contributed significantly to the emerging nationalistic and imperialistic competition between the European great powers; on the other, it also complicated the internal process of national integration within the heterogeneous new nation-state.

It was characteristic that the Prussian/"small-German" unification was created not only by the German national movement from below but also by the strongest territorial state within Germany from above.[32] In principle, this state form signified an easternization of Germany, in both geographical and political senses. Thus the aims of the German national movement were not realized by the more constitutionally and liberally oriented West German territorial states, but by the militarily strongest and most absolutist state power at the eastern periphery "from outside" and through a "revolution from above." This had an impact on two dimensions of the geopolitical structure of the German nation-state in particular: its ethnic-territorial and its political-geographical bases.

Every plan for nationally unifying the German-speaking population confronted particular difficulties because of their spatial dispersion and only partial integration into the traditional European state structure.

Within this context, the Prussian/"small-German" nation-state was a construction clearly more limited, and for the other European powers more acceptable, than any "great-German" solution corresponding more to the ethnic-cultural base and idea of German nationalism.[33] As a consequence, however, the ethnic Germans in the Habsburg Empire in particular were excluded from Germany. Although this consequence was gradually accepted in the *Kaiserreich* through the process of national integration, there remained a latent tension between the original ethnic-cultural great-German nationalism and the small-German realization of the German nation. This tension was to manifest itself in the form of German irredentism following the dissolution of the Habsburg Empire after the First World War.[34]

The small-German form of unification, despite its name, contained some great-German as well as traditional and dynastic components. Thus, with the annexation of Alsace-Lorraine, an ethnically German and French population politically oriented predominantly to France was included in the German nation-state.[35] As in the case of the Danish population in northern Germany, great-German nationalism and the dynastic-military interests of Prussia went hand in hand. At the same time, the Prussian unification of Germany implied the inclusion of an important part of the Polish population in the Prussian eastern provinces.[36] Thus, in a small-German sense, the ethnic-territorial borders of the German Empire were not sufficiently limited. Consequently, these borders represented the bases for both an increasing virulence of ethnic-national conflicts inside Germany and a growing nationalistic competition for power between Germany and the other European nation-states.

The Prussian/"small-German" solution implied a more authoritarian and centralized nation-state that aggravated the internal and external problems originating from the ethnic-territorial construction.[37] As a "revolution from above," this form of unification established a semi-constitutional absolutist regime in which constitutional institutions were not able to control the monarchical executive effectively. Hence the authoritarian traditions of political culture were strengthened in the long run, but the democratic and pluralistic components in state and society were weakened.[38] At the same time, the traditional federal-decentralized structure of the German states, although not completely dissolved, was decisively transformed by the weight of Prussia in the

German Empire and its corresponding authoritarian centralism. The traditional form of a polycephalic federation was replaced by a more monocephalic structure that complicated the national integration of the differing regional identities.[39]

As a consequence, three structural problems of the German nation-state became aggravated, displaying their explosive effects in the era from the *Kaiserreich* to the rise of the national socialist regime. First, ethnic conflicts became more virulent, because the nationalistic policy of Germanizing ethnic minorities, especially the Poles in the Prussian East, could be implemented more easily within an authoritarian framework.[40] Second, the Prussian-dominated German unification exacerbated the religious oppositions so characteristic of the German regions. In contrast to the traditional balance of Catholics and Protestants, the Catholic population was now forced into a minority position.[41] The authoritarian hegemony of predominantly Protestant Prussia led to discrimination against the Catholic minority, which had a negative long-term effect on the integration of the Catholic population into the German nation-state. At the same time, Jewish emancipation remained restricted and ambiguous.[42] Third, the social conflicts accompanying capitalist industrialization were exacerbated because authoritarian control, social discrimination, and political exclusion prevailed against democratic forms of conflict regulation. This strategy of negative integration tightened the bond between the state and the middle classes, thereby excluding large parts of the working class.[43]

In sum, the ethnic-territorial and geopolitical bases of the German Empire, created by the symbiosis between German nationalism and Prussian absolutism and basically effective until the rise of the Nazi regime, exacerbated the problems of internal integration and external international balance. Structural problems of domestic policy aggravated the conflicts in foreign policy, and vice versa. Still, despite its importance, the geopolitical structure of the German Empire represents only one explanatory dimension for the rise of the destructive nationalistic power potentials during this period.

Geoeconomic Dynamics of the German Empire

The transformation of the traditional European balance of power by the political centralization of a formerly dispersed, weak center was particularly significant in the economic growth of unified Germany. In a relatively short time, the German economy developed from a "moderately backward" part of the European semiperiphery to a developed center of the European core.[44] Because of its economic growth, by the First World War this new center had attained a dominance vis-à-vis the West European nation-states and, even more pronounced, vis-à-vis Eastern Europe. Yet, as the period of crisis and stagnation between the two world wars demonstrates, this growing economic power had structural limits within the European power grid.[45]

At the same time, this power shift occurred within a global context. Europe, accompanied by the exceptional economic rise of the United States, cemented its industrial and imperialistic hegemony over the entire world.[46] Expansion of the world economy entailed global imperialist and colonial conquest and domination, but these developments were inextricably intertwined with nationalist power struggles in Europe itself. This competition provoked imperialist competition on the world markets, and vice versa. Within this global context, the rise of a dynamic and increasingly dominant center of economic power in the middle of Europe exacerbated the nationalist and imperialist competition for power.[47]

In what ways did the geoeconomic dynamics of the German Empire have an impact on the transformation of the economic center-periphery structures in Europe? To begin with, the population of the German Empire grew at a faster rate. For instance, the populations of the European core countries of Germany (35 million), France (36 million), and Great Britain (21 million) changed from a ratio of approximately 3:3:2 in 1850 to roughly 3:2:2 in 1913 (66, 41, and 40 million, respectively).[48] In other words, Germany's population developed in this period into a decisively dominant one within the European matrix.[49]

In similar ways, the economic growth patterns shifted the power relations between these three countries. In the same period, the German gross national product grew from $10.4 to $49.8 billion, the French from $11.9 to $27.4 billion, and the British from $12.6 to $44.1 billion.[50] The basis of this enormous shift was the above-average growth of German industrial production and productivity. For example, Germany's share in world manufacturing output was only 4.9 percent in 1860 compared to France's 7.9 percent and Britain's 19.98 percent, but this ratio was reversed around 1913, when Germany led European production marginally with a share of 14.87 percent; Great Britain fell behind with 13.60 percent; and France fell even further behind with only 6.1 percent.[51]

At the same time, these shifts in favor of the German Reich were accompanied by important changes in domestic and foreign market structures. Great Britain dominated the world markets as well as continental European markets until 1870, but then was challenged increasingly in both markets and began to lose its dominance on the European continent, particularly to Germany. So, for instance, Great Britain's national share in industrial goods was 50 percent on the world market in 1870, Germany's 12 percent and France's 10 percent. But by 1913 the British share was 31.8 percent, with Germany at 25.6 percent and France at 13 percent.[52]

Geographical shifts in international trade patterns also developed. British exports of industrial products to Europe were now clearly surpassed by German exports. Here, the increasing conquest of the German domestic market by Germany's own production, as well as growing markets of German exports to Eastern, Southeastern, and Mediterranean Europe, played a major role. In 1913, 75 percent of German exports, compared to 30 percent of British ones, went to Europe.[53] A parallel development challenged traditional British dominance in the sphere of capital exports in Europe. With respect to the volume of capital exported in 1913, Great Britain was clearly leading with $19.5 million (43 percent), compared to France with $9 million (20 percent) and Germany with $5.8 million (13 percent).[54] However, in 1913 Great Britain invested only 5 percent of its capital exports in Europe, whereas France and Germany concentrated more than 50 percent there.[55]

Although the geoeconomic change in favor of Germany between 1871 and 1914 was dramatic, it does not explain the rapid intensification of nationalist economic competition during this period. In this respect, the economic institutions in which this change occurred played a crucial role. The basic organization that shaped and supported the modernization of relatively backward countries in the context of British industrial hegemony remained the nation-state. Even when the economic network crossed borders and was interregionally intertwined, the industrialization of latecomers followed the framework of the national economy.[56] The economy was supposed to increase national power, and in this sense its development was fundamentally shaped by economic nationalism.

This economic nationalism was also crucial for the economic development of the German Empire, which had a strong tradition of a mercantilist-absolutist economic policy.[57] In Germany, mercantilism had first emerged as a developmental policy of the absolutist state. The state later provided an arsenal of political measures for rapidly industrializing Germany, and continued to support German industry even after it had achieved international competitiveness. As a result, Germany's national economic policies aggravated international competitive struggles.

The turning point for neomercantilism in Germany was the transition to a tariff system institutionalized at the beginning of the depression in the late 1870s.[58] This system was intended to protect the German domestic market for German industry and East Elbian agriculture. At the same time, it served as a support for German economic competition on European markets, thus exacerbating national polarization within Western and Eastern Europe. On the one hand, the free trade-oriented northwestern European countries were confronted with increasingly difficult access to the German market for their industrial goods. On the other hand, the countries of the East European semiperiphery and periphery were limited in agrarian export opportunities that were vital for financing their own belated process of industrialization. In these ways, the dynamics of Germany's economic growth and its neomercantilist, protectionist strategy decisively contributed to the political polarization that led to the First World War.

Germany's defeat in the First World War thus signified a transition period during which German economic power was considerably reduced. The loss of former German territories and colonies, and of assets and markets overseas, together with domestic economic crises resulting from the war led to a decisive leveling down of the relatively dominant prewar position of the German economy. Notwithstanding Germany's comparative economic recovery in the second half of the 1920s, the former dynamics in terms of population increase, economic growth, and market expansion could not be resumed. The great powers in Europe, which were even in global decline, were again *al pari* in economic terms.[59]

In this international context, the German economy had two options: either integrate into the world market or resume the protectionist-mercantilist tradition.[60] With the outbreak of the Great Depression of the 1930s, the protectionist orientation again prevailed. Supported by crisis-stricken industries and completely uncompetitive agriculture, the concept of Mitteleuropa was taken up, renewing the principles of the neomercantilist protective system—only for a larger area that included the lands of the former Habsburg Empire. Under the globally changed conditions of competition, Mitteleuropa was supposed to protect a Central European market dominated and reserved for German industry in competition against the North American, British, and Soviet economic regions.[61] The autarkic economy, rearmament strategy, and warfare pursued by the national socialist regime made this economic option crucial for neomercantilist Central European German hegemony. However, the subsequent totalitarian-racist struggle for *Lebensraum* in Eastern Europe fundamentally transcended the economic aims of the Mitteleuropa concept.[62]

Political-Cultural Bases of the German Empire

Neither geopolitical structures nor geoeconomic dynamics linked with decisive transformations of the European center-periphery matrix were sufficient to bring on two world wars or national socialism. Nor did the intensified nationalist and imperialist competition for power have to culminate in those major catastrophes of the first half of the twentieth century. The political and economic changes only provided the structural conditions under which such historical developments became possible. The determining factor was how the German society reacted to them. In this respect, the political-cultural bases of the German nation-state and the patterns of national identity formation were crucial.[63]

In order to explain the internal origins of the national socialist regime in Germany, the thesis of the German *Sonderweg* has focused especially on the unevenness between the economic and political processes of modernization within the German Empire.[64] As a consequence of the aborted liberal democratic revolution in 1848, so the main thesis goes, rapid capitalist development was not accompanied by a parallel process of liberal democratization. Instead, the semiconstitutional authoritarian state remained dominated by the traditional aristocracy, particularly the Prussian Junker class. This social and political order remained intact in many ways after the First World War, thus facilitating the rise of the national socialistic regime. In disputing the *Sonderweg* thesis, critics questioned the legitimacy of applying an ideal-typical model of Western modernization to German development, insisted on the relative modernity and bourgeois character of society and state, and stressed the historical complexity and alternative potentials of the *Kaiserreich*.[65] In explaining the rise of the national socialist regime, these critics referred less to the political and social order of the *Kaiserreich* and concentrated more on the political and economic constellations of the Weimar Republic.

But these contradictory positions are not necessarily mutually exclusive simply because they begin with different methodological presuppositions. Thus the *Sonderweg* thesis retrospectively finds causes for the later rise of national socialism in conditions created by the formation of the German nation-state. In this sense, it analyses the *Kaiserreich* from a structural-historical perspective. In contrast, critics oriented toward a narrative social history insist on the differences between the *Kaiserreich* and the Weimar Republic, emphasizing the contingent circumstances of the latter as responsible for the rise of the Third Reich. From the perspective taken here, one needs to ask how political culture and national identity formation were related to geopolitical and geoeconomic structures and developments of the German Empire in the era between the *Kaiserreich* and the Weimar Republic, and how they contributed to the rise of the national socialist dictatorship.

Corresponding to the symbiosis of the German national movement and the Prussian authoritarian state, German national identity and political culture were based on the specific ethnic, cultural, and democratic sentiments and values of German nationalism, and were shaped by the military ethos of the traditional elites who were able to transform the national aspirations of the German nation-state into reality. Both sources had a decisive impact on political culture and national consciousness from the *Kaiserreich* up to the Weimar Republic, though the particular form and extent of their influence depended on historical circumstances.

German nationalism as it had developed during the nineteenth century represented an ethnic-linguistic-cultural phenomenon identified with the territorially based German *Kulturnation* and oriented toward its unification as a nation-state. But it was at the same time a liberal democratic nationalism, directed against the dynastic separation and absolutism of the German-speaking regions. Both components constituted German nationalism.[66] Hence, it is problematic to reduce Western and German nationalisms to opposing ethnic-cultural and political-constitutional ideal-types.[67] Nevertheless, the constitutional-democratic components of German nationalism were on the whole more ambiguous and less dominant; the romantic-cultural components carried more weight in reaction to foreign hegemony, especially French hegemony. At the same time, the identification with a powerful state became stronger, because only through a strong state was the unification of a German nation-state possible—or so it seemed.

This political-cultural shift toward national sentiments romanticizing German culture and idealizing a powerful state became even more pronounced after the unification of Germany by Prussia, which contributed considerably to the strengthening of politically authoritarian attitudes at the expense of liberal democratic ones. With the unified nation-state finally realized but "threatened" from inside as well as outside, these elements hypostasized German culture as unique and superior.[68] At the same time, as a means of protecting German nationhood, identification with the aristocratic war ethos of the traditional elite became more intense.[69] Moreover, both components contained a strong Protestant-Lutheran cast, emphasizing the outward-directed cultural mission and the inward-directed pietist belief in authority.[70] In contrast, the liberal democratic components were weakened. Thus national liberalism as the main pillar of German unification "from below" increasingly lost out to new political movements and parties that articulated the religious, social, and ethnic conflicts so characteristic of Imperial Germany. Over time, the political base for a more democratic constitutionalization of authoritarian state structures became smaller, not least because further constitutionalization seemed to threaten the strong state at a time when it was confronted with increasing social and national conflicts.

The internal shift in the components of German political culture was characteristically combined with a mental shift of German nationalist attitudes toward other nations. Toward the more liberal democratic and developed capitalist Western Europe, originally seen to be superior, the antiliberal, antimaterialist, and romantic-cultural *ressentiment* increased.[71] Conversely, vis-a-vis the more backward Eastern Europe, the romanticizing, cultural-imperialist, and Germanizing-colonialist components intensified.[72] These characteristic elements of German nationalism, shaped either by religion or secular religion, came together in the "mind of 1914" as the ideological corollary of the German two-front war.[73]

Only against the background of these moral sentiments can one understand how the German defeat in World War I, the democratic-reformist November revolution, and the imposed Versailles peace treaty were experienced by a large part of the population as national humiliation and treason. Wounded nationalism was essentially at the core of the political difficulties and weaknesses of Weimar democracy.[74] From the perspective of German nationalism, Weimar democracy was the result of foreign intervention and represented a weak and disunited Germany. The alternative national identity embodied in democratic institutions could not prevail against the dominant nationalistic mood. On this basis, a chiliastic nationalism emerged that, supported by the economic crisis and the remaining authoritarian structures in state and society, sought the salvation of Germany. Anti-Semitic national socialism was by no means the sole possible outcome of German nationalism. As the most radical chiliastic variant, however, it was able to mobilize most of the other nationalist forces and determine the course of the "German revolution" that established a totalitarian dictatorship.[75]

Division, Reconstruction, and Unification, 1945–1992

Configurational Restructuring of Germany within Europe

With its defeat in World War II, Germany completely lost its central power position in Europe.[76] In a sense, Europe returned temporarily to the earlier weak center with strong fringes. Instead of attaining hegemony in Europe, Germany became militarily occupied, territorially divided and reduced, demographically decimated, economically destroyed, and nationally demoralized. At the same time, Europe had finally lost its global hegemony as a result of its self-destruction in both world wars. The process of decolonization brought the worldwide domination of the European powers to an end. The global power balances shifted toward the victorious peripheral superpowers of European civilization: on the one side, the United States as the pole of civil society in the West; on the other side, the Soviet Union as the pole of state autocracy in the East.

Germany's fate in this period essentially depended on the future course of European development. The renewal of Europe as a region more or less equal to both superpowers was conceivable only by overcoming the traditional European state order based on a fragile equilibrium of competing nation-states and destructive mobilization of nationalistic sentiments.[77] Only a process of European unification—whatever its concrete arrangements for military union, political cooperation, concentration of economic resources, and transnational cultural interconnections—could realistically manage such a renewal. *Nolens volens,* such a construction of Europe required solution of the German question.[78] Any repetition of the post–World War I experience would have paralyzed Europe forever. The demilitarization and military control of Germany had to be accompanied by its political, economic, and cultural integration into a renewed Europe. Only then could any future nationalistic restoration of Germany be presented and its political and economic potential channeled into a restrengthened Europe. The geopolitical dilemma of post–World War II Europe within the global world order thus afforded Germany the opportunity to begin anew.

However, the form and course of European renewal, including the controlled reconstruction of German society and state, were soon determined by the sovietization of Eastern Europe and the resulting East-West conflict.[79] Both Europe and Germany now became divided. Central Europe, and in its middle both parts of Germany, became the peripheral frontiers between the two hostile superpowers. The intended renewal of Europe through an overarching process of European cooperation and integration became restricted to Western Europe, whereas Eastern Europe was subjected to the Soviet communist system by military, political, and ideological force. At the same time, the division of the German nation-state became cemented through the foundation of the West German Federal Republic and the counterfoundation of the East German Democratic Republic. With this, the German question was solved, or at least brought to a standstill. The division of Europe by the cold war essentially determined the processes of European renewal and German reconstruction.

Western Europe, under the umbrella of the United States, slowly moved toward cooperation and integration. The concrete forms and actual course of West European development represented a mix of divergent conceptions regarding more loosely federal versus more centralized, or more European versus more Atlantic, forms of cooperation and integration.[80] Nevertheless, over time Europe moved toward a deepening and widening transnational framework that concentrated its growing economic and political power within the global order. Within this framework, West Germany could regain a limited national sovereignty, became politically and economically intertwined with Western Europe, and was even permitted some military potential. This framework enabled the gradual renewal and reconstruction of the West German economy, society, and state. At the same time, it prepared the reconstitution of a German position of relative dominance within the West European core.

Meanwhile, Eastern Europe was fitted into the imperial framework of the Soviet Union and separated from Western Europe. The region was violently torn from its traditional political and economic course. The Soviet imperial framework also implied a form of transnational integration,[81] but here the structure of military, political, and administrative institutions served primarily the hegemonic interests of the USSR. In reaction to this, the state-socialist regimes preserved more strongly the traditional nation-state and nationalism.[82] At the same time, the imposed transnational division of labor reflected the economic interests of the Soviet economy, redirecting East European industrial development to Soviet economic structures. Within this framework, East Germany was far more limited in its ability to regain any sort of national sovereignty. However, the construction of East Germany's economy, society, and state under Leninist auspices resulted in the growing strength of its position within the Soviet bloc.

However unequal the conditions in Western and Eastern Europe, they nevertheless provided stable international relations in which the gradual regeneration and reconstruction of Europe could take place, however divergent its forms in the East and the West. Along with these processes of development, the power matrix of the postwar era, with the weak European center divided between the superpowers at the fringes of the European civilization, slowly changed. Through its economic and political rise, Western Europe began to carry more weight vis-à-vis the Atlantic hegemon. Eastern Europe, based on its growing political and economic functions for the Soviet Empire, also increased its power vis-à-vis the USSR—a factor that in the end decisively contributed to the fall of Soviet communism. At the same time, the power differential between democratic capitalist Western Europe and bureaucratic socialist Eastern Europe grew steadily, delegitimizing the alternative communist industrialization model. With the collapse of the Soviet order, Europe returned to the world stage as one of the centers of global power. Meanwhile, however, Europe's divided reconstruction has considerably changed its prewar center-periphery structures. At the same time, due to the rise of Japan and other East Asian regions, the relative decline of the hegemonic position of the United States, and the changing role of the former Soviet Union, this world stage has been transformed decisively.[83]

Within this transformed European and global context, German unification has renewed Germany's position of relative dominance in Europe. United Germany again represents the most populous, economically most advanced, politically most weighty, and at least potentially the strongest military power between Western and Eastern Europe. In this sense the German question, dormant between 1949 and 1989, has been revived. However, the divided reconstruction of the German nation-state in a divided Europe decisively transformed the social bases and international configurations of the reunited German nation-state. The parameters of the German question have changed decisively. What historical continuities and discontinuities affect united Germany's position and future position in the new Europe?

Geopolitical Reconstructions of the German Nation-State

Despite the deep ruptures in German national history in the twentieth century, German unification revealed the basic continuity of the German nation-state as founded in 1871.[84] Even when dismembered in the postwar era, the West German Federal Republic was undertaken as a provisional state in the expectation of a united Germany, and the East German Democratic Republic was similarly understood as a first step to a united, albeit socialist Germany. Under the cold war system, however, this provisional division turned out to be unexpectedly durable. Over time, the formation of separate state identities was clearly under way, enabling a mutual de facto recognition of both German states—without giving up the idea of a common German nation. On the basis of this continuing national sentiment and identity, the second German unification became possible. The continuity of a historically grown national community was obviously stronger than the formation of partial identities.

But the divided reconstruction of Germany in the postwar era has revealed a major discontinuity from the era of the German Empire. Within West Germany, a basic Westernization of the German nation-state took place and, with it, a break from the traditional German *Sonderweg* of authoritarian modernization. This break was first accomplished in the democratic capitalist redirection of West German development. In contrast, East German bureaucratic socialist development continued basic features of the traditional German "special path." But in the end, the GDR revolution, the collapse of the GDR, and German unification resulted in the Westernization of East Germany as well. Although united Germany is and will not be a simple extension of West German society and state to East Germany, the conditions of East German transformation are clearly set by the West German model.

This Westernization of the German nation-state has implied a major change in its geopolitical base. In ethnic-territorial terms, Germany's geographical center position in Europe was shifted to the West as an immediate consequence of the defeat in World War II. With the parallel westward shift of Poland, Germany lost about one-fourth of its former state territory in the East. One-half formed first the Western zones of occupation and then West Germany, and the remaining fourth made up first the Soviet zone and then East Germany.[85] This westward geographical shift had several crucial implications. To begin with, as a result of the separation of the former Eastern Prussian provinces and the expulsion of most Germans from Central and Eastern Europe, the traditional ethnic-national mix and conflict zones in the East disappeared.[86] The center of the Federal Republic was now in the western and southern parts of the German nation, and as a consequence, the more Western federal and democratic traditions of the German society dominated. The center of East Germany, by contrast, was formed around the central provinces of former Prussia as a territorial basis for the reproduction of the German authoritarian state. Further, the division of Germany resulted in equal status of Protestantism and Catholicism in the

West German society, whereas East Germany became overwhelmingly Protestant. Finally, the migration of millions of German refugees and expellees from the former Prussian Eastern provinces, Eastern Europe, and also East Germany to West Germany had opposite effects on the demographic structure of the two parts of Germany. In West Germany a massive ethnic mobilization, intermixing, and interregional integration of Germans took place—not to mention the later influx of non-German immigrants. In East Germany, by contrast, the traditional ethnic structure of prewar Germany was to a great extent preserved.

As a consequence, united Germany possesses a much higher congruence between nation and state compared with the era of the German Empire.[87] With its recognition, however belated, of the Eastern border with Poland as well as of the abandonment of compensatory claims to Czechoslovakia, however half-hearted, united Germany has accepted its ethnic-territorial recomposition in the postwar era. This recognition has been carried through by the conservative liberals rather than the social democratic liberals against the political will of the traditional elite, as in the case of the Versailles Treaty. For the first time in German history, there is not only a clear-cut ethnic-territorial border to the West, but to the East as well—even taking into account the remaining German ethnic minorities in Poland and other East European countries. As a result of the ethnic-territorial consolidation of the German nation, the basis for a renewal of nationalistic conflicts of this sort between Germany and its European neighbors has been destroyed.

The divided reconstruction and final unification of Germany resulted in the Westernization of the German nation-state. The liberal constitutional democratization of German state structures was first carried through in West Germany. Helped by the delegitimization of any militarist nationalism after World War II,[88] the German democratic political forces under Western control rebuilt the institutional framework of parliamentary democracy.[89] West German democracy aimed at correcting the major political-institutional shortcomings of its Weimar predecessor. In particular, the Basic Law reduced the president to representational tasks, institutionalized a stronger control of the chancellor by the Bundestag (lower house of the federal parliament) and the Bundesrat (upper house), limited the number of parties by introducing the 5 percent clause, and created the Bundesverfassungsgericht (Constitutional Court) as the supreme body of constitutional surveillance. The

West German party system basically reproduced the Weimar political spectrum, although the moderate middle was now much stronger and the nationalist or communist positions were considerably weakened. In addition, reversing the authoritarian state centralism of the past, the regional-federal component was decisively strengthened. Thus, the eleven (originally fifteen and, after the entry of the Saar, sixteen) Länder in the federally constituted Bundesrat formed a considerable counterweight to the centrally constituted Bundestag.[90] From this perspective, West Germany was a "state without a center."[91]

In contrast, East Germany under Soviet imperial hegemony underwent a thorough political Easternization which continued the basic features of the German authoritarian path of modernization in a specific bureaucratic communist form.[92] The starting conditions of political development in East Germany, however, were barely different from those in West Germany. Militarist nationalism was thoroughly delegitimized, the political will to overcome the past by democratization was widespread, and the Weimar party spectrum reemerged as well. However, through Soviet military control and on the basis of strong currents of German socialism, the emerging political system of the GDR institutionalized a specific form of Soviet totalitarian rule.[93]

Even compared to other East Central European communist regimes, East Germany was characterized by an encompassing political-administrative control over state, economy, and society. Thus the party system was rearranged as the unique "bloc system" where the SED—formed out of the forced merger of the Communists and Social Democrats—surrounded itself by a ring of loyal parties. In addition, the traditional federal order was dissolved in favor of a bureaucratic state centralism, contributing to both the particular coherence and the weakness of the GDR state. In contrast to other East Central European communist regimes, in the GDR no independent counterelite could form.[94] As a consequence, the GDR revolution was unable to renew the state in an alternative form. Instead it simply collapsed.

German unification in 1989–90, in the form of an enlarged Federal Republic, finally accomplished the political-institutional Westernization of the whole of Germany.[95] Instead of a compromise between the two German states, all major components of the West German political system were taken on by East Germany.[96] To begin with, upon entering the Federal Republic, the GDR was dissolved by restoring the former federal structure in the form of the five new Bundesländer. Then, the integral parts of West German democracy were transferred with only minor modifications, including the West German Grundgesetz (Basic Law) or constitution, the parliamentary institutions, and the party system. In addition, all major state institutions—including the legal and administrative system, the military and police structures, and the cultural and educational bodies—were reconstructed along West German lines. All in all, the incorporation of East Germany into the West German democratic, parliamentary, and federal order removed the last institutional remnants of the authoritarian-conservative route of modernization in Germany.

At the same time, the political-institutional Westernization of the German nation-state has been closely connected with Germany's incorporation into the transnational Atlantic and West European frameworks. In this respect, West Germany's integration into the Western alliances and Western Europe provided the model for a united Germany. This integration was originally motivated by the determination of the Western Allies to contain a nationalist Germany, but in fact it turned Germany into one of the main pillars of the Western institutional framework. To begin with, under the precarious conditions of the cold war, West Germany regained a limited but increasingly important position within the Atlantic military alliance. In addition, the European Economic Union and later the European Community, with its central bureaucracy in Brussels, furthered West Germany's economic growth, leading at the same time to a greater dependence of these institutions on West German economic resources.[97] Moreover, within the emerging framework of West European political institutions, West Germany could regain not only a limited national sovereignty but increasing political weight in European decision making. Further, the West German federal order became a guiding model for the process of West European unification, because it provided a structure of graded or scaled sovereignties that made European integration attractive for the smaller and ethnically more pluralistic nation-states.[98]

The incorporation of the GDR into the enlarged Federal Republic was accompanied by its immediate inclusion in the Atlantic and West European institutional frameworks. On the military level, united Germany became a member of NATO, limited only by some minor concessions to the strategic interests of the still-existing Soviet Union. On the economic and political levels, united Germany was accepted as a full member of the European Community without the usual transitional steps of accommodation. The West and East European apprehensions of Germany's potentially independent course as an economic and political hegemonic power in the center of Europe gave way to the Maastricht Treaty that attempted to accelerate the process of West European unification.

Thus, German unification in 1989–90, in contrast to that in 1870–71, was not carried through in opposition to the European state order and power balance, but in concord with the European state system.[99] In geopolitical terms, the German question seems to have found a stable answer through the ethnic-territorial consolidation, political democratization, and Western—particularly West European—integration of the German nation-state. The renewed political power position of united Germany in the center of Europe seems to be reconciled, at least for the time being, with its European neighbors. The degree to which this geopolitical solution will hold also depends on the second parameter of the German question: the geoeconomic base of the German nation-state.

Geoeconomic Reconfigurations of the German Nation-State

In contrast to the nationalist and imperialist structures of the German economy in the era between 1871 and 1945, the postwar divided reconstruction of the German economy took place in close interconnection with transnational economic blocs. The West German economy became particularly intertwined with the West European economy, gradually regaining a position of dominance in the globally rising West European core.[100] The East German economy slowly advanced to become one of the most developed economies in the Soviet bloc.[101] Unification brought these economies together and recreated the German economic center position between Western and Eastern Europe. In which ways has the divided reconstruction and reunification of the German economy reshaped Germany's geoeconomic role?

In contrast to the geoeconomic dynamics of Imperial Germany, West Germany's regained position of relative dominance was not characterized by large developmental discrepancies with other West European economies. Although West Germany's economic growth in the first half of postwar reconstruction until the 1960s was exceptional, in the second half in the 1970s and in the 1980s it was roughly similar to that of other West European economies.[102] One reason for this growth pattern was West Germany's relatively low starting level after the war and the subsequent readjustment to normal European growth conditions after the famous "economic miracle." Another source of growth was the extraordinary population boom, which began with the flow of East European expellees and East German refugees and continued with an increasing number of Mediterranean immigrant workers. Thus the population grew rapidly from 43 million to 59 million between 1946 and 1965, but only slightly thereafter; by 1988 the population was only 61 million. The number of foreigners, meanwhile, increased from 1 million in 1970 to 5 million in 1988.[103] With this demographic growth, the Federal Republic finally reached almost the same population level as the German Reich in 1913. However, its population had decreased considerably compared to that of Great Britain, France, and Italy, since these countries had in the meantime increased their populations almost to the German level.[104]

In addition, Germany's growth in industrial production and productivity played a decisive role in its regaining relative economic dominance in Western Europe. For instance, from 1950 to 1970 West Germany's gross national product grew from $46 million to $159 million, whereas that of France increased from $47 million to $134 million and that of Britain from $47 million to $115 million in the same period.[105] In a parallel movement from 1953 to 1980, West Germany's industrial potential (measured as an index on the basis of Great Britain in 1900 = 100) grew from 180 to 590, whereas that of France increased from 98 to 362 and that of Great Britain from 258 to 441 in the same period.[106] An even more obvious illustration of this trend is the respective share in total European exports in 1970; here, the West German share was 22.8 percent, the French 10.6 percent and the British 11.3 percent.[107] Considering the decisive growth of the West European economy as a whole, however, these parameters do not signify any tendency toward Germany's hegemonic position over the other European nations; they indicate the gradual stabilization of the relative dominance of the West German position within the West European economy.[108]

At the same time, the geographical center of West Germany's foreign trade was clearly concentrated in West Europe. For instance, in 1984 almost 50 percent of West German foreign trade was exchanged with the European Community. The same held true for most other West European countries, whose share of foreign trade with the European Community moved between 40 percent and 60 percent in the same year.[109] A novel form of an international division of labor developed in which the different stages of production were linked cross-nationally. Larger West German corporations shifted parts of their production to the peripheral European countries, using their cheap labor instead of utilizing more expensive production locations in West Germany. In contrast to West European trade, East European markets played only a marginal role for West Germany. Even so, West Germany held the leading position in foreign trade and investment compared with the other advanced industrial societies.[110]

All these parameters signify great integration of the West German economy into Western Europe between 1945 and 1989, compared with 1871 to 1945, demonstrated particularly by the increased international trade and capital investments between the West European countries and even more by a novel West European division of labor and integration of production. As a result, nationalized economic competition—so characteristic of the era between 1871 and 1945—lost its significance. Sectoral, technical, and scientific interrelations and dependencies cut across national borders. Thus two crucial components of economic nationalism were decisively altered. First, the agrarian pattern of competition that determined national oppositions and hostilities between Germany and its neighbors, especially the East European countries between 1871 and 1945, was transcended and replaced by a cross-national competitive pattern, in which the German economy complemented the European agrarian regions, especially those of Southern Europe.[111] Second, economic competition based on traditional industries lost its nationalistic structure and became interconnected in a multisectoral, multifunctional division of labor that increasingly included the South and West European semiperiphery and periphery.[112]

The East German economy also developed relatively well compared to other East Central and East European countries, but in almost complete separation and protection from world market competition. Compared to the economic and technological starting conditions of West Germany immediately after World War II, those of East Germany were not substantially different.[113] Industrial regions in Saxony and Thuringia, the Berlin region, and the Baltic seaports were at the same level of development as West German counterparts; they had suffered the same degree of destruction during the war. Only with the division of Germany and Europe did the East German economy significantly deteriorate. To begin with, separated from West Germany, East Germany lost not only its traditional West German and West European markets, but also core industries like coal and steel. In addition, the Soviet Union dismantled many industrial plants as war reparations. Moreover, East Germany lacked any investment push like the Marshall Plan in West Germany. Finally, the politically repressive socialist transformation of GDR society, accompanied by economic expropriation, resulted in a growing mass emigration, particularly of the educated middle class, scientific-technical specialists, and skilled workers. Before the construction of the Berlin Wall, 3 million people out of an original 20 million inhabitants left East Germany.

Yet the East German economy in the 1960s and 1970s showed conspicuous growth. One of the crucial preconditions of this "second German economic miracle" was the construction of the Berlin Wall, which shut down the ruinous exit of the East German work force. In addition, central administrative control and planning based on the largely nationalized industry and collectivized agriculture enabled a stabilization and acceleration of production. Reflected in the five-year plans, this was made possible by systematically expanding heavy industry in preference to consumer goods and by increasing wages. But this type of growth favored quantitative expansion of traditional industries over modernization and innovation; and, the significantly improved consumption levels, including the encompassing social security system in the 1970s and 1980s, were accompanied by economic stagnation, technological lag, and ecological pollution as well as reliance on international credit. As a result, the GDR's economic growth in the 1980s steeply declined, thus eroding the legitimacy of the socialist system's claim to be superior to Western capitalism.

In contrast to the West European transnational market integration of production, the Council for Mutual Economic Assistance in Eastern Europe represented an administrative-coordinating framework for adjusting East European production to the economic and military interests of the Soviet Union.[114] As a consequence, the East European countries preserved their traditional national economies and, with respect to foreign trade, were oriented one-sidedly to the economic structure of the Soviet center.[115] The GDR had one of the most advanced econo-mies in the Soviet bloc,[116] but this Soviet-induced development was sub-stantially misdirected. It bound East Germany's economic structure to the Stalinist form of industrialization that expanded late nineteenth-century European industrialization rather than adjusting and catching up to the competitive standards of the world market.[117] Correspond-ingly, the East German economy developed primarily traditional indus-tries like steel and coal, machine tools, and petrochemistry, rather than investing in modern competitive technologies and sectors. The true state of the East German economy came to light when finally con-fronted directly with West German and world market competition.

With the fall of communism and German unification, the diverging paths of economic development in Western and Eastern Europe as well as in West and East Germany have been reconnected, and the tradi-tional economic unevenness between Western and Eastern Europe has been restored. Even worse, the misdevelopment of Eastern Europe has aggravated traditional economic power differentials. The united Ger-man economy has gained not only economic weight but a vast East Eu-ropean space of economic opportunities. The crucial question is what long-term power shifts in the geoeconomic position of united Germany will be brought about by this sea change, once the economic recon-struction of the East German economy is complete.[118]

A substantial economic power gain of united Germany's economy is decisively restricted by the severe construction difficulties of the East German part. In contrast to the other East European countries, the abrupt incorporation of the East German economy into the West Ger-man and West European framework has resulted in the immediate and complete collapse of traditional economic structures in East Germany under the pressure of undampened world competition.[119] The sudden exclusive orientation to Western products, the widespread collapse of the East European markets, and the gradual rise of wages to West Ger-man levels left the East German economy no chance of survival. Within two years, its gross national product, industrial production, and em-ployment were cut in half. Only massive state intervention—in the form of tax waivers, financial transfers, public investments, and indus-trial policy—enabled a slow, albeit partial, economic recovery. The West German economy, supplied overnight with East German markets and workers, experienced a sudden and overheated economic boom which first created a huge state deficit and then swung back into a deep recession. In addition, global economic shifts and sectoral East European competition, especially in agriculture, textiles, coal, and steel, have had a structural impact. For the time being, united Germany's economy seems to be rather weakened than strengthened.

In the long run, however, the enormous financial transfers from West to East Germany—on average about $100 billion each year—represent huge investments in infrastructure, industrial production, and work force.[120] For the East German economy this amounts to nothing less than a total economic and technological renovation along West German lines. Thus a substantial long-term increase of German economic power can be expected. This can be demonstrated with some statistical indicators. United Germany has increased to 80 million inhabitants, not counting the 6 million foreigners, an increase of Germany's share in the population of the European Community from 19 percent to 23 percent.[121] Germany's GNP as a share of the European Community's economy will grow from 25 percent in 1985 (as the added total of East and West Germany) to 28 percent in 1995 and finally 30 percent in the year 2000.[122] Germany's share in European foreign trade and investment will increase proportionally.

This substantial growth of economic power does not signify Germany's return to its hegemonic position in Europe in the historical sense, but represents a limited power gain in the position of dominance characteristic of the West German economy before unification. In fact, this relative dominance will be reduced in the long term by two major countertendencies. First, even if Germany accepted a medium-level immigration rate of 300,000 per year, its population would decline to 73 million in the year 2025, whereas that of its neighbors would still increase slightly.[123] A corresponding relative decline in the German lead in terms of GNP, industrial production, and foreign trade will be likely. Second, the planned enlargement of the European Community to the north, in the center, and to the east would imply a reduction of Germany's relative weight within the Community.[124]

With the opening of the East European markets, the gravity of the German economic position of relative dominance moves more to the east. As a result, united Germany's growing economic weight is directly confronted with the misdeveloped and backward East European economies. The economic unevenness and dependence between Germany and Eastern Europe will thus continue to be particularly pronounced. German foreign trade and investment clearly dominate the East European markets.[125] Already before unification, West and East German trade had the largest share in Eastern Europe including the Soviet Union. After unification, this trend continued, except that the East German share now decreased rapidly, whereas the West German share increased decisively.[126] Certainly, the East European markets, despite their growing share, will not represent an alternative for the German economy to its West European markets; Germany's East European foreign trade is only one-tenth its trade with Western Europe.[127] The trade and investment of other European countries, the United States, and increasingly Japan with Eastern Europe counterbalance the German influence.[128] Nevertheless, given the successful economic reconstruction of the East German economy on the highest Western technological levels and the partial modernization of the East Central European economies, one can expect united Germany's strong economic dominance vis-à-vis Eastern Europe and Eastern Europe's strong dependence on the German center.[129]

However, this emerging dominance will not constitute a renewed German economic-nationalistic hegemony. The relationships between united Germany and Eastern Europe will follow the integrated core-periphery matrix of the West European economy. The planned association of the East Central European countries with the European Community will create structural problems similar to those encountered previously in the South European countries.[130] As a consequence of the similar importance of agriculture, raw materials, and textiles in these countries, the main competitive struggle will be between the East European and the South European semiperipheries and peripheries, whereas their economic relations to the West and Central European core countries will be complementary. In this context, the German economy will be interested in balancing its relationships with all European semiperipheries and peripheries, rather than repositioning itself in a one-sided shift to Eastern Europe. United Germany, like West Germany before it, will function as the major engine of the deepened and enlarged European Community including the East, precisely because the German economy benefits the most from this development. East Central Europe, like Southern Europe previously, will participate in this European development in the form of partial and dependent modernization.

Changes in the Geocultural Base of the German Nation-State

Ethnic-territorial consolidation, political-institutional democratization, and European economic integration represent basic institutional changes in the geopolitical and geoeconomic bases of the German nation-state within Europe between 1945 and 1992. These changes, however, are not independent of their cultural contexts. The question remains to what extent and how the traditional geocultural base of the German nation-state has changed in this period. In this respect, the changes in German nationalism and political culture are of particular importance.

As a reaction to the hypertrophy of nationalism in the Third Reich and its disastrous consequences, the foundations of traditional German ethnic-cultural nationalism with its state-power orientation were shaken in the immediate postwar period. Despite the basic continuity of national identity, its authoritarian and cultural components were decisively undermined.[131] Aspirations toward democratization and international reconciliation predominated over nationalistic sentiments of military revenge or cultural superiority. In this sense, German nationalism after World War II differed essentially from the humiliated and resentful nationalism that emerged after World War I. This break in the structure of German nationalism affected the development of national sentiment and political culture in both parts of Germany.

In West Germany, national consciousness became increasingly connected not only with constitutional-democratic values but also a deeply ambiguous patriotism.[132] On the one hand, there was a continuing positive national identity that felt betrayed by the "misuse" of the German national idea by the Nazi regime. On the other, there was a developing negative identity that, after the Holocaust, denied the possibility of any positive identification with the German national heritage. As a corollary, the unbroken identification with German history, language, and culture was increasingly contested by a critical rejection of the constitutive components of German national identity. The developing contrast of these two sentiments was crucial for West German history, often sharpening into a fundamentalist opposition of irreconcilable attitudes.

In connection with the changing national sentiments, a gradual democratization of West German political culture developed.[133] In the immediate postwar period, beneath the institutionalized political democracy, various forms of political authoritarianism were still widespread, and in the first phase of the Federal Republic until the 1960s they were bound to the emerging democratic state. Supported by the successful economic reconstruction, a sort of patriarchal identification with liberal democracy emerged.[134] But in the second phase of the Federal Republic in the 1970 and 1980s, these patriarchal structures were increasingly contested. Despite their connection with reemerging socialistic and nationalistic ideologies at the political fringes, political pluralism and participatory democracy developed more thoroughly.[135]

This growing democratic identity based on an ambiguous national consciousness was accompanied by changing attitudes in West Germany toward its European neighbors. Within the context of West European integration, an increasing identification with (Western) Europe developed.[136] Perhaps to compensate for its contested nationalism, the West German tendency to identify with Europe was characteristically more pronounced than in other West European countries. As a corollary, the traditional sentiments of superiority and resentment against Western civilization receded. In contrast, West German attitudes toward Eastern Europe contained more traditional nationalist sentiments.[137] Through the experience of expulsion of populations, territorial loss, and East German socialism, widespread feelings of revanchism and anticommunism were only gradually overcome by reconciliatory and pragmatic sentiments. Thus, West German identification with Western Europe preserved German sentiments of superiority against Eastern Europe.

In East Germany, despite the break with the extremist and militarist nationalism of the past, traditional structures of German national sentiments and political culture were preserved rather than changed.[138] Within the socialist-authoritarian GDR regime, German nationalism was reproduced in two forms. First, GDR socialism itself represented a sort of "negative nationalism" that aspired to the reconstruction of the entire German nation as a socialist state.[139] Second, German national identity and nationalism served as a counteridentity in reaction to the bureaucratic-totalitarian structures of Leninism. As long as the inner German border was still open, this counteridentity became manifest in the growing flow of emigration to West Germany. When the border was closed, German nationalism turned into a widespread latent sentiment that quickly came to the surface when the wall fell in 1989.[140]

Within the context of the GDR's socialist-bureaucratic system, the traditional German authoritarian political culture was preserved as well.[141] The hegemonic socialism itself represented a transformed German idealistic authoritarianism. Based on an antifascist socialist morality, it produced a widespread legitimacy and loyalty particularly in the leading political class. At the same time, the traditionally German "unpolitical culture" that combined state piety with state obedience was reproduced. Under these circumstances, discontent and rebelliousness were manifested either by leaving the GDR or by retreating privately into the "niche society," rather than through open political opposition. As a consequence of the reproduction of German authoritarian nationalism, the GDR revolution was predominantly a "national revolution" rather than a "democratic revolution."[142] The major forces at work were mass emigration and the demand for unification, rather than a democratization of the GDR itself.[143]

With the reproduction of authoritarian nationalism in East Germany, traditional nationalistic attitudes toward Germany's European neighbors were preserved. Regarding Western Europe, GDR Marxism and its images of imperialism nourished traditional resentments against Western civilization, capitalism, and liberal democracy. At the same time, rejection of GDR Marxism often led to an uncritical identification with Western capitalism—an identification which played a decisive role in the transition process from communism to a capitalist market society. Regarding Eastern Europe, "socialist internationalism" under the auspices of Soviet imperial rule did not change traditional German nationalism. Underneath the ritual invocation of socialist friendship, feelings of superiority and resentment against the less developed East remained alive.

With unification, both diverging patterns of German national consciousness and political culture have not only come together but also confront each other directly. Despite the ethnic-territorial consolidation and political-institutional democratization of united Germany, the cultural processes of creating a democratic and united nation raise sub-stantial problems. Although a return to any traditional form of German authoritarian nationalism is unlikely, unification has revived some na-tionalistic and authoritarian components of German political culture.

First, unification has resulted in a kind of renationalization of Ger-man political culture.[144] To begin with, the national sentiments dur-ing unification, compared with the previous ambiguous forms of West German identity, reflected a novel German patriotism connected with some romantic undertones and some self-assertive overtones.[145] In the political and intellectual debate on unification, the struggle between national and "postnational" positions was renewed.[146] After the initial euphoria, the practical difficulties of unification brought the histori-cally rooted differences between the Western and Eastern parts of the nation to the surface. As a result, budding national pride changed to national self-doubt and mutual resentment.[147] In the context of the structural inequality of unification, the two forms of German identity clashed. The West Germans feel legitimized in their restructuring of the nation according to their own successful model. The East Germans feel colonized, insisting that their legacy be respected. For the time being, the struggle for a reunited national identity strengthens nationalistic self-preoccupation and self-definition. As a consequence, attitudes to-ward immigrants and ethnic minorities in both parts of Germany have become more restrictive and hostile.

Second, unification has also resulted in a certain retraditionalization of German political culture. On the West German side, the comprehen-sive imposition of West German political and economic institutions on East Germany has strengthened partriarchical political attitudes at the cost of participation and pluralism. On the East German side, the politi-cal-cultural reactions to the incorporation of East Germany into the West German system have been characterized predominantly by a con-tinuation of the previous political authoritarianism. Patriarchical over-identification with the West German state, apathetic disappointment with democratic politics, and resentful, aggressive attitudes outweigh democratic participatory forms of political culture. Under the condi-tions of partial modernization and massive social dislocation, the East German chances of following the West German example of political de-velopment are slim. A substantial stabilization of political authoritarian attitudes in East Germany is more likely. This has an impact on the over-all German political culture as well.

Finally, the tendencies discussed above also influence German atti-tudes toward Europe. The prior West German identification with West-ern Europe and active pro-European policy are being reshaped in a more German nationalistic way. The rise of patriotic sentiments and popular neonationalism corresponds to a more egoistic German European Com-munity policy.[148] Nevertheless this will not change the basic German commitment to the European Community. Regarding Eastern Europe, the picture is more ambiguous.[149] A desire for reconciliation and the idea of a European civilizing mission intermingle with traditional feel-ings of superiority, resentment, and fear of an increasing "flood of for-eigners" from the East. In balancing these sentiments, German politics attempts to integrate the closest Eastern neighbors into the European Community and to use them as a *cordon sanitaire* against imagined threats from farther east. The danger is that a strongly nationalistic Ger-many would delay a process of mutual German–East European under-standing like the one that took place between Germany and Western Europe earlier—a reconciliation badly needed in the face of the tragic past, and given the economic and political inequality of the present.

Conclusion

I have outlined a historical-sociological analysis of the continuities and discontinuities of the geopolitical, geoeconomic, and geocultural bases of the German nation-state. This analysis has compared the internal conditions of Germany, in relation to Europe, for the periods of its foun-dation and development (1871 to 1945) and division, reconstruction, and reunification (1945 to 1992). The results of this comparison are summarized below.

1. In terms of ethnic-territorial structures, the geopolitical basis of the German nation-state has been characterized by the relative weight of its population and its pronounced heterogenity, intermixture, and boundlessness vis-à-vis the adjacent ethnicities and nationalities in the middle of Europe. Under these preconditions, the foundation of the German Empire excluded a variety of ethnic Germans and included sev-eral non-German ethnic groups. Accordingly, the national structure of

the German Empire complicated internal national integration and exacerbated external nationalistic conflicts. By contrast, the present German nation-state is characterized by a high degree of ethnic-national consolidation, as a consequence of the destruction of the ethnic intermixture to the east. The potential for nationalistic conflicts is decisively reduced, but the ethnic conflict potential within German society, under the conditions of continuing pressure and the need for immigration, is and will remain relatively high.

Regarding political-institutional structures, the geopolitical basis of the German nation-state has been determined by its political weight and power potential in the center of the European state system. The foundation of the German Empire resulted externally in a decisive aggravation of political imbalances within the European state system, and internally in an exacerbation of the conflicts between the authoritarian-centralized and the traditionally federal-decentralized and the more democratic-constitutional structures. These represented pivotal preconditions for the sharp polarizations and oscillations between authoritarian and democratic political movements and regimes in the era from 1871 to 1945. By contrast, the political power potential of the German nation-state today is mediated in two basic ways: externally through transnational integration into the West European community, and internally through constitutional democratization and federalization. Both signify an essential balancing of the political power differentials between the German nation-state and the surrounding European state system.

2. Since Germany has become a predominantly industrial society, the geoeconomic basis of the German nation-state has been characterized by a position of relative dominance in the center of West-East European developmental unevenness. This economic power differential has been based particularly on Germany's technological lead, productivity, work discipline, and size of work force. Under conditions of nationalistic power competition in a globally hegemonic Europe, the foundation of the German Empire greatly exacerbated the economic and imperialist struggle between the European great powers. On the basis of its position of relative dominance, the German Empire attempted twice to build up a nationalistic position of hegemony over continental Europe. In both cases, this irrational hubris led to a temporary leveling down of Germany's dominant position.

By contrast, united Germany's position of relative dominance today is situated within the fundamentally changed structures of the world economy. The nationalistic-imperialistic competition of national economies within European world hegemony has been replaced by a globalized world economy in which only an economically united Europe is able to compete with other leading regional economic blocs. This global change transforms Germany's position of relative dominance within the European center-periphery matrix. The German economy is increasingly interconnected with the surrounding European countries and regions—technically, scientifically, industrially, and financially. Eastern Europe will eventually be associated and perhaps incorporated into a Westernized Europe in concentrically enlarging circles. In relation to Central and Eastern Europe, Germany's dominance will be especially pronounced, because of its geographical proximity and advanced state of development. But rather than reconstituting nationalistic relations of dependence, this will result in the dependent and partial modernization of East Central Europe.

3. The geocultural basis of the German nation-state has here been understood as the conceptions of German national identity and political culture within the European web of national identities and political cultures. In this regard, Germany has been located in the middle between the more politically determined nations in the West and the more ethnic-culturally determined nations in the East. In addition, Germany has been located in the middle between the Protestant countries to the North and the Catholic countries to the South. The fact that both boundaries cut through Germany has aggravated its problems of national and political integration. The foundation of the German Empire under Prussian Eastern hegemony exacerbated both conflict lines. The ethnic-cultural and authoritarian-Protestant components of German national identity pushed back the democratic constitutional and the more ethnically and religiously pluralistic components. This involution enabled, under specific historical circumstances, the rise and institutionalization of an extreme, chiliastic-racist and totalitarian nationalism.

By contrast, the ethnic-cultural basis of the unified German nation-state today is tightly linked with democratic constitutional components. Religious conflict lines, cultural-romantic hypostatization, and authoritarian-militaristic attitudes have largely disappeared. Instead, the pragmatic buildup of antinationalism in West Germany in reaction to the previous extreme nationalism is converging with the renewed national patriotism strengthened by the entrance of East Germany. It is true that in this context, the impact of a growing radical neonationalism at the political fringe is being felt. However, the renationalization and retraditionalization of German political culture and national identity are clearly limited, because overwhelmingly the political spectrum is characterized by democratic constitutional and European orientations and sentiments. Nevertheless, these sentiments go hand in hand with a more pronounced ethnic-cultural closure of European identity, in which Catholic East Central Europe is included, but non-European (mostly Islamic) and East European (Christian Orthodox) regions are excluded.

4. It is clear that the changing components of the German question reemerging with German unification have been stronger than the persistent elements. As a European nation-state, united Germany is again the most populous, the most advanced technically and economically, the most politically influential, and the most potentially significant militarily. Despite this historical continuity, however, the geopolitical, geoeconomic, and geocultural forms of Germany's position of relative dominance within Europe have essentially changed. The ethnic-territorial consolidation of the German nation-state is combined with its transnational integration and federal decentralization. The rising economic power of the German nation-state is linked with European mediation and international globalization of the German economy. And despite the increasing renationalization and retraditionalization of German political culture and national identity, the legitimacy of parliamentary democracy and European integration, though contested in its forms, has remained essentially unchanged. Even though the practical process of German unification and the materialization of a more balanced reciprocity between Germany and its Eastern neighbors will raise many problems, the German question, at least in the traditional sense, seems to be basically solved for the foreseeable future.

NOTES

1. See especially Ralf Dahrendorf, *Reflections on the Revolution in Europe* (London: Chatto and Windus, 1990); Ivo Banac, ed., *Eastern Europe in Revolution* (Ith-

aca: Cornell University Press, 1992); Daniel Chirot, ed., *The Crisis of Leninism and the Decline of the Left* (Seattle: University of Washington Press, 1991); Kazimierz Poznanski, ed., *Constructing Capitalism: The Reemergence of Civil Society and Liberalism* (Boulder: Westview Press, 1992); Stephen Graubard, ed., "Europe . . . Central Europe . . . Eastern Europe," *Daedalus* 119:1 (1990) and Stephen Graubard, ed., "The Exit from Communism," *Daedalus* 121:2 (1992); Charles Tilly, *European Revolutions, 1492–1992* (Oxford: Blackwell, 1993).

2. See especially David Calleo, *The German Problem Reconsidered: Germany and the World Order, 1870 to the Present* (Cambridge: Cambridge University Press, 1978); Wolf Gruner, *Die deutsche Frage: Ein Problem der deutschen Geschichte seit 1800* (Munich: Beck, 1985); Dirk Verheyen, *The German Question: A Cultural, Historical, and Geopolitical Exploration* (Boulder: Westview Press, 1991).

3. For example, Andrej Markovits and Stefan Reich, "Modell Deutschland and the New Europe," *Telos* 89 (1991): 45–64; Dahrendorf, *Reflections*, chap. 4; Paul Stares, ed., *The New Germany and the New Europe* (Washington, D.C.: Brookings Institution, 1992).

4. An excellent historical overview is John Breuilly, ed., *The State of Germany: The National Idea in the Making, Unmaking and Remaking of a Modern Nation-State* (London and New York: Longman, 1992).

5. Dahrendorf, *Reflections;* Paul Kennedy, *Preparing for the Twenty-first Century* (New York: Random House, 1993), pp. 270ff.: Paul Kennedy, "Germany in Europe: Half a Hegemony," *New Perspective Quarterly* 10:1 (1993): 35–38.

6. The starting point of this vehement debate was Hans-Ulrich Wehler, *The German Empire, 1871–1918* (Leamington Spa, U.K., and Dover, N.H.: Berg, 1985; *Das deutsche Kaiserreich*, Göttingen, 1973), and the critique of David Blackbourn and Geoff Eley, *The Peculiarities of German History: Bourgeois Society and Politics in Nineteenth-Century Germany* (Oxford: Oxford University Press, 1984; *Mythen deutscher Geschichtsschreibung*, Frankfurt/M., 1980). See the recent accounts of Jürgen Kocka, "Deutsche Geschichte vor Hitler: Zur Diskussion über den 'Deutschen Sonderweg,'" in Jürgen Kocka, *Geschichte und Aufklärung* (Göttingen: Vandenhoeck & Ruprecht, 1989), and Richard Evans, "The Myth of Germany's Missing Revolution," *New Left Review* 149 (1985): 67–94.

7. Calleo, *German Problem Reconsidered.*

8. This is also the premise of the comparative approach by John D. Stephens, "Democratic Transition and Breakdown in Western Europe, 1870–1939; A Test of the Barrington Moore Thesis," *American Journal of Sociology* 94:5 (1989): 1019–77, and Dietrich Rueschemeyer, Evelyne H. Stephens, and John D. Stephens, *Capitalist Development and Democracy* (Chicago: University of Chicago Press, 1992).

9. Especially Stein Rokkan, "Dimensions of State Formation and Nation-building: A Possible Paradigm for Research on Variations in Europe," in Charles Tilly, ed., *The Formation of National States in Western Europe* (Princeton: Princeton University Press, 1975), pp. 562–600; Stein Rokkan and Derek W. Urwin, *Economy, Territory, Identity: Politics of West European Peripheries* (London: Sage, 1983); Stein Rokkan and Derek W. Urwin, eds., *The Politics of Territorial Identity* (London: Sage, 1982); see also Peter Flora, "Stein Rokkans Makro-Modell der pol-

itischen Entwicklung Europas: Ein Rekonstruktionsversuch," *Kölner Zeitschrift für Soziologie und Sozialpsychologie* 33:3 (1981): 397–436.

10. M. Rainer Lepsius, "Die Bundesrepublik Deutschland in der Kontinuität und Diskontinuität historischer Entwicklungen: Einige methodische Überlegungen," in Werner Conze and M. Rainer Lepsius, eds., *Sozialgeschichte der Bundesrepublik Deutschland: Beiträge zum Kontinuitätsproblem* (Stuttgart: Klett-Cotta, 1983), pp. 11–19.

11. "Paradoxically the history of Europe is one of center formation at the periphery of a network of strong and independent cities: this explains the great diversity of configurations and the extraordinary tangles of shifting alliances and conflicts." Rokkan, "Dimensions," p. 576. On the specific multipolarity of European history see Samuel N. Eisenstadt, *European Civilization in Comparative Perspective* (Oxford: Oxford University Press, 1987). See also Max Haller, "The Challenge for Comparative Sociology in the Transformation of Europe," *International Sociology* 5:2 (1990): 183–204. See also the further development of Rokkan's analysis by Charles Tilly, *Coercion, Capital, and European States, AD 990–1990* (Cambridge, Mass.: Blackwell, 1990) and Michael Mann, *The Sources of Social Power,* vol. 1 (Cambridge: Cambridge University Press, 1986).

12. Rokkan, "Dimensions," pp. 578–79.

13. Immanuel Wallerstein, *The Modern World-System* and *The Modern World-System II* (New York: Academic Press, 1974, 1980); Daniel Chirot, *Social Change in the Modern Era* (San Diego: Harcourt Brace Jovanovich, 1986).

14. Chirot, *Social Change;* Daniel Chirot, ed., *The Origins of Backwardness in Eastern Europe* (Berkeley: University of California Press, 1989).

15. Geoffrey Barraclough, *The Origins of Modern Germany* (New York: Norton, 1984); Mary Fulbrook, *Concise History of Germany* (Cambridge: Cambridge University Press, 1990).

16. Rokkan, "Dimensions"; Tilly, *Coercion, Capital, and European States, AD 990–1990;* Paul Kennedy, *The Rise and Fall of the Great Powers* (New York: Random House, 1987). Particularly on Germany: Michael Hughes, *Early Modern Germany, 1477–1806* (Philadelphia: University of Pennsylvania Press, 1992).

17. Eric Hobsbawm, *The Age of Revolution, 1789–1848* (London: Weidenfeld and Nicolson, 1962). Immanuel Wallerstein, *The Modern World System III* (New York: Academic Press, 1989).

18. Alexander Gerschenkron, *Economic Backwardness in Historical Perspective* (Cambridge: Harvard University Press, 1962); Dieter Senghaas, *The European Experience: A Historical Critique of Development Theory* (Leamington Spa, U.K., and Dover, N.H.: Berg, 1985); Chirot, *Origins of Backwardness.*

19. Hans-Ulrich Wehler, *Deutsche Gesellschaftsgeschichte, 1700–1815,* and *1815–1848/49,* 2 vols. (Munich: Beck, 1987); Thomas Nipperdey, *Deutsche Geschichte, Bürgerwelt und Starker Staat* (Munich: Beck, 1984); James Sheehan, *German History, 1775–1866* (Oxford: Oxford University Press, 1989).

20. Gruner, *Die deutsche Frage;* Kennedy, *Rise and Fall.* See also Gordon Craig, *Europe since 1815* (New York: Dryden Press, 1974), chap. 1.

21. David Landes, *The Unbound Prometheus: Technological Change and Industrial Development in Western Europe from 1750 to the Present* (Cambridge: Cam-

bridge University Press, 1969); Wehler, *Gesellschaftsgeschichte Deutschlands;* Sydney Pollard, *Peaceful Conquest: The Industrialization of Europe, 1760–1970* (Oxford University Press, 1981); Hubert Kiesewetter, *Industrielle Revolution in Deutschland, 1815–1914* (Frankfurt/M.: Suhrkamp, 1989).

22. Kiesewetter, *Industrielle Revolution;* Willfried Spohn, *Weltmarktkonkurrenz und Industrialisierung Deutschlands, 1870–1914* (Berlin: Olle & Wolter, 1977).

23. Comparative approaches to German nationalism: Peter Alter, *Nationalismus* (Frankfurt/M.: Suhrkamp, 1985); Rogers Brubaker, *Citizenship and Nationhood in France and Germany* (Cambridge: Harvard University Press, 1992); Werner Conze, *Gesellschaft, Staat, Nation: Gesammelte Aufsätze* (Stuttgart: Klett-Cotta, 1992); Bernd Giessen, ed., *Nationale und kulturelle Identität: Studien zur Entwicklung des kollektiven Bewusstseins in der Neuzeit* (Frankfurt/M.: Suhrkamp, 1991); Liah Greenfeld, *Nationalism: Five Roads to Modernity* (Cambridge: Harvard University Press, 1992); Hans Kohn, *Prelude to Nation-States: The French and German Experience* (Princeton: Van Nostrand, 1967); George Mosse, *The Culture of Western Europe* (Boulder: Westview Press, 1988); Hans-August Winkler, ed., *Nationalismus* (Königstein/Ts.: Athenaeum, 1985), especially Theodor Schieder, "Typologie und Erscheinungsformen des Nationalstaates in Europa," pp. 119–37. More generally, see Ernest Gellner, *Nations and Nationalism* (Oxford: Blackwell, 1983), and Anthony Smith, *National Identity* (Reno: University of Nevada Press, 1992).

24. Gruner, *Die deutsche Frage,* chap. 4; Dieter Langewiesche, in Breuilly, ed., *The State of Germany;* Langewiesche, "Reich, Nation und Staat in der jüngeren deutschen Geschichte," *Historische Zeitschrift* 254 (1992): 341–81; Hagen Schulze, "Europe and the German Question in Historical Perspective," in Hagen Schulze, ed., *Nation-Building in Central Europe* (Leamington Spa, U.K., and Dover, N.H.: Berg, 1987), pp. 183–96.

25. Robert Berdahl, "Der deutsche Nationalismus in neuer Sicht," in Winkler, ed., *Nationalismus,* pp. 138–54; James Sheehan, "What Is German History?: Reflections on the Role of the Nation in German History and Historiography," *Journal of Modern History* 53 (1981): 1–23.

26. Gerschenkron, *Economic Backwardness;* Landes, *Unbound Prometheus;* Kiesewetter, *Industrielle Revolution in Deutschland;* Spohn, *Weltmarktkonkurrenz und Industrialiserung Deutschlands,* pp. 318ff.

27. Langewiesche, "Reich, Nation und Staat"; Nipperdey, *Deutsche Geschichte, 1800–1866;* Sheehan, *German History;* Hagen Schulze, *Der Weg zum Nationalstaat: Die deutsche Nationalbewegung vom 18. Jahrhundert bis zur Reichsgründung* (Munich: Deutscher Taschenbuch Verlag, 1985).

28. Calleo, *German Problem Reconsidered;* Gruner, *Die deutsche Frage;* Kennedy, *Rise and Fall.*

29. See the sharp polemic of Hans-Ulrich Wehler, *Entsorgung der Vergangenheit?: Ein Polemischer Essay zum "Historikerstreit"* (Munich: Beck, 1988), pp. 174ff.; but compare, for example, the critical review of Paul Kennedy (1987) by Klaus Hildebrandt in *Historische Zeitschrift* 250 (1990): 347–56.

30. Sheehan, "What Is German History?"

31. This is emphasized by Thomas Nipperdey, *Deutsche Geschichte, 1866– 1918: Machtstaat vor der Demokratie* (Munich: Beck, 1992); and Werner Conze,

"Staats- und Nationalpolitik: Kontinuität und Neubeginn," in Conze and Lepsius, eds., *Sozialgeschichte*, pp. 441–67.

32. Schulze, *Der Weg zum Nationalstaat*, pp. 119ff.; Dieter Langewiesche, "Revolution von oben?: Krieg und Nationalstaatsgründung in Deutschland," in Dieter Langewiesche, ed., *Revolution und Krieg: Zur Dynamik historischen Wandels seit dem 18. Jahrhundert* (Paderborn: Schöningh, 1989), pp. 117–33.

33. Langewiesche, "Reich, Nation und Staat," and William Carr, "The Unification of Germany," in Breuilly, ed., *The State of Germany*, pp. 80–102.

34. On the dialectical development of German and Austrian national identities see Langewiesche, "Reich, Nation und Staat," p. 376; Barbara Jelavich, *Modern Austria: Empire and Republic, 1815–1986* (Cambridge and New York: Cambridge University Press, 1987).

35. Hans-Ulrich Wehler, *Probleme des deutschen Kaiserreichs* (Göttingen: Vandenhoeck & Ruprecht, 1972); Thomas Nipperdey, *Deutsche Geschichte, 1866–1918*, 2:282–86.

36. Nipperdey, *Deutsche Geschichte, 1866–1918*, 2:266–81; W. Hagen, *Germans, Poles, and Jews: The Nationality Conflict in the Prussian East, 1772–1914* (Chicago: University of Chicago Press, 1980).

37. Wolfgang Mommsen, *Der autoritäre Nationalstaat* Reinbek: Rohwolt, 1990); Nipperdey, *Deutsche Geschichte, 1866–1918*, vol. 2; Otto Pflanze, ed., *Innenpolitische Probleme des deutschen Kaiserreichs*; Wehler, *Das deutsche Kaiserreich*. For a comparative perspective see Michael Mann, *The Sources of Social Power*, vol. 2 (Cambridge: Cambridge University Press, 1993).

38. This, of course, is the adamant critique of Max Weber; see Wolfgang Mommsen, *Max Weber: Gesellschaft, Politik und Geschichte* (Frankfurt/M.: Suhrkamp, 1974); Wolfgang Mommsen, *The Political and Social Theory of Max Weber* (Chicago: University of Chicago Press, 1989).

39. Derek W. Urwin, "Germany: From Geographical Expression to Regional Accommodation," in Rokkan and Urwin, eds., *The Politics of Territorial Identity*, pp. 165–250.

40. Klaus Bade, *Population, Labour, and Migration in 19th and 20th Century Germany* (Leamington Spa, U.K., and Dover, N.H.: Berg, 1987); Hans-Ulrich Wehler, *Krisenherde des Kaiserreichs, 1871–1918* (Göttingen: Vandenhoeck & Ruprecht, 1970).

41. Thomas Nipperdey, *Deutsche Geschichte, 1866–1918: Arbeitswelt und Bürgersinn* (Munich: Beck, 1990): Thomas Nipperdey, *Religion im Umbruch: Deutschland, 1871–1918* (Munich: Beck, 1989).

42. George Mosse, *German Jews Beyond Judaism* (Cincinnati: Hebrew Union College Press, 1985). Reinhard Rurup, *Emanzipation und Antisemitismus* (Göttingen: Vandenhoeck & Ruprecht, 1975); Uriel Tal, *Christians and Jews in Germany, 1870–1914* (Ithaca: Cornell University Press, 1975).

43. Ira Katznelson and Aristide Zolberg, eds., *Working-Class Formation: Nineteenth-Century Patterns in Western Europe and the United States* (Princeton: Princeton University Press, 1986); Jürgen Kocka, *Lohnarbeit und Klassenbildung* (Göttingen: Vandenhoeck & Ruprecht, 1983); Seymour M. Lipset, "Working-Class Radicalism and Reformism," in his *Consensus and Conflict* (New Brunswick:

Transaction Books, 1985); Carlos Waisman, *Modernization and the Working-Class: The Politics of Legitimacy* (Austin: University of Texas Press, 1982): also Willfried Spohn, "Religion and Working-Class Formation in Imperial Germany, 1871–1914," *Politics and Society* 19:1 (1991): 109–32.

44. For an excellent account of the nineteenth-century German pattern of industrialization, see Richard Tilly, "Germany," in Richard Sylla and Gianni Toniolo, eds., *Patterns of European Industrialization: The Nineteenth Century* (London: Routledge, 1991), pp. 175–97.

45. Kennedy, *Rise and Fall;* George Modelski, *Long Cycles in World Politics* (Seattle: University of Washington Press, 1987); Senghaas, *The European Experience.*

46. Eric J. Hobsbawm, *The Age of Capital, 1848–1875* (Cambridge: Cambridge University Press, 1975) and *The Age of Empire* (New York: Pantheon Books, 1989).

47. See especially Paul Kennedy, *The Rise of the Anglo-German Antagonism, 1860–1914* (London and Boston: Allen and Unwin, 1980), and my own study *Weltmarktkonkurrenz und Industrialisierung Deutschlands, 1870–1914* (Berlin, 1977).

48. Spohn, *Weltmarktkonkurrenz und Industrialisierung Deutschlands,* p. 97.

49. Kennedy, *Rise and Fall,* p. 199.

50. Paul Bairoch, "Europe's Gross National Product: 1800–1975," *European Economic History,* 1976, p. 281. The figures are in 1960 U.S. dollars and prices.

51. Paul Bairoch, "International Industrialization Levels from 1750 to 1980," *European Economic History,* 1984, p. 296.

52. Spohn, *Weltmarktkonkurrenz und Industrialisierung Deutschlands,* pp. 150ff.

53. Calculated from I. Svennilson, *Growth and Stagnation in the European Economy* (Geneva, 1954), pp. 176ff.

54. Ivan T. Berend and György Ranki, *The European Periphery and Industrialization, 1780–1914* (Cambridge and New York: Cambridge University Press, 1982), p. 75.

55. Spohn, *Weltmarktkonkurrenz und Industrialisierung Deutschlands,* pp. 158ff.; Berend and Ranki, *European Periphery,* pp. 77–79.

56. The interregional interconnections are stressed by Sidney Pollard, *Peaceful Conquest: The Industrialization of Europe, 1760–1970* (Oxford: Oxford University Press, 1981); the role of the state is emphasized by Gerschenkron, *Economic Backwardness;* see also the comparative discussion in Berend and Ranki, *European Periphery.*

57. The economic dimension of German nationalism is emphasized by Harold James, *A German Identity, 1770–1990* (New York: Routledge, 1989).

58. Hans Rosenberg, *Grosse Depression und Bismarckzeit* (Berlin, 1967); Spohn, *Weltmarktkonkurrenz und Industrialisierung Deutschlands,* pp. 239–55.

59. Kennedy, *Rise and Fall,* chap. 6.

60. Knut Borchardt, *Grundriss der deutschen Wirtschaftsgeschichte* (Göttingen: Vandenhoeck & Ruprecht, 1978); Dietmar Petzina, *Die deutsche Wirtschaft in der Zwischenkriegszeit* (Wiesbaden: Steiner, 1977); Alfred Sohn-Rethel, *Ökonomie und Klassenstruktur des deutschen Faschismus* (Frankfurt/M.: Suhrkamp, 1973).

61. Friedrich Naumann, *Central Europe* (London, 1916); Diethard Behrens, "Kontinuitäten deutscher Europapolitik?" in *Prokla, Zeitschrift für kritische Sozialwissenschaft* 75 (1989): 10–28; Rudolf Jankowski, "Die aktuelle Mitteleuropadiskussion in historischer Perspektive," *Historische Zeitschrift* 247 (1988): 529–40.

62. Michael Burleigh, *Germany Turns Eastwards: A Study of Ostforschung in the Third Reich* (Cambridge and New York: Cambridge University Press, 1990).

63. In this sense it is problematic when Calleo, *German Problem Reconsidered*, does not take internal aspects of Germany's political development into consideration.

64. The *Sonderweg* thesis (see note 6) was originally formulated by Thorstein Veblen, *Imperial Germany and the Industrial Revolution* (New York: Viking Press, 1946); Ralf Dahrendorf, *Gesellschaft und Freiheit in Deutschland* (Munich: Piper, 1964); Barrington Moore, *Social Origins of Dictatorship and Democracy* (Boston: Beacon Press, 1966).

65. Blackbourn and Eley, *Peculiarities of German History*.

66. Breuilly, ed., *The State of Germany*; Mosse, *Culture of Western Europe*, pp. 65–85; Nipperdey, *Deutsche Geschichte, 1866–1918*, 2:250–65. See also Nobert Elias, *Studien über die Deutschen* (Frankfurt/M.: Suhrkamp, 1990).

67. This is the tendency in the otherwise excellent studies of Brubaker, *Citizenship and Nationhood*, and Greenfeld, *Nationalism*.

68. George Mosse, *The Crisis of German Ideology: Intellectual Origins of the Third Reich* (New York, 1964; reprint, Fertig, 1981); Helmuth Plessner, *Die verspätete Nation: Über die politische Verführbarkeit des bürgerlichen Geistes* (Frankfurt/M., 1974).

69. Elias, *Studien über die Deutschen*.

70. Koppel S. Pinson, *Pietism as a Factor in the Rise of German Nationalism* (New York, 1934), and *Modern Germany* (New York: Macmillan, 1966).

71. Elias, *Studien über die Deutschen*; Mosse, *Culture of Western Europe*; Rudolf von Thadden, "Aufbau nationaler Identität: Deutschland und Frankreich im Vergleich," in Bernd Giessen, ed., *Nationale und kulturelle Identität*, pp. 493–510.

72. Burleigh, *Germany Turns Eastwards*.

73. Wolfgang Mommsen, "Der Geist von 1914: Das Programm eines 'politischen Sonderwegs' der Deutschen," in Wolfgang Mommsen, *Über die Deutschen und die deutsche Frage* (Munich: Piper, 1990), pp. 87–106.

74. Karl Dietrich Bracher, *The German Dictatorship: The Origins, Structure, and Effects of National Socialism* (New York: Holt, Rinehart, and Winston, 1970); Rainer Lepsius, *Extremer Nationalismus: Strukturbedingungen vor der Nationalsozialistischen Machtergreifung* (Stuttgart: Klett, 1966); Kurt Sontheimer, *Antidemokratisches Denken in der Weimarer Republik: Die Politischen Ideen des deutschen Nationalismus, 1918–1933* (Munich, 1968).

75. Mosse, *Crisis of German Ideology*; James M. Rhodes, *The Hitler Movement* (Stanford: Hoover Institution Press, 1980).

76. Kennedy, *Rise and Fall*.

77. Johann Galtung, *Europe in the Making* (New York: Crane Russak, 1989); Derek Urwin, *Western Europe Since 1945* (London, 1985): Derek Urwin, *The Community of Europe: A History of European Integration Since 1945* (London and New York: Longman, 1991).

78. Gruner, *Die deutsche Frage*.

79. Wilfried Loth, *Ost-West Konflikt und deutsche Frage* (Munich: dtv, 1989); Ernst Nolte, *Deutschland und der Kalte Krieg* (Stuttgart: Klett-Cotta, 1985).

80. Urwin, *Western Europe Since 1945* and *The Community of Europe*.

81. Janos Kornai, *The Socialist System: The Political Economy of Communism* (Princeton: Princeton University Press, 1992), especially pp. 355–59; Kazimierz Poznanski, *Technology, Competition, and the Soviet Bloc in the World Market* (Berkeley: Institute of International Studies, University of California, 1987).

82. Ernest Gellner, "Ethnicity and Faith in Eastern Europe," *Daedalus* 119:1 (1990): 279–94; Smith, *National Identity*; Erhard Stölting, *Eine Weltmacht zerbricht: Nationalitäten und Religionen in der UdSSR* (Frankfurt/M.: Eichorn, 1991); Charles Tilly, "Ethnic Conflict in the Soviet Union," *The Working-Paper Series*, no. 106 (New York: Center of Studies of Social Change, 1991).

83. Robert Gilpin, *The Political Economy of International Relations* (Princeton: Princeton University Press, 1987); Kennedy, *Preparing for the Twenty-First Century*.

84. Breuilly, ed., *The State of Germany*; Mary Fulbrook, *The Divided Nation: A History of Germany* (Oxford: Oxford University Press, 1991), chap. 9.

85. Christoph Klessmann, *Die doppelte Staatsgrundung: Deutsche Geschichte, 1945–1955* (Göttingen: Vandenhoeck & Ruprecht, 1986); Mommsen, *Nation und Geschichte*; Hans-Peter Schwarz, *Vom Reich zur Bundesrepublik* (Neuwied and Berlin: Luchterhand, 1966); Dieter Thränhardt, *Geschichte der Bundesrepublik Deutschland* (Frankfurt/M.: Suhrkamp, 1986).

86. Rainer Lepsius, "Die Bundesrepublik Deutschland in der Kontinuität und Diskontinuität der deutschen Geschichte"; Klessmann, *Die doppelte Staatsgründung*.

87. See generally, Gellner, *Nations and Nationalism*; Smith, *National Identity*.

88. William Sheridan Allen, "The Collapse of Nationalism in Nazi Germany," and Peter Alter, "Nationalism and German Politics after 1945," in Breuilly, ed., *The State of Germany*, pp. 141–76; David Conradt, "Changing German Political Culture," in Gabriel A. Almond and Sidney Verba, eds., *The Civic Culture Revisited* (Boston and Toronto: Little, Brown, 1980), pp. 212–72.

89. David Conradt, *The German Polity* (New York: Longman, 1989); Ernst Fraenkel, *Deutschland und die westlichen Demokratien* Frankfurt/M.: Suhrkamp, 1991).

90. Derek Urwin, "Germany: From Geographical Expression to Regional Accommodation," in Rokkan and Urwin, *The Politics of Territorial Identity*.

91. Gordon Smith, William Paterson, and Peter Merkl, *Developments in West German Politics* (London: Macmillan, 1989).

92. Volker Berghahn, *Modern Germany: Society, Economy, and Politics in the Twentieth Century* (Cambridge: Cambridge University Press, 1987); David Childs, *The GDR, Moscow's German Ally* (London: Unwin Hyman, 1988); Fulbrook, *Divided Nation*; Gert-Joachim Glaessner, *Die andere deutsche Republik* (Opladen: Westdeutscher Verlag, 1989); Klessmann, *Die doppelte Staatsgründung*; Sigrid Meuschel, *Legitimation und Parteiherrschaft in der DDR* (Frankfurt/M.: Suhrkamp, 1992); Dietrich Staritz, *Geschichte der DDR, 1949–1985* (Frankfurt/M.: Suhrkamp, 1985); Hermann Weber, *Geschichte der DDR* (Munich: Deutscher Taschenbuch Verlag, 1989).

93. Meuschel, *Legitimation und Parteiherrschaft,* part 1: Weber, *Geschichte der DDR,* chap. 3; Staritz, *Geschichte der DDR,* part 2.

94. On the GDR elite see Christian P. Ludz, *The Changing Party Elite in East Germany* (Cambridge: MIT Press, 1972).

95. Bruno Schoch, ed., *Deutschlands Einheit und Europas Zukunft* (Frankfurt/ M.: Suhrkamp, 1992); Stares, ed., *The New Germany and the New Europe.*

96. The emphasis on West German elite nationalism and East German economic nationalism is one-sided; for example see Claus Offe, "On the Tactical Use Value of National Sentiments," in *Critical Sociology* 17:3 (1990): 9–16; also Jürgen Habermas, *Die nachholende Revolution* (Frankfurt/M.: Suhrkamp, 1990).

97. Urwin, *The Community of Europe;* S. Bulmer and W. E. Paterson, *The Federal Republic of Germany and the European Community* (London, 1987).

98. Rainer M. Lepsius, "Beyond the Nation-State: The Multinational State as the Model for the European Community," *Telos* 91 (1992): 57–76; Ludger Kuhnhardt, "Federalism and Subsidiarity," *Telos* 91 (1992): 77–86; Urwin, "German Federalism as a Model for the European Community."

99. Wolf Gruner, "Germany in Europe: The German Question as Burden and as Opportunity," in Breuilly, ed., *The State of Germany,* pp. 201–23; Stares, ed., *The New Germany and the New Europe.*

100. Kennedy, *Rise and Fall,* pp. 413–37; Urwin, *Western Europe Since 1945.*

101. Poznanski, *Technology, Competition, and the Soviet Bloc.*

102. Wolfgang Abelshauser, *Wirtschaftsgeschichte der Bundesrepublik Deutschland, 1945–1980* (Frankfurt/M.: Suhrkamp, 1983); Volker Berghahn, *Modern Germany;* Borchardt, *Grundriss der deutschen Wirtschaftsgeschichte;* Hans Jaeger, *Geschichte der Wirtschaftsordnung in Deutschland* (Frankfurt/M.: Suhrkamp, 1988).

103. Berghahn, *Modern Germany,* p. 271.

104. OECD, *Main Economic Indicators, 1986:* In 1985 Great Britain had 56 million, France 55 million, and Italy 57 million inhabitants.

105. Bairoch, "Europe's Gross National Product: 1800–1975," p. 303.

106. Bairoch, "International Industrialization Levels," p. 299.

107. Bairoch, "European Foreign Trade," p. 14.

108. Christian Deubner, Udo Rehfeldt, Frieder Schlupp, "Deutsch-französische Wirtschaftsbeziehungen im Rahmen der weltwirtschaftlichen Arbeitsteilung: Interdependenz, Divergenz oder strukturelle Dominanz," in Robert Picht, ed., *Deutschland, Frankreich, Europa: Bilanz einer schwierigen Partnerschaft* (Munich: Piper, 1978), pp. 91–136.

109. Allan M. Williams, *The Western European Economy: A Geography of Post-War Development* (London: Hutchinson, 1987), p. 39.

110. Michael Kaser, "The Economic Dimension," in Edwina Moreton, ed., *Germany Between East and West* (Cambridge and New York: Cambridge University Press, 1987), pp. 123–40.

111. Allan Williams, ed., *Southern Europe Transformed* (London: Harper and Row, 1984).

112. Ibid.; Urwin, *The Community of Europe.*

113. Berghahn, *Modern Germany,* chaps. 5 and 6.

114. Kornai, *The Socialist System,* pp. 355ff.

115. Berghahn, *Modern Germany;* Gert Leptin, *Die deutsche Wirtschaft: Ein Ost-West Vergleich* (Opladen: Westdeutscher Verlag, 1970); Gert Leptin, *Economic Reform in the GDR Economy* (London, 1978).

116. Kaser, "The Economic Dimension."

117. Daniel Chirot, "What Happened in 1989?" in Chirot, ed., *Crisis of Leninism.*

118. Kennedy, *Preparing for the Twenty-First Century,* pp. 270ff.

119. Michael Kreile, "The Political Economy of the New Germany," in Stares, ed., *The New Germany and the New Europe,* pp. 71–79.

120. Ivan Szelenyi, "Social and Political Landscape, Central Europe, Fall 1990," in Banac, ed., *Eastern Europe in Revolution,* pp. 25–241, especially pp. 234ff.

121. Reinhard Rode, "Deutschland: Weltwirtschaftsmacht oder überforderter Euro-Hegemon?" in Schoch, ed., *Deutschlands Einheit und Europas Zukunft,* pp. 203–28, here p. 212.

122. Anne-Marie Le Gloannec, "The Implications of German Unification for Western Europe," in Stares, ed., *The New Germany and the New Europe,* pp. 251–78, here p. 258.

123. Otto Johnson, ed., *World Almanac 1993,* pp. 132–33.

124. Kennedy, *Preparing for the Twenty-first Century,* chap. 12.

125. Andras Inotai, "Economic Implications of German Unification for Central and Eastern Europe," in Stares, ed., *The New Germany and the New Europe,* pp. 279–304.

126. Ibid.

127. Le Gloannec, "Implications of German Unification"; and Inotai, "Economic Implications."

128. Inotai, "Economic Implications."

129. Kennedy, *Preparing for the Twenty-First Century,* chaps. 11 and 12.

130. Williams, *Southern Europe Transformed;* Senghaas, *The European Experience.*

131. Peter Merkl, "A New German Identity," in Gordon Smith, William Paterson, Peter Merkl, and Stephen Padgett, eds., *Developments in German Politics* (Durham: Duke University Press, 1992), pp. 327–48.

132. Allen, "The Collapse of Nationalism," Alter, "Nationalism and German Politics," and Conradt, "Changing German Political Culture."

133. Schwarz, *Vom Reich zur Bundesrepublik.*

134. Conradt, "Changing German Political Culture."

135. Peter Pulzer, "Political Ideology," and Peter Merkl, "A New German Identity," in Smith et al., eds., *Developments in German Politics,* pp. 303–26 and 327–48.

136. Alter, "Nationalism and German Politics."

137. Gunter Trautmann, ed., *Die hässlichen Deutschen?: Deutschland im Spiegel der westlichen und ostlichen Nachbarn* (Darmstadt: Wissenschaftliche Buchgesellschaft, 1991).

138. Mary Fulbrook, "Nation, State and Political Culture in Divided Germany, 1945–90," in Breuilly, ed., *The State of Germany,* pp. 177–200.

139. Meuschel, *Legitimation und Parteiherrschaft,* part III.4.

140. Albert Hirschman, "Exit, Voice, and the Fate of the German Democratic Republic," *World Politics* (1992): 173–202.

141. Meuschel, *Legitimation und Parteiherrschaft,* part III.

142. Sigrid Meuschel, "Revolution in der DDR: Versuch einer sozialwissenschaftlichen Interpretation," in Wolfgang Zapf, ed., *Modernisierung moderner Gesellschaften* (Frankfurt/M.: Campus, 1991).

143. Hirschman, "Exit, Voice, and the Fate of the German Democratic Republic"; Norman Naimark, " 'Ich will hier raus': Emigration and the Collapse of the German Democratic Republic," in Banac, ed., *Eastern Europe in Revolution,* pp. 72–95; Helmut W. Smith, "Socialism and Nationalism in the East German Revolution, 1989–1990," *Eastern European Politics and Societies* 5:2 (1991): 234–46.

144. John Breuilly, "Nationalism and German Unification," in Breuilly, ed., *The State of Germany,* pp. 224–38.

145. Merkl, "A New German Identity."

146. Stephen Brockmann, "The Unification Debate," in *New German Critique,* Winter 1991, pp. 3–30.

147. On the following see especially Merkl, "A New German Identity."

148. Klaus Gottstein, ed., *Integrated Europe?: Eastern and Western Perceptions of the Future* (Frankfurt/M.: Campus, 1992).

149. Ibid.; Schoch, ed., *Deutschlands Einheit und Europas Zukunft;* Trautmann, *Die hässlichen Deutschen.*

German Economic
Penetration in
East Central Europe
in Historical Perspective

Ivan T. Berend

In December 1990, the German Volkswagen company bought 31 percent of the shares of the single most important Czech industrial firm, Skoda, in Mladá Boleslav, forty miles northeast of Prague, for $333 million. According to reports in the spring of 1993, it invested $163 million in the company and planned to add another $313 million in 1994. The initial agreement estimated that this landmark investment would amount to $6.3 billion over seven years, acquiring 70 to 75 percent of Skoda's shares.[1] When fully realized, the transaction would be the largest cross-border investment in European history.

"Fears of German economic domination of the region also abound," reported the *New York Times*. "Germany is now central Europe's largest trading partner, with a volume of about $10 billion with Poland and the former Czechoslovakia and about $5 billion with Hungary last year."[2] Is the unforgettable history of the 1930s repeating itself, and a new, enlarged German *Grossraumwirtschaft* again in the making? Is it the mysterious fate of East Central Europe that the region must face a traditional and continuous German *Drang nach Osten?* Is the region subject to a geopolitical determination which always reappears in certain historical situations?

Without pretending to answer these questions, I am going to analyze the history of German–East Central European economic connections.

Core-Periphery Relations and Regional Blocs

The concept of a world economy suggests a close relationship between a number of "national" economies. Since the participants of the world system are not equal in scope and strength, there is, according to several highly diverse interpretations, a kind of subordination and dependence in the system in addition to an unquestionable interdependence. Many theories of the world economy—ranging from the late nineteenth- and early twentieth-century socialist concepts of imperialism put forth by Karl Kautsky, Rosa Luxemburg, Nikolai Bukharin, and Vladimir Lenin to the post–World War II concept of Raul Prebisch and Immanuel Wallerstein of the "core-periphery" structure of the modern world system—have rejected, albeit in different ways, the classical and neoliberal theories of a harmonious world market of equal partners capable of realizing a "comparative advantage." Instead, these analysts characterize international economic links between nonequal partners as a system of domination and subordination, where all advantages accumulate on one side and all disadvantages on the other.

There is no place here to summarize and criticize the different concepts. It is, however, necessary to define my own interpretation at the outset. "Core" and "periphery" are, in fact, historical categories with ever-changing references. Certain peripheral areas catch up, while certain parts of the core break off and lose their central character. As stated in a book I wrote with Gyorgy Ranki:

We thus understand by "periphery" an area dependent on the "core." In a peripheral country, the economy, foreign trade, balance of payments, and production develop tied to, influenced by and subordinated to the core countries. The relationship is fundamentally an unequal one and benefits the core. It is often destructive of the periphery; *but it can also be an inducement to development, serving—under appropriate conditions—to lift the area from its peripheral position.*[3]

This statement was based on the analysis of the nineteenth-century European economic process, but is certainly even more applicable to the twentieth-century world economy. It should be added that core-periphery interpretations often simplify the complex pattern of the world economy by talking about a Western core and several—Latin American, East Central European, Asian, and African—peripheries. According to this abstraction, the modern world system reflects the pattern of the solar system with a star (the sun) at its core and several planets on its periphery.

The reality, however, particularly in the twentieth century, is of an order whose structure is much more complex. Instead of the solar system as a model, I suggest the universe, which consists of several solar systems, several star-suns with their own planets. The universe of the modern world system thus has several cores with their own peripheries.

Hence, in addition to the general abstraction of a single core, or Western world,[4] with its peripheries on all of the continents, one should differentiate between at least two additional levels of core-periphery relations when describing the structure of the modern world economy:

1. Inside each single "national" economy there are several small cores—developed cities, metropolises surrounded by economically connected villages. (The metropolis-village parable was used by Nikolai Bukharin to describe the world economic system in 1915.) These are, however, intra- and not inter-country relations.

2. Inside each single continent and subcontinent, or more precisely, historical-geopolitical region, there are regional cores with their own peripheries. To mention a few examples: the nearly self-sufficient Habsburg Empire had a "Cisleithan" core (the Austrian-Czech lands) and Hungarian, Dalmatian, and Bukovinian peripheries from the sixteenth century on. During the same period, each colonial empire reproduced core-periphery relations with a European "Fatherland core"; and Asian, African, and other colonies acting as peripheries. The United States became the core of the American continent, with its Latin American "backyard," by the late nineteenth century. In the twentieth century, Japan definitely played the role of a regional core, with its continental Asian backyard. And a united Germany, from the last third of the nineteenth century on, emerged as a core with her *Südosteuropäische* backyard.

Historical Antecedents

There are, of course, certain historical antecedents and geopolitical determinants of the central role of Germany. They go back to the early centuries when German tribes, who were excellent warriors, appeared in Europe and represented a permanent danger for their neighbors. In his famous description and analysis of "Germany" written in A.D. 98, Tacitus, while intending to present a sharp contrast between the increasingly decadent and declining Romans and the free, puritan, tough, and rising Germans, was both impressed and shocked by their attitudes and characteristics: "The Germans transact no business, public or private, without being armed," and "think it base and spiritless to earn by sweat what they might purchase with blood."[5] He also stressed the emancipation of the German youth "from paternal rule [which] dedicates him to the service of the state. Henceforth war becomes the freemen's chief and proper work. . . ."[6]

The various German states or empires had traditional military and empire-building ambitions, and the territories and countries east of Germany were among their primary targets. *Drang nach Osten,* or advance toward the East, was a leitmotif of German political ambitions throughout the Middle Ages. The newly founded Hungarian kingdom faced its first attack by foreigners in the early eleventh century, and this came from Germany. The Baltic area was conquered by the German Teutonic knights, and Russia was saved only by the successful resistance of Alexander Nevski.

Another expression of German interests was a permanent immigration into the region: the Saxons appeared in Transylvania, and most of the first Hungarian towns were established by German *hospes,* or guests, as early as the thirteenth century. Indeed, German became the common language of urban settlements in Hungary. In the eighteenth century, mass German peasant immigration populated the western and central parts of Hungary, which had been left deserted after Ottoman occupation and a series of struggles for independence in the sixteenth and seventeenth centuries. In the nineteenth century, roughly four million immigrants were attracted by opportunities on the Russian frontier, and most of the settlers in the backward but awakening empire were Germans.

German settlement throughout East Central Europe and Russia fueled the *Völkisch,* the pan-German idea of the late nineteenth century of uniting *staatsfremde* Germans—those who lived in foreign, non-German states—into an enlarged German empire.

From Spheres of Influence to the "Mitteleuropa" Plan

Based on traditional historical connections which made several countries of East Central Europe a part of a German "cultural sphere," the Wilhelminian Reich, in an intense rivalry with France, began to build its political alliance system and economic stronghold in the region beginning in the last third of the nineteenth century. A latecomer compared to other Western rivals, Germany emerged as the most industrialized country in Europe at the turn of the century, and attempted to join the exclusive "Club of Colonial Empires." Germany felt it lacked an important national status symbol, since it did not possess a colonial empire. As Heinrich von Treitschke confessed in 1887, "Each great nation at the height of her power decides to make some mark on the barbaric lands. . . . Those who do not participate in this great rivalry will play a miserable role in the coming epoch. Colonialization became a matter of life and death for the great nations."[7]

However, Germany met with strong resistance from Britain and France, the leading colonial empires of the age, and thus had to start in a more modest way: it began by swallowing only those areas that were available. The Reich emerged as the third biggest capital exporter in the world behind Great Britain and France, representing 13 percent of exported capital in 1914. Although the role of Britain and France was much larger, with 43 and 20 percent respectively, Germany became the dominant financier of East Central Europe. Britain's capital exports were mainly channeled toward her colonial empire (46 percent) and the United States (21 percent), while Europe received only 5 percent of her investments in 1914. An ambitious France directed 38 percent of her capital exports toward the French colonies, as well as Egypt, Turkey, and overseas territories, while an insignificant amount (11 percent) went to Central Europe and the Balkans. France did, however, place 27 percent of her investments in Russia in the hope of strengthening an important ally against Germany.

With limited opportunities for colonial investment activity, most of Germany's capital exports were earmarked for Europe. Most attractive to German investors were Austria-Hungary, the Balkans, Turkey, and Russia. The first two areas received more than 37 percent of German capital exports to Europe, and approximately another 15 percent went to Russia. Germany became the main financier of the Hungarian banks, as well as the initiator and builder of the famous Orient Express and the railroad system of the Balkans.

An ambitious German military-bureaucratic and financial elite, however, considered Southeastern Europe a springboard toward the Middle East and India, which would allow Germany to beat her rivals in their own colonial heartland. This was the main motive behind planning a major war and launching a blitzkrieg to defeat Western rivals and conquer Eastern and colonial territories, following the ingenious military doctrine of the Prussian war machine. Austria-Hungary, Italy, Romania, Bulgaria, and Turkey joined the Reich in this venture, expressing their strong ties and assumed joint interests.

In the middle of a temporarily successful war effort, Friedrich Naumann proposed the establishment of a German-led "Mitteleuropa" federation with Austria-Hungary, Romania, Serbia, and Bulgaria (Switzerland and Holland would also join from the West). The liberal Naumann called for a democratic federation of sovereign states where the central leading legislative and executive bodies would be formed by the delegates of the member nations—a position for which he was attacked by pan-German fundamentalists.

At the same time, however, Naumann argued for German leadership of the federation: "Based on our strength and experiences we are driven by higher goals: we ourselves seek to be the Core." To create a Mitteleuropa that is competitive and strong enough, it needed, added Naumann, "the neighboring agricultural territories . . . and certain linguistic unity and united military institutions."[8] At the Vienna session of the Österreichisch-Deutscher Wirtschaftsverein on June 18, 1915, Naumann, in a debate with the Hungarian minister Gustav Gratz, stated: "it is understandable that certain nations seek to industrialize . . . but this attempt is mistaken, since what the Hungarians want today will probably be required by other nationalities tomorrow."[9] Naumann left no doubt that not only would Germany not give up its colonial ambitions, but through the creation of a German-led Mitteleuropa, it would emerge as one of the four leading powers of the world.

A major step in realizing this plan was the agreement signed between Germany and Austria-Hungary on May 12, 1918, which created a customs union and strengthened economic cooperation. However, the German Mitteleuropa plan and colonial superpower ambitions collapsed with Germany's military defeat in the fall of the same year. Moreover, Germany lost a great part of its previous acquisitions, and the interests of its wartime enemies were ruthlessly imposed by the Versailles Treaty. Germany not only lost Alsace-Lorraine and the few colonies acquired before the war, but was forced to pay war compensation and accept strict limitations on its armed forces. Germany's potential ally, Austria-Hungary, was destroyed and, under the banner of the "right of self-determination," several peoples of East Central Europe realized belated national revolutions. Several small and highly vulnerable independent countries attempted to defend their mutually conflicting national interests. France, the strongest continental power after World War I, sought to guarantee its political and military interests in Germany's former "backyard" by "Balkanizing" the area and building up its own sphere of influence. A humiliated Germany was knocked out of the race for world power and domination.

Southeastern Europe and the Nazi 1930s

Although temporarily successful, the attempt to weaken and isolate Germany was a deadly miscalculation. Emerging out of the ruins of a crisis-ridden economy and Weimar democracy, a rebellious and aggressive Nazi Germany immediately posed as the savior of other humiliated nations. Hitler inherited a compact set of proto-Nazi ideologies and skillfully borrowed the entire legacy of right-wing, anti-Semitic pan-German nationalism, including the theories of Arthur Moeller van den Bruck. The prophecies of van den Bruck, elucidated in his 1923 treatise, *Das Dritte Reich,* transformed the current class struggle into one against Jews and external enemies, and defined "the new national mission of German socialism . . . as leading the oppressed nations and showing them how to live."[10]

Indeed, the desperate peoples of East Central Europe, dismayed by their failure as independent nations to modernize based on the Western example before the war, humiliated by their defeat in the war and by the draconian peace that followed, and devastated by the Great Depression, were particularly inclined to follow a new messiah. Thus the road toward German penetration into East Central Europe was paved.

In the 1930s and during World War II, Germany successfully built up a *Grossraumwirtschaft* (a closed, isolationist regional economic block with Southeastern Europe), independent from the world economy. There were several reasons it did so. First, Hitler had immediately begun preparing for war. In addition to developing industries of strategic importance and embarking on a rapid rearmament, the Nazis sought to ensure the economic and foreign trade basis of a new blitzkrieg as well. In September 1934, under the direction of Hjalmar Schacht, the *Neuer Plan* was thus initiated. An important element of this Four Year Plan was the establishment of a regional system of self-sufficiency, based on bilateral agreements between Germany and the countries of East Central Europe. Under strict state control, the Nazi government meticulously planned the quantity and direction of German foreign trade. The central principle was the creation of a trading bloc with nearby agricultural and raw material producing countries, where Germany could purchase most of its import requirements with its own products, and not with its diminishing supply of foreign currency. Besides economic considerations, Hitler sought to be prepared for an Allied naval blockade by ensuring food and strategic raw material imports from neighboring countries by safe ground transportation.

The Southeast European countries offered a "natural" backyard for Germany. They had the surplus foodstuffs and several important raw materials indispensable for the German war economy and transportable via nearby, blockade-free overland routes. In addition, the agrarian states in Southeastern Europe were suffering the most from the Great Depression, with export possibilities evaporating and agricultural prices declining dramatically. The agricultural "scissors effect" increased to such a striking degree that their terms of trade plummeted roughly 30 percent in the first three years of the 1930s. Moreover, the countries of the region fell into a debt crisis, became insolvent in the summer of 1931, and lost most of their hard currency reserves. Hence, the Southeast European countries were ready to run into the embrace of Nazi Germany.

In a letter to Hitler written a few weeks after the Nazis seized power, Hungarian Prime Minister Gyula Gömbös complained: "Hungarian agricultural products . . . are practically unable to reach German markets. . . . I should like to ask you to make a government decision that Germany will assist our agricultural exports. . . . Agricultural exports are not only an economic issue for me but a political one as well, and if you appreciate it, it would strengthen my political direction."[11]

Hitler sent a positive answer a week later, promptly dispatching Dr. Werner Daitz, head of the Foreign Trade Department of the Nationalist Socialist Party, to Budapest and inviting Gömbös to Berlin. On June 16, 1933, Prime Minister Gömbös visited Berlin as a "private person" and met with Hitler. Between July 14 and 22, 1933, German and Hungarian trade delegations began discussions in Berlin and prepared the modification of the 1931 trade agreement of the two countries. "It became clear already in the beginning of the talks," reported Ambassador Masirevich to the Hungarian government at the end of the session, "that the primary aim of the German government was to grant concessions to Hungary that may be characterized as giving a helping hand, while at the same time serving . . . German interests."[12]

The German cabinet made its decision in January 1934: "The goal of Germany in signing the trade agreement," it frankly stated in the secret document, "is strongly and inseparably to link the Hungarian economy to the German one through increasing trade."[13] On February 21, 1934, the agreement was signed, thus opening a new chapter in German and East Central European trade. The German-Hungarian trade agreement, with its new, special arrangements that were attractive to the agricultural states of Southeastern Europe, became a model for follow-up agreements with the other countries of the region.

The German government radically changed its former policy of agricultural protectionism, established by the so-called Bülow tariff of 1925 and strengthened during the Great Depression. Breaking away from its previous policy, Germany committed itself to accepting large deliveries of grain, livestock, meat, and lard by providing a special import quota for them. Hungary, on the other hand, opened its markets for German industrial products and decreased its tariffs by 20 to 30 percent for German textile, paper and other consumer goods, machinery, and so forth. Hungary also provided import quotas for German products in fields where imports had been entirely banned since 1931.

In addition to opening its markets to special bilateral import quotas, Germany, as a second novelty of the agreement, guaranteed partial repayment of its high agricultural tariffs. For this, a 15 million mark government fund was established. The Hungarian government could thus pay a subsidy for all exported commodities, which for wheat was 4 to 6 pengö and for lard 74 pengö per quintal. The Hungarian government paid 22 million pengö altogether in annual export subsidies, which would be repaid by Germany. This did not mean real financial sacrifice for Germany, since the Hungarian government guaranteed the opening of German assets in Hungary that had been frozen along with all other foreign assets in the summer of 1931. Because of these subsidies, however, the price of Hungarian agricultural goods on the German market was above world market prices.

There was a third major novelty in the agreement: the patterns did

Germany's Role in the Foreign Trade of Southeastern Europe

Country	Export to Germany as a % of total exports		Imports from Germany as a % of total imports	
	1933	1937	1933	1937
Bulgaria	36.0	43.1	38.2	54.8
Hungary	11.2	24.1	19.6	26.2
Romania	16.6	19.2	18.6	28.9
Yugoslavia	13.9	21.7	13.2	32.4
Greece	17.9	31.0	10.2	27.1

not use hard currency in their bilateral trade and paid for purchases with goods; only at the end of the year were differences in value settled by currency payments. (This so-called clearing system had been used already in 1932, when Austria and Yugoslavia signed their own clearing agreements.) Germany consistently applied this barter type trade system with the East Central European countries, which, like Germany, suffered from a notorious lack of hard currency.

In the Hungarian trade agreement, Germany made a further gesture by granting that only 90 percent of the Hungarian deliveries would be covered by German deliveries, while the remaining 10 percent was to be available for the Hungarian National Bank for buying hard currency or goods sold on the world market for hard currency alone. As a consequence, German-Hungarian trade dramatically increased. Hungarian exports to Germany doubled from 11 percent to 22 percent of the country's total exports in a single year, 1933–34.

The agreement signaled a general trend: Germany opened its doors to the agrarian countries of the region by making preferential agricultural exports possible. The German-Hungarian trade agreement, which was the first of its kind, became a model for trade agreements with other countries of the region. In May 1934, Germany signed a trade agreement with Yugoslavia, followed by Bulgaria, and, in March 1935, Romania. As a result, the region established strong economic ties with Germany, as the accompanying table shows.[14]

The share of German exports earmarked for Southeastern Europe increased from 2.8 percent to 9.4 percent between 1933 and 1937, while imports from the region rose from 4.7 percent to 10.5 percent during the same period. The region became the most important supplier to Germany of certain agricultural products and raw materials. Wheat imports jumped from 2.4 to 36.9 percent, corn from 6.8 to 32.9 percent, meat from 7.0 to 35.0 percent, lard and bacon from 0.1 to 31.0 percent, timber from 24.5 to 35.0 percent, ores from 2.9 to 28.9 percent, and bauxite from 37.2 to 62.1 percent of total German imports.

The German government and its propaganda often emphasized the selfless assistance that Germany offered to crisis-ridden East Central Europe. As Ernst Wagemann, president of the German Economic Research Institute, wrote in 1939, no country "could help more than Germany, which included [these countries] into the process of her stormy economic development."[15] "Germany was the only industrialized country," added Hermann Gross in 1938, "to give generous help to the Southeast European agrarian countries with preferential treatment and increased imports of the products of these countries."[16] In reality, Nazi Germany systematically built up the *Grossraumwirtschaft* as an inseparable part of its war preparations and expansion. In 1934, Deputy Minister Hans Ernst Posse clearly declared that the time had arrived "to consider as goal number one of our economic policy to incorporate the German economy into her organically developing *Grossraumwirtschaft.*"[17]

David Kaiser was certainly right in maintaining that "the first battle of World War II" was won by Hitler in the 1930s, when shortsighted Western policies that excluded economic cooperation allowed the Southeast European region to be incorporated into the German *Lebensraum.* Although the East Central European countries gained some short-term advantages as a result of this—such as access to the protected German market with guaranteed preferential treatment on prices, which helped them immensely in overcoming the particularly severe impact of the Great Depression in the region—they paid a very high price for it. German economic policy secretly ensured that its trade partners were financially contributing to the war preparations. It had already become clear at the end of 1934 that huge German debts were accumulating in the clearing accounts, since they had not delivered the goods to cover Southeast European imports. In three years, between 1934 and 1936, the German debt to Hungary amounted to 46 million pengö. Germany's clearing debts were as high as nearly 500 million marks for the entire region at the end of 1936. The poor countries of East Central Europe thus were contributing to financing German rearmament efforts.

Furthermore, the trade agreements forced the countries of the region to increase food and raw material exports to Germany. The world market situation began to change from the mid-1930s on. World market prices increased (by 70 percent for wheat, 150 percent for corn, 100 percent for meat between 1933 and 1937), and exports became partly possible again for hard currency. "Our grain exports," stated an internal report of the Hungarian Ministry of Foreign Affairs in 1937, "are more advantageous to other countries than Germany. Italy pays 70% hard currency and important raw materials . . . Switzerland offered 25% in hard currency."[18]

In the fall of 1936, Germany opened a new chapter of her war preparations in the framework of the Four Year Plan directed personally by Hermann Göring. A rapid rearmament was coupled with the creation of a self-sufficient regional bloc in case of renewed war. Nazi Germany thus began to force her partners to deliver more than the quantities agreed upon in 1934. In October 1936, Göring arrived in Budapest and demanded more agricultural, particularly grain, exports. "In the given situation," noted Göring, "it is flatly impossible for Hungary to leave Germany in the lurch."[19] During the preparation of a new trade agreement, the German delegation presented a kind of ultimatum: "the prerequisite of the continuation of negotiations" was a statement of the Hungarian trade delegation that their country was ready to deliver "1 million quintals of wheat," thus revising its previous statement "to deliver only 10% of her export surplus, and a maximum of 500,000 quintals."[20]

East Central Europe Incorporated into the German War Economy

After the Anschluss and the Munich agreement—that is, in 1938–39—the German positions became much stronger vis-à-vis East Central Europe, and Hitler began to realize his ambitious goal of a total incorporation of East Central Europe as a subordinated *Ergänzungswirtschaft* into the German war economy. An ever-increasing part of agricultural and raw material production was delivered to Germany. A quarter of a century after Friedrich Naumann's ambitious dream, Nazi Cabinet Minister Walther Funk, responsible for the economy, declared the German plans to be based on a position of power: whoever had political power in Europe had the right to establish a new economic order, and the other countries must "adjust their economies to our demands."[21] In a *Kontinenteuropäische Grossraumwirtschaft unter Deutscher Führung,* one of the major plans formulated, Europe would be divided into three zones: a satellite Southeastern Europe, an occupied Western Europe, and a conquered and absorbed Soviet Union, Poland, and Czech lands.

In the spring of 1941, the interim chargé d'affaires in Berlin sent a detailed confidential report to the Hungarian Minister of Foreign Affairs summarizing the information on Nazi economic policy in a reorganized Europe he had received from a semiofficial spokesman of the German Minister of Foreign Affairs. According to the plan, the Southeast European countries would have "to conform to their national circumstances," and industrialization

was incompatible with the agricultural character of these countries. . . . Simultaneously with the political revision, the Southeast European states must also conform their economies to the demands of the continental economy. . . .Their agricultural production should be directed by the needs of the other parts of the continent; the main products are to be cereals and oil-seeds; supplementing these, other industrial crops are to be grown as well, and to process them, agricultural industry may develop. . . . The production of raw materials will be supplemented by their local processing into semi-finished products . . . using hydraulic power.

Chargé d'affaires Szentmiklossy added:

We can be prepared for . . . German interference in Hungarian industry. . . . [W]e have already seen signs that, with respect to the development of the agricultural branches of industry, the Germans are aiming at "directed cooperation," which means that they will direct development in this field to suit the needs of the German market through constant interference. . . . Lastly, they will prevent the establishment of industries inconvenient from the German point of view . . . and will establish ones judged useful with the help of German capital and German holdings.[22]

István Bethlen, Hungary's prime minister in the 1920s, clearly recognized a new chapter of German expansionism when analyzing the bilateral economic negotiations of 1939. As he put it at a session of a parliamentary commission:

During the talks we had recently, our negotiating partner repeatedly warned us "Don't keep insisting on Hungarian industry. . . . You are an agrarian country, be a country of peasants and sell us your agricultural products; we shall supply you with industrial goods. . . ." This means total economic dependence, total economic penetration by Germany; it can lead to nothing but political dependence.[23]

The continuous German demand for deliveries of East Central European agricultural "surpluses" to the Reich was ruthlessly realized. The German administration in the occupied territories requisitioned an increasing proportion of the declining production. There were 370,000 tons of grain confiscated and delivered to Germany from Poland in 1940; the quantities increased to 700,000, 1.2 million, and 1.5 million tons in 1941, 1942, and 1943 respectively. The occupying armies carried off 10 million tons of food from Yugoslavia during the four years of occupation. Moreover, in the later years of the war, even the satellite countries of Southeastern Europe were forced to restrict their domestic consumption in order to satisfy German demands. In the summer of 1942, the daily bread ration in Hungary was decreased to 15 dekagrams (5.3 ounces), whereas in Germany it was 28.6 dekagrams (10.1 ounces).

In addition to agricultural products, the exports to Germany of existing raw materials of strategic importance were increased. In the early years of the war 60 percent of Romanian oil production, more than 6 million tons in 1938–39 and over 5 million tons in 1940–44, was delivered to Germany. Hungarian manganese ore and bauxite production doubled during the war years (the latter reaching nearly 1 million tons in 1943), and 60 percent of the total output went to Germany. Moreover, according to an agreement signed in 1942, the Hungarian government agreed that "for 25 years, beginning August 1, 1942 . . . Hungary will permit the export of 1 million tons of bauxite to Germany, and will levy neither tariffs, nor any other duties on this export."[24]

By the end of 1941, with the collapse of the German Blitzkrieg before Moscow, the industrial capacities of these countries were also used, and in certain fields even developed, in the service of the German war economy. Because of the Allied bombing of Germany, a "decentralization" of the armament industry, particularly in aircraft production, led to the establishment of new firms in the incorporated Polish territories. The German Steyer Werke founded an airplane engine factory in Maribor, Yugoslavia, in 1942. A major joint program of 1 billion pengö to undertake serial production of Messerschmitt fighters was signed with Hungary at the end of 1941. The Hermann Göring Werke penetrated into the entire area and assumed an important position in Romanian heavy industry, including the Malaxa complex and the Resita iron-steel works and coal basin. The Göring Werke participated in Bulgarian strategic road construction and, in the last stage of the war, bought the largest Hungarian steel and engineering company of Manfred Weiss on the island of Csepel. More and more leading economic positions were concentrated in the hands of German firms located in East Central Europe. Prime Minister Pál Teleki of Hungary pointed out in a 1939 confidential letter, at the beginning of German aggressive penetration: "The German Empire possesses such vast and widespread interests in our country, that she can control and, what is more, influence all of Hungary's economic life through these interests."[25]

Indeed, the region became an *Ergänzungswirtschaft* (an additional economic unit) of the German war economy, trading almost entirely with Germany alone. The German share in Hungary's foreign trade, which ranged between 20 and 25 percent during the 1930s, jumped to 50 percent in 1938–39, to nearly 60 percent in 1941, and more than 70 percent in 1944. Romania, Bulgaria, and the newly created satellite states of Slovakia and Croatia had an even higher rate of 75 to 80 percent. As a clear sign of subordination, most of Southeast European deliveries were not covered by German payment or deliveries, and, as a leading official of the German Ministry of Finance stated in 1942, "The bulk of the Hungarian consignments . . . should in fact be regarded as a contribution to the common war effort."[26]

German debt to Hungary increased from 140 million marks in 1941 to 1 billion in 1943. The debt grew by an additional 1.5 billion marks by 1944, including the cost of the German occupation of Hungary, which was paid for by the Hungarians. "We are, in fact, lending the German treasury 60 percent more than we lent to the Hungarian treasury," noted the president of the Hungarian National Bank during a hearing of a parliamentary commission in April 1943.[27]

Economic relations with other East Central European states followed a similar pattern. Germany's debt of 210 million marks to Bulgaria increased to 680 million in 1943. Bulgaria's total financial contribution to Germany, including the cost of German troops stationed in the country, reached 1.2 billion marks in September 1944. Germany accumulated a debt of 1 billion marks even to small "independent" Slovakia between 1939 and 1944. Romania's financial support, including occupation costs, amounted to 2 billion marks.

An occupied, economically incorporated, subordinated, and looted East Central Europe became an inseparable part of the German *Lebensraum* during World War II. The end of the war and the total defeat of Nazi Germany, however, closed this chapter of successful German penetration and occupation of East Central Europe.

Germany and East Central Europe after 1989

The aggressive Sovietization of East Central Europe, including the division of Germany and the creation of satellite East Germany, entirely changed Germany's relationship to East Central Europe in the postwar period. German economic ties were radically severed, and previous German economic positions were taken over by the Soviet Union. German ownership in the former Axis countries such as Hungary, Romania, and Bulgaria became a part of German war compensation to the Soviet Union and served as a basis of creating the so-called Soviet-Hungarian and Soviet-Romanian joint ventures, the economic strongholds of Soviet domination. Germany itself was transformed and became part of the North Atlantic Treaty Organization and emerging European Community.

The economic strength and geopolitical position of a newly united Germany after the collapse of state socialism in East Central Europe and the Soviet Union, however, immediately opened a new chapter in relations between Germany and East Central Europe. Trade relations that were insignificant in the 1950s, 1960s, and early 1970s were rejuvenated after the new Ostpolitik of the Bundesrepublik and the Helsinki Agreement in 1975. During the 1980s, Germany became the most important Western trade partner of a number of East Central European countries. West Germany's share of Hungarian exports and imports reached 15 and 23 percent respectively in 1985. In Polish trade, however, its share was only 9 percent.

CMEA and Soviet trade, though gradually declining, still definitely remained the most important factor for all of the East Central European countries, amounting to between 40 to 80 percent of their foreign trade until 1988. Poland, Romania, and Hungary were among those countries with a lower percentage of CMEA trade, while Bulgaria and Czechoslovakia represented the other extreme. In the case of Hungary, Poland, and Romania, which began the reorientation of their trade in the 1970s, the percentage share of Soviet trade remained as high as 28, 24, and 31 percent respectively in 1988. In Czechoslovakia and Bulgaria, this share was 43 and 61 percent respectively. Six East Central European CMEA countries had an average trade share of 40 percent with the Soviet Union and an additional 22 percent with each other.

The crisis and collapse of state socialism and its isolationist regional trade agreement system, the Council for Mutual Economic Assistance, dramatically changed the economic position of Germany in the region after 1989. Germany embarked on an impressive trade expansion to occupy former Soviet positions in the area. Although East Central European trade sharply declined and the region's role in world trade dropped by nearly one-third between 1988 and 1990, German imports from East Central Europe increased from 19 to 26 billion DM, or nearly 38 percent. Germany's imports from Czechoslovakia and Poland increased by 76 and 79 percent respectively, in three years. German exports to Yugoslavia and Poland increased by nearly 30 percent. Romanian exports declined by one-half, but German exports to Romania increased by 40 percent.

Since Germany had become the most important importer of East Central European products, the pioneers of market transition—Poland, Hungary, and Czechoslovakia—drastically altered their export orientations. The total exports of the three countries to the West increased by 81, 54, and 39 percent respectively between 1988 and 1990. "The exports of Czechoslovakia, Hungary and Poland to the rapidly growing German market," reported the *Economic Survey of Europe* in 1992, "accounted for some 40–50 per cent of the increment of their total exports to the West during 1988–1991."[28] Between 1988 and 1992, Germany became the single biggest trading partner of postcommunist East Central Europe, as the accompanying table shows.

Germany thus gained a leading position in East Central European trade, with roughly one quarter of exports and imports of the countries of the region. In almost all cases, the German role in foreign trade was

Foreign Trade with Germany

Country	% of total exports		% of total imports	
	1985	1992	1985	1992
Bulgaria	2	11	4	22
Czechoslovakia	5	23	4	20
Hungary	15	27	23	25
Poland	9	29	9	27
Romania	8	25	3	11
Russia (Soviet Union)	6	25	5	33

Note: The 1985 figures represent the Federal Republic of Germany.
In the 1992 columns, the Romanian and Bulgarian figures are for 1990.
Sources: national and United Nations statistics.

greater than in 1937 and surpassed the level reached by the Soviet Union in the decades of Soviet domination over these countries.

Germany assumed an equally determinant position in providing credits to and investing in East Central Europe. While most of the Western countries were reluctant to assist, Germany took the initiative and exploited its geopolitical advantage, knowledge, and tradition regarding the markets of the region. In addition, Germany's role was especially important in supplying crucial aid in the earliest stage of transition. While foreign aid provided rather insignificant support for East Central European transformation generally, amounting to only 14 percent of assistance to the pioneering countries of the region, Germany guaranteed 72 percent of Hungarian and 40 percent of Polish bilateral grants. In fact, over 40 percent of Western bilateral financial assistance came from Germany during the first three years of the transition. Germany was particularly active in Czechoslovakia, Hungary, and Poland, committing 62, 54, and 31 percent of all bilateral assistance respectively.

In the first years of transition, Germany emerged as the most important single direct capital investor in East Central Europe. German companies financed 40 percent of foreign capital investment in both Russia and Poland, 30 percent in Czechoslovakia, and 20 percent in Hungary. According to a report of the German Bundesbank in the spring of 1993, Germany has been the number one financial supplier of East Central

Europe since the beginning of 1990, providing 113 billion DM to the region, including half the assistance to the successor states of the former Soviet Union.

German credit and investment, however, slowed in 1991–92, since the economic consequences of the German unification and the need for investment in former East Germany exhausted the potential of German capital exports. During the first three years of transition, 400 billion DM—about $255 billion—were transferred from West to East Germany. Until 1991, German investments surpassed all others in Hungary, reaching $800 million, but they were overtaken by American investors in 1992. In the spring of 1993, American private investment totaled $1.8 billion in the country.

To illustrate the most recent trends, there were 719 transactions (including purchasing of firms, founding joint ventures, etc.) totaling $27.9 billion from September 1991 to September 1992. While the United States, with 219 transactions totaling $8 billion, assumed first place ahead of Italy and Great Britain, Germany dropped to fourth place with 80 transactions and $2.5 billion. German assistance after 1989, including private investments, lost its previous momentum, though it still played a leading role in the Czech Republic, Hungary, and Poland. The East Central European countries today complain more often about the lack of German capital investments than the danger of German economic domination.

The unprecedented rise of German economic penetration in East Central Europe after 1989 thus slowed significantly. A successful economic unification of the two Germanies will certainly take longer than was imagined. In one to two decades, however, a consolidated and much stronger Germany, which would be by far the richest nation in Europe and one with over 80 million inhabitants, may launch an even more aggressive economic attack to reconquer its traditional sphere of influence.

Although German economic penetration in post-1989 East Central Europe was rather strong, allowing Germany to regain its core position in the region, the historical situation is very different compared to post-1871 and post-1993 period. To draw a simple parallel with previous times would be entirely superficial and mistaken. After the 1871 unification, as Willfried Spohn has argued, an "Easternized," Prussian-led Germany began a nationalist-imperialist adventure. Since the new unification, a "Westernized" Germany has been searching for its place in a new European framework. There is no attempt to build a nationalist empire, and German politics is oriented primarily to the European Community and not to a *Mitteleuropa-Grossraumwirtschaft*. The aggressive drive to regain dominant economic positions is mostly motivated by economic interests to expand markets and exploit relatively cheap labor costs in the region (which range from one-sixth to one-tenth those of Germany).

In addition, trade connections with capital investment by Germany may help to initiate a domestic economic revival and restructuring in East Central Europe. As the history of various peripheries clearly reflects, in an advantageous domestic economic-political and social environment, core-periphery contacts may help the periphery to catch up with the core. In other cases, however, the same economic ties will serve only the core's interests. German economic penetration to East Central Europe holds the potential for both alternatives. It is uncertain yet whether the present German economic position in the region will help some of the region's countries to catch up or if it will become a basis for the renewed building of a German *Grossraumwirtschaft*. The future development of the European Community, the degree to which Germany becomes the predominant power in Europe, and the success or failure of the transformation of the different East Central European countries themselves will determine the future of German relations with the region.

In the long run, a positive scenario would be the integration of a part, or more precisely, of the Western rim of East Central Europe, into the Community. As a negative scenario, however, we cannot exclude the possibility of the traditionally peripheral region of East Central Europe becoming the backyard of a rising German superpower.

NOTES

1. However, Dr. Milan Smutny, a spokesman for the factory, was quoted in the spring of 1993 as saying that "by 1997 [Volkswagen] will have built an entire new factory with a total investment of more than $3 billion." *New York Times,* April 30, 1992, p. A7.

2. Ibid.

3. Ivan T. Berend and György Ranki, *The European Periphery and Industrialization, 1780–1914* (Cambridge and New York: Cambridge University Press, 1982), p. 9 (italics added).

4. Regarding the early modern period and even the age of the Industrial Revolution, it was certainly valid to speak about a northwestern European core. From the late nineteenth century on, the "Western core" and the "East-West" and "North-South" dichotomies have been valid abstractions but not historical-geographical definitions. The southernmost South Africa in this upside-down world belongs, for example, to the economic "North," just as Japan does to the "West." Similarly, Cuba became a part of a political "East" while Turkey and Greece joined the "West."

5. *The Works of Tacitus*, the Oxford Translation, vol. 2, ed. Henry G. Bohn (London, 1854), pp. 303, 305.

6. *Cornelii Taciti de Germania*, ed. Henry Furneaux (Oxford: Clarendon Press, 1894), p. 25.

7. Heinrich von Treitschke, *Politics* (London, 1916), 1:115–16.

8. Friedrich Naumann, *Mitteleuropa* (Berlin, 1915), pp. 54ff.

9. Cited by Károly Irinyi, *A Naumann-féle "Mitteleuropa"-tervezet és a magyar politikai közvélemény* (Naumann's "Mitteleleuropa" Plan and Hungarian Political Views) (Budapest: Akadémiai Kiadó, 1963).

10. Cited by Rohan d'O. Butler, *The Roots of National Socialism, 1783–1933* (London: Faber and Faber, 1941), p. 264.

11. Deutsche Zentral Archiv (DZA), Potsdam. AA. Abt.-I.41288. ". . . wir alte rassenschutzlerische Kameraden," concluded Gömbös in a letter written in German, "die uns in derselben Weltanschauung, und auch auf der wirtschaftlichen Linie verstehen und uns gegenseitig unterstützen werden." Letter dated April 22, 1933.

12. The report of the Hungarian ambassador on July 23, 1933. Hungarian State Archive (hereafter HSA), Foreign Ministry, Department of Economic Policy, German File (Magyra Országos Levéltár, Külügyminiszterium, Gazdaságpolitikai Osztály, Német dosszie), 640.cs.I/2.967/4 adm. res.

The archive documents of DZA and HSA cited in this chapter were first published in I. T. Berend and György Ránki, *Magyarország a fasiszta Németország "élet-terében," 1933–1939* (Hungary in the *Lebensraum* of Nazi Germany, 1933–39) (Budapest, 1960); and I. T. Berend and György Ránki, "Hungary in the Service of the German War Economy during the Second World War," in Berend and Ránki, *Underdevelopment and Economic Growth* (Budapest: Akadémiai Kiadó, 1979).

13. DZA, Potsdam. AA. Abt.-II.41288.

14. Antonin Basch, *The Danube Basin and the German Economic Sphere* (New York: Columbia University Press, 1943), p. 192.

15. Ernst Wagemann, *Der Neue Balkan* (Hamburg, 1939), pp. 119–21.

16. Hermann Gross, *Die wirtschaftliche Bedeutung Südosteuropas für das deutsche Reich* (Stuttgart and Berlin, 1938).

17. H. E. Posse, *Möglichkeiten der Grossraumwirtschaft: Die nationale Wirtschaft*, vol. 2 of K. Andresen, *Die Deutsch-Ungarischen Wirtschaftsbeziehungen und das Problem ihrer engeren Ausgestaltung* (Rostock, 1935), p. 86.

18. HSA, Foreign Ministry, Economic Policy Department. German File 641. I-3-A, April 12, 1937.

19. Ibid., 1937/5. 377/a, November 28, 1936.

20. Ibid., 641. I-3-A, April 12, 1937.

21. György Ránki, *The Economics of the Second World War* (Vienna and Cologne: Böhlau Verlag, 1993).

22. HSA, Foreign Ministry, Economic Policy Department. Res. 466–1941.

23. HSA, Parliamentary Commissions. Protocol, vol. 17, p. 84.

24. HSA, Foreign Ministry, Economic Policy Department. Res. 30-1942.

25. HSA, Foreign Ministry, Economic Policy Department. German File, Res. 358-1939.

26. HSA, Foreign Ministry, Economic Policy Department. Records of the Hungarian-German negotiations, 1942.

27. HSA, Minutes of the Parliament's 42 Commission, April 8, 1943, vol. 31, p. 384.

28. *Economic Survey of Europe, 1991–92* (New York: United Nations, 1992), p. 78.

Germany's Policy Toward the Disintegration of Yugoslavia

Aleksa Djilas

In the summer of 1991, Germany broke ranks with the United States and the European Community and began an intense campaign for the immediate and unconditional international recognition of Slovenia and Croatia, the two seceding republics of the Yugoslav federation. During the subsequent civil war in Yugoslavia, the German government—if anything, surpassed by an important section of German public opinion and the German media—uncritically supported Slovenes and Croats as democratic and "Western," while condemning Serbs as defenders of communism, and describing their policies as an expression of inferior Byzantine and "Eastern" civilization.

While Serbian actions in Croatia and Bosnia-Herzegovina undoubtedly deserve the severest censure, the German inability to be at all critical of the anti-Serbian nationalism of the seceding republics demonstrates a revival of traditional German views and prejudices about Yugoslavia and the Balkans in general. These attitudes were once a part of German nationalism as it developed between German unification in 1871 and the beginning of the First World War. Indeed, this period is much more important than that of the Third Reich for uncovering the origins of Germany's attitudes and policies toward the disintegration of Yugoslavia.

The media in Serbia that are controlled by President Slobodan Milošević's nationalistic government claim that Germany has aspirations similar to those it had during the Second World War; yet the overwhelming majority of Germans reject neo-Nazism and have nothing in common with its racist ideology. On the other hand, pre–First World War German nationalistic sympathies and antipathies are very much alive, and judging by their intensity during the disintegration of Yugo-slavia, are likely to become a potent political force. They will be mod-erated by Germany's liberal democratic institutions, which are vigorous if not deeply rooted. Nonetheless, overcoming German nationalism will be a great challenge to European integration.

After the unification of Germany in 1871, Austria-Hungary and Ger-many were the only two empires in Central Europe. Their alliance in 1879 was the first modern great-power alliance, and it permanently dis-rupted the relatively stable relations among the great powers that had prevailed until then. It was the direct cause of the formation of other great-power alliances: France with Russia, France with Britain, Britain with Russia.

Austria-Hungary and Germany were allies as well as rivals. Of the two, Austria-Hungary was the weaker. Not only was the German army much more powerful than the Austro-Hungarian army, but German in-dustry and banks were also stronger. Austria-Hungary resented German supremacy, but could do little to challenge it.

The First World War increased German influence in Austro-Hungarian affairs. In 1917, for example, Germany was making deci-sions in the Balkans, but Austria-Hungary had no influence on German policies toward its conquests in Western Europe. In the spring of 1918, Charles I, who had become the emperor after Francis Joseph's death in November 1916, put the Austro-Hungarian army under the supreme command of the German Kaiser. (In reality it was commanded by Hin-denburg and Ludendorff.[1]) This move was made because of German pressure and could perhaps be considered the first Anschluss.

During the First World War, Germany threatened the independence not only of Austria-Hungary but of its other allies, the Ottoman Empire and Bulgaria—in much the same way it threatened the independence of its adversaries. In general, Germany pursued a policy of limiting the sovereignty of all countries in Central Europe and in the Balkans. The German Reich wanted to be able permanently to exploit Balkan eco-nomic wealth, especially mineral deposits (coal, copper, etc.), which were particularly rich in Serbia. Romanian oil was also a sought-after commodity. In order to achieve this, Serbia and the Balkans were to be-come *Ergänzungswirtschaftsraum* (a complementary economic area) of the German economy. In the second half of the Great War, Germany suffered shortages of the natural resources needed to wage war and became obsessed with the idea of economic autarky. Consequently, its interest in the Balkans increased. But at no time during the war did the Reich succeed completely in its plans for the economic exploitation of the Balkans.[2]

Austria-Hungary's hostility toward Serbia was much greater than Germany's, especially after 1903. In May of that year, a military conspiracy overthrew Serbia's ruling Obrenović dynasty, and the Karadjordjević dynasty came to the throne. Serbia soon shed its previous dependence on Austria-Hungary and turned toward Russia. Its politicians were not motivated by any sort of pan-Slavic Russophilia. Rather, the regime needed Russia—and also the Entente (Britain and France)—for protection from Austria-Hungary and for support of their struggle for the unification of Serbs and South Slavs.

The Dual Monarchy of Austria-Hungary perceived Serbia as an obstacle to its old ambition to gain control (preferably through conquest) of the central and southwestern part of the Balkan Peninsula. But the "new Serbia," where parliamentary democracy was making progress, was also a threat to the monarchy's internal unity, because it increased the growth of the independence movements among the South Slavs (Croats, Serbs, Slovenes) under Austro-Hungarian rule. The Austrian press was more hostile and contemptuous toward Serbia than toward any other country, and Serbia repaid in kind. Serbia and Austria-Hungary each considered the other its greatest enemy.

The Habsburg Monarchy had been seriously challenged by the French Revolution and Napoleon, by the Revolution of 1848, by the defeat in Italy in 1859, and finally by another defeat at the hands of Prussia in 1866. Desperate to reestablish its legitimacy, it looked for some successes in foreign policy and war. The first steps were the occupation of Bosnia-Herzegovina in 1878—it had been given to the monarchy by the Congress of Berlin earlier that year—and then its formal annexation in 1908. Many Serbs both inside and outside Serbia who believed that Bosnia-Herzegovina should unite with Serbia were convinced that the great powers, and in particular the two Central European ones, were extremely unjust, and began to talk of the "curse of the Berlin Congress."[3]

Austria-Hungary did not know what to do with Serbia either before or during the First World War, but it never imagined Serbia as an independent country. Rather, it always supported Bulgarian territorial pretensions toward Serbia, and aimed to annex some territory for itself as well. After the Central Powers conquered Serbia and Montenegro in 1915, Austria-Hungary considered the possibility of restoring their statehood, even their unification, but only as vassal states. Some plans argued that Serbia and Montenegro should be ruled by a Habsburg prince; all plans called for the overthrow of the Karadjordjević dynasty, because it was a champion of Serbian and South Slav unification and independence.

Divisions existed within the Dual Monarchy itself over policy toward Serbia and the South Slavs. Hungarians wanted to preserve the dualism established by the Ausgleich (compromise) of 1867. They therefore opposed the incorporation of too large a part of Serbia into the Dual Monarchy, because this would have strengthened the Serbs and South Slavs within the monarchy, thereby increasing their chances of establishing parity with Hungarians and German Austrians, who believed that there were already too many Slavs in Austria-Hungary.

Imperialist ambitions gained strength in Germany and Austria in the last quarter of the nineteenth century. In both states the pan-German right pushed a vaguely defined program for *Drang nach Osten* (including the southeast). This presumed annexations and the creation of vassal states in large areas of Southeastern Europe and the Middle East. In some German plans "Mitteleuropa" was envisioned to include all territory between the North Sea and the Persian Gulf. Viewed in the context of the *Drang,* Serbia was seen as a potential bridge to Asia and world hegemony.

Since Germany and Austria-Hungary were federal states largely ruled by the nobility, they considered annexations as achievable as they had been before the growth of modern national consciousness. They demanded from other states almost feudal submission, and were ready to divide up territories without consideration for the language, nationality, or wishes of the population. At the same time they themselves were largely or partly modern nation-states with national languages, cultures, and political leaders. A particularly strong contrast existed between Germany's national ideology with its modern view of the German right to unity and national political will, and Germany's anachronistic view of other nations, whose right to determine their national politics was not recognized.

During the First World War, both Germany and Austria-Hungary tried to exacerbate the conflict between Croats and Serbs in order to weaken their movement toward South Slav unification. They therefore chose to interpret it as a conflict between two fundamentally different and mutually exclusive civilizations. The Croats were characterized as part of a superior Western civilization, based on Catholicism and the tradition of the Roman law. The Serbs were seen as belonging to an Eastern civilization, based on Orthodoxy and Byzantine political traditions. This pseudoscientific simplification further argued that the division between the East and the West dated from the year 395, when the Roman Empire was divided into its western and eastern parts. Many articles and books were published trying to prove the inferiority of the Byzantine civilization and consequently of all contemporary countries influenced by it.[4]

Germany and Austria-Hungary's strong sense of cultural superiority over the "East" in general and toward the Balkans in particular imbued these two countries with a sense of mission. Their need to dominate was therefore directed not only toward the political and economic sphere but toward the cultural sphere as well. They thus developed elaborate theories—philosophical, cultural, economic, and geostrategic—to justify conquest. It could perhaps be said that no nationalism in European history had as large and thorough an ideological underpinning as German nationalism did before the First World War.

Before the end of the war many people in Western Europe and in the United States (including, some of the time, the British Prime Minister Lloyd George and the American President Woodrow Wilson) believed that Austria-Hungary should be preserved, after first being transformed into a genuine federation.[5] They were convinced that if the Dual Monarchy disintegrated along with Russia—where revolution had broken out in February 1917—a political vacuum would be created in Central Europe, and Germany would fill it and dominate the successor states of the monarchy.[6] The Habsburg monarchy, for so many centuries a barrier to the Turkish thrust toward the West, was now meant to be a barrier to German expansion in the other direction.

Serbia opposed any restoration of Austria-Hungary. Basing its political thinking on concepts typical of Central and East European nationalism, Serbia believed that a state could have only one set of political goals and that those goals were determined by the national will, which itself was rooted in the nation's character, history, and interests. The political goals pursued by a multinational state would be those of the strongest nation—in the case of Austria-Hungary, those of the German Austrians. Serbia claimed that German Austrians would ally with Hungarians to repress other nations, and that a restored Austria-Hungary, rather than being a barrier to German expansion, would, because of German predominance within its borders, open the way for the German Reich to move east and southeast toward Constantinople and the Persian Gulf.

Considering the nature of the relationship between the state and the nation in Central and Eastern Europe, Serbia was probably right when it refused to believe that a restored Austria-Hungary could ever guarantee equality to all its nations. But it failed to realize that Yugoslavia, which Serbia was at that time struggling to create, would also be multinational and would have similar problems. Serbia was also mistaken in thinking that the small nation-states of Central Europe which were successors of Austria-Hungary would be capable of containing Germany after the war. But then, considering the power of Germany, could any regional arrangement have been strong enough to contain it? Even with the determined support of Britain, France, and Russia, this would have been a difficult task. And at many crucial moments in the period between the two world wars such support would be lacking.

In 1913, Berlin did not allow Austria-Hungary to intervene against Serbia, which had emerged from the Balkan Wars too powerful for the Dual Monarchy's taste. After the June 1914 assassination of Archduke Francis Ferdinand in Sarajevo, the Germans undoubtedly pushed Austria-Hungary into the war. During the First World War, although the Germans fought the Serbs, they respected them, and even complimented them on their martial valor. During the occupation of Serbia, the Serbs were afraid of the German troops and despised those from Austria-Hungary.

In the post-1918 debates in Germany about who was responsible for the outbreak of the war, the Serbs were considered among the most guilty, together with the British and the Russians. German anti-Serbian sentiment increased after Hitler's ascent to power in 1933. His Serbophobia, rooted in the years of his youth spent in Vienna, was virulent.

As a result, Nazi ideology became permeated with anti-Serbian sentiment. In this respect Germany remained under the ideological influence of Austria-Hungary.

One of the major goals of German foreign policy after the Nazis came to power was to destroy the alliances among the Central and East European states (Little Entente, Balkan Entente). Hitler pursued this policy because small states could easily be made vassals of Germany. Yugoslavia was to be destroyed, and Croatia's struggle for independence supported. The right of nations to self-determination was frequently invoked by the Nazis, for example in connection with the Sudeten Germans and Slovakia, to achieve this end. In the 1930s no country in the world insisted as much as Germany on the right of nations to self-determination.

Germany's primary aim was to tie these countries economically to itself. It therefore supplied them with industrial goods and capital in exchange for their agricultural products and raw materials, offered them a favorable rate of exchange, and helped them to deal with the economic crisis. A trade agreement with Yugoslavia was concluded in May 1934. From 1936 until 1939, 30 percent of Yugoslav exports went to Germany, and 35 percent of Yugoslav imports came from Germany.[7] Yugoslavia's trade balance with Germany was positive. Yet it was a dangerous dependence, especially after the Anschluss, when Germany and Yugoslavia had a common border. Germany planned, after making these countries economically dependent, to subjugate them either by making them vassals or through conquest. In pursuing these plans Germany was clearly continuing its First World War policy of making the Balkans a complementary economic area.

Germany's international role has been enlarged in the last few years not because of its unification in 1990, but because of the Soviet withdrawal from Eastern and Central Europe and the weakening of American influence in Western Europe. In fact, unification, because of the economic and political difficulties it causes, is a burden for Germany. The country has become more powerful not because it was enlarged but because it was unbound. The fall of communism has created a power vacuum in the center of Europe, much like the one in the period between the two world wars. And once again Germany is trying to fill it.

There are, of course, also differences between the current situation and the interwar period. European countries—Germany included—now have much stronger liberal democratic institutions. Russia is much more integrated into European political processes. And isolationism is unlikely to triumph in the United States to the extent it did after the First World War.

Yugoslavia neither particularly feared nor opposed German unification. As Audrey Helfant puts it, "At the federal political level, the Yugoslav reaction to German unification was one of cautious welcome, with caution predominating in the early part of the process, and welcome later."[8] Yugoslavia opposed NATO membership for a united Germany, however, arguing that unification should take place by overcoming the cold war division of Europe. When unification proceeded faster than Yugoslavia expected, they accepted it, emphasizing that they respected the right of nations to self-determination. At the time of German unification, some 600,000 Yugoslavs (mostly unskilled and semi-skilled workers and their families) were living in the Federal Republic. A disproportionate number of them were Croats. Unification did not endanger the position of these *Gastarbeiter,* nor did it weaken economic relations in general between Yugoslavia and Germany.

During 1990, Yugoslavia's first post–Second World War free elections were held in all six republics. The Slovene election, in April, was the first; Croatia followed in May. In both Slovenia and Croatia the communists lost and noncommunist governments were formed. It soon became obvious that the two republics were intent on secession from the Yugoslav federation. Although they spoke for a while of confederal arrangements, their insistence on having an independent foreign policy and armed forces clearly showed that they wanted complete independence. In the context of this bid for new political arrangements, Slovenia and Croatia maintained that they had traditionally been a part of Europe, while other nations of Yugoslavia had not. They proceeded to make independent foreign policy moves to link themselves with other European countries. They pursued with particular zeal the policy of integration into Central Europe, which in practice meant seeking cooperation with Austria and Germany. Insisting on their Central European heritage and culture, they tried to distance themselves from the "Balkan" part of Yugoslavia. In other words, Central Europeanism was a part of their secessionist ideology. In the media in Croatia and Slovenia there was a revival of pseudoscientific theories arguing that Slovenes and Croats were not Slavs.[9]

Neither Slovenia nor Croatia favored any kind of integration with Europe based on the continued existence of Yugoslavia. This was the main reason they were suspicious of the Pentagonale, the grouping of five countries—Italy, Austria, Hungary, Czechoslovakia, and Yugoslavia—founded in 1989 on the initiative of the Italians. (Czechoslovakia, in fact, joined only in May 1990.) The main goals of the Pentagonale were economic, with particular stress on transportation. But it was also an Italian attempt to counterbalance the German influence in Central Europe. Italy had in general expressed support for Yugoslav integration into Europe, but had insisted on a unified Yugoslavia.

After the victory of Croatian nationalists in the election of May 1990, Croatia was considered by many Serbs as a reincarnation of the Second World War fascist Croatia. But Germany was not at this time considered a Fourth Reich. The Milošević-controlled media in Serbia started attacking Germany only after it began supporting Croatia some time in the summer of 1991. Since that time Serbs have been saying that the Fourth Reich is rising, and that the Serbs are a barrier against its design. It has not been explained precisely why this role should be played by the Serbs, and not some other nation that had also previously fought against Germany, such as the French or the Poles.

Ever since the end of the Second World War the majority of Serbs have had a deep mistrust of Germany. This persisted, for example, even during Germany's most nonnationalistic period when Willy Brandt was chancellor. (Brandt made a very successful visit to Yugoslavia in 1973, and German loans followed.) In the 1970s, more educated Serbs began to accept West Germany as a genuinely democratic country, well integrated into Europe and friendly to Yugoslavia and Yugoslavs. There were still doubts, however, about the stability of German democracy, and about what would happen if Germany were suddenly united and allowed to pursue a genuinely independent foreign policy.

Until summer 1991 the German government, and in particular its Foreign Minister Hans-Dietrich Genscher, were among the most resolute Western defenders of a unified Yugoslavia. They considered the continued existence of Yugoslavia the foundation of peace in Southeastern Europe. However, when civil war broke out in Yugoslavia in

June 1991, generating widespread public support in Germany and Austria for the recognition of Croatia and Slovenia, the German government began to see the unity of Yugoslavia as an obstacle to peace.

The German government briefly continued to support the preservation of Yugoslavia, but insisted that this must be achieved through peaceful means. Yet the only way to preserve the unity of the country and avoid escalation of hostilities was for the Yugoslav army to disarm by force all paramilitary units, particularly the Croatian and Serbian ones. However, this action was not taken and hostilities escalated. Germany then announced that it would recognize Slovenia and Croatia if the fighting continued, invoking the right of nations to self-determination. This encouraged Slovenia and Croatia to continue fighting, and decreased the chances for an armistice. When the fighting in Slovenia ceased in late summer and the Yugoslav army withdrew, Germany continued demanding recognition for Slovenia, at the same time maintaining its demand for the recognition of Croatia, where the war was still raging.

Beginning in the summer of 1991, there were demands in Germany for Western economic and military aid to Croatia and even for military intervention on its side. Professor Kalefleiter from Kiel University, for example, an influential intellectual figure on the German right, argued on September 13, 1991, in *Rheinischer Merkur* that Germany should supply the Croats with the most modern military technology, like Leopard II tanks and the Patriot air defense system.[10] In autumn the Catholic Church in Germany became very active on Croatia's behalf. And German businessmen and banks played a crucial role in supplying Croatia with weapons, although there was a United Nations embargo on exports of military material to any of the combatants in the Yugoslav civil war.

Germany's demands for immediate recognition of Slovenia and Croatia created a division within the European Community. All member states except Denmark opposed the German request. They were joined in their opposition by the U.S. State Department. Although not quite certain how to deal with the Yugoslav civil war, Europeans and Americans were advocating a comprehensive solution.

Germany put enormous pressure on fellow members of the European Community, especially on the British and the French, to recognize Slovenia and Croatia. Germany claimed that Croatia's president, Franjo

Tudjman (Tuđman), was simply a West European Christian Democrat, declaring that Croatia's treatment of its Serbian minority satisfied European standards (although a European Community commission had found differently). Germany thus decided not to notice Croatian predatory interests in Bosnia-Herzegovina. As Misha Glenny points out:

In July [1991], after the war in Croatia had already broken out, President Tuđman stated publicly that the solution to an all-out war in the crumbling Yugoslavia was the division of BiH [Bosnia-Herzegovina] between Croatia and Serbia. This meant that while Germany was busy lobbying on behalf of the Croatian leader for the recognition of Croatia, citing the dual principles of self-determination and inviolability of present borders, Tuđman was openly advocating that these lofty ideals be ignored in the case of BiH.[11]

The Bosnian government in fact opposed the recognition of Slovenia and Croatia. Their secession would leave Bosnia-Herzegovina inside rump Yugoslavia, where it would have to choose either to be dominated by Serbia or to secede and risk provoking the rebellion of its Serbs and Croats and its potential dismemberment by Serbian and Croatian forces.

The Maastricht agreement of December 1991 was a step toward a further integration of the European Community, including a common European foreign policy. The Europeans, in particular the French and the British, were keen to avoid an open confrontation with Germany which would have endangered the agreement. So when Germany threatened to proceed with recognition on its own, they followed the German lead. The recognition of Slovenia and Croatia was announced by the European Community just before Christmas, and then extended in January 1992.

After recognition, there was an eruption of pro-German sentiment in Croatia. Streets, squares, and even restaurants were named after leading German and Austrian politicians, mostly with their consent, and the newly composed song "Danke Deutschland" was performed on Zagreb television. Milošević's propaganda was in a triumphant mood, claiming that the act of recognition was further proof of an anti-Serbian alliance between the "Fourth Reich" and "fascist" Croatia. But even those Serbs who opposed Serbian expansion found German policy intolerable, because it was designed to prevent the creation of greater Serbia, yet was tolerant and even supportive of the creation of greater Croatia. It also seemed that Germany wanted to punish the Serbs, not for what they were doing but for what they were—for their Balkan cultural and historical heritage and Orthodox faith—while Croats were being rewarded for being Central Europeans and Roman Catholics.

The recognition of Slovenia and Croatia was Germany's most independent foreign policy move in its postwar history. Instead of being constructive, the policy has proved to be divisive. Instead of Europe preserving Yugoslav unity, as many Yugoslavs had hoped it would do, the disintegration of Yugoslavia has supplied proof that Europe was never truly united. Recognition of Slovenia and Croatia, in fact, affected European unity more than it did Yugoslav disintegration.

In general, both the proponents and opponents of recognition have exaggerated its effects on the course of events in Yugoslavia. It is nonsense to claim, as the German Foreign Ministry does, that there would have been no war in Croatia if it had been recognized sooner. The causes of the Croatian war were the mistreatment by the Croatian government of its Serbian minority, and the policy of the Serbian government which incited the Croatia's Serbs to rebel and steered the Yugoslav army to come to fight on their side. Earlier recognition of Croatian independence would not have removed any of these causes. Nor was the war in Croatia stopped by recognition, as many Germans and Croats believe. Fighting did indeed cease after recognition was extended, but this was because United Nations special envoy Cyrus Vance negotiated a cease-fire after both sides had come to the conclusion that they could only lose through more fighting. In the case of Slovenia, fighting stopped many months before recognition.

But if Germany does not deserve credit for saving Croatia and Slovenia, does it deserve blame for the civil war in Yugoslavia? It does, but only partially. Its support for Croatia and Slovenia delayed the armistice, but was not the main cause of fighting. As far as Bosnia-Herzegovina was concerned, recognition of Slovenia and Croatia left Bosnia-Herzegovina inside a truncated Yugoslavia dominated by Serbia and in this way pushed it to seek independence. Moreover, the promise of early recognition increased the hopes of separatists in Bosnia-Herzegovina that the West would protect it after secession.

Bosnia-Herzegovina seceded from Yugoslavia in March 1992 and was internationally recognized several weeks later by the European Community and the United States (which also then extended recognition to Slovenia and Croatia). Civil war immediately broke out. But as in the case of Croatia, the main cause of war was a deep internal disunion between the three constituent communities—Muslims, Serbs, and Croats—and the land-grabbing policy of Serbia and Croatia. Considering the tensions inside Bosnia-Herzegovina, it was surprising that the war did not break out sooner. Germany's responsibility, therefore, was mainly in exacerbating existing divisions and conflicts, rather than in creating new ones.

Why did Germany press for recognition? The debate about the motives behind Germany's policy toward the disintegration of Yugoslavia has been even more intense than the debate about the effects of the policy. Economic explanations are frequently proposed, but seem weak. Germany could, after all, have dominated all of Yugoslavia economically. It did not need to divide it into smaller units. Political motives seem more plausible. Germany will find it much easier politically to dominate Slovenia and Croatia than all of Yugoslavia. These two countries are considerably smaller than Yugoslavia, and therefore less likely to resist German leadership. And they also have less reason to resist, since their historical memories of Germans and Germany are much less painful than those of the Serbs. Croatian nationalism, in particular, has in some historical periods seen Germany and Austria as its protector.

In Vienna there are influential public figures who speak of Slovenia becoming a tenth *Bundesland* of Austria through a peaceful change of borders. But the majority of Austrians give no support to such plans; they do not want almost two million members of a Slav nation to become citizens of Austria. Most leading Austrian politicians express great reservations even about looser political arrangements such as a Central European or Danubian federation, welcoming only common economic and cultural projects. Indeed, many more Austrians would prefer closer bonds with Germany and Western Europe than with Slovenia.[12]

While Germany's motives in promoting the recognition of Slovenia and Croatia were undoubtedly political, this does not mean that Germany was acting according to a plan—although most Serbs believe that to be precisely the case. Germany's efforts to draw Slovenia and Croatia into its sphere of influence were largely unpremeditated. It was, after all, the media and public opinion that began supporting Slovenes and Croats at the expense of Serbs long before the German government did.

In the German media the amount of hostility to the Serbs was much greater than anywhere else in the West.[13] It seems that the German national consciousness has not freed itself from traditional clichés about democratic, Central European, civilized Croats and Slovenes, and despotic, Balkan, Byzantine, barbarous, and primitive Serbs. These clichés are part of the general belief that there are insurmountable differences in the culture, politics, mentality, and way of life between the "inferior" East and the "superior" West. A corollary of these views is a belief that Germany as the most powerful West European country should be the champion of Europe's values and its leader. Under the guise of the defense of Western democratic values and human rights during the disintegration of Yugoslavia, traditional German nationalistic prejudices reappeared.

On July 3, 1991, when the West still supported Yugoslavia, the *Frankfurter Allgemeine Zeitung* declared that recent developments have shown "that Serbo-Yugoslavia is not a civilized country."[14] A *Schadenfreude* about the disintegration of Yugoslavia entered the media and has remained there to this day.[15] In addition, the whole history of Yugoslavia since its creation in 1918 began to be reinterpreted in very negative terms. The interwar Kingdom of Yugoslavia, while undoubtedly Serbian-dominated and oppressive toward non-Serbs, began to be described as horrifying, and accused without any evidence of pursuing genocidal policies. In the same vein, it was argued that during the Second World War communist-led Partisans, predominantly Serbian, supposedly murdered more unarmed civilians than did the armed occupiers, with those killed being mostly Croats, Slovenes, or members of the Albanian or German minorities. Tito, it was claimed, founded his rule on *Menschenvernichtungsaktionen,* for which he used the Serbs. And communist Yugoslavia, which in fact took pains to abolish Serbian predominance, was accused of retaining the "Serbian master-race chauvinism" of prewar Yugoslavia. It was further claimed that communism in general had no support in Yugoslavia except among the Serbs, and that the Yugoslav army was "Serbo-communist."

According to the German media, present-day Slovenia was a small freedom-loving republic. Slovenia received such acclaim perhaps because Slovenes were Germanized through history more than other South Slavs: "The Slovenes, a nation which, because of its sense of order has tended to be obedient toward its rulers, adapted to the German domination and culture."[16] Not only did Germany give complete support to the unconditional international recognition of Slovenia and Croatia immediately after their declaration of independence in June 1991, but it often insisted that the Albanians in the province of Kosovo, which was a part of Serbia, also had the right of secession. At the same time the Serbian leadership was accused of having an "oriental" understanding of law and state, and the Serbian state of being un-European. Once the war started, only the Serbian generals and politicians were seen as war criminals, and it was demanded that Serbia should be made to pay reparations to Slovenia and Croatia.

Serbian crimes committed during the war in Croatia and Bosnia-Herzegovina were compared to those of the Nazis. All territories captured by the Serbs were regarded as "lost to Europe," and Serbia was proclaimed an uncivilized state that should be disarmed by the "civilized West." As the war progressed, there were lamentations that Germany, because of its international reputation and the prohibitions of its own constitution, could not send troops to fight on the Croatian side. Later demands were made for the German air force to participate in the bombardment of Serbian positions in Bosnia-Herzegovina.

The extreme bias with which, in the name of Western values, most German media supported Slovenes and Croats and castigated Serbs suggested that mythologizing ethnocentrism, the main source of every nationalism, was still alive in Germany. Needless to say, Germany was not attempting to create the Fourth Reich, as the Serbs would have it. But through spontaneous reactions based on inherited and deeply rooted assumptions of who is "like us" and who is "the other," Germany promoted the creation of two conservative, nationalistic, pseudo-democratic, and—in the case of Croatia—aggressive states.

Germany is now trying to enlarge its political, economic, and cultural influence in Slovenia and Croatia, to the point of limiting their sovereignty. One is reminded of Germany's policies during the First World War when it tried to dominate all countries in Central Europe and the Balkans.[17] Germany is always careful to play the role of protector of Slovenia and Croatia in the international arena. In the summer of 1993, for example, it warned the Croatian government not to start an offensive against Serbian-held territories of Croatia (in most of which Serbs are a majority) and criticized it for its role in dismembering Bosnia-Herzegovina. Yet when the British and French proposed that

Croatia should be punished for its misdeeds in Bosnia-Herzegovina by the imposition of an embargo on international commerce and air traffic similar to the one imposed in May 1992 on Serbia and its ally Montenegro, Germany came to Croatia's aid and blocked the recommendation.

What do such conflicts between Germany and its European allies portend for the future of Europe? Some believe that they have irreversibly damaged the process of European integration, and that the next international crisis will create an open split. But it is still possible for Germany to overcome its disposition—demonstrated during the civil war in Yugoslavia—to perceive other nations in positive and negative stereotypes, express passionate sympathies and antipathies for them, and pursue partisan policies when they are in conflict. Since the Second World War, Germans have made a major and mostly successful effort to "overcome the past" and purge their political and intellectual life of any vestiges of national socialism. A similar exertion in rational and critical analysis of its nationalistic prejudices, which were mostly formed before the First World War, will undoubtedly be as beneficial.

NOTES

1. Istvan Deak, *Beyond Nationalism: A Social and Political History of the Habsburg Officer Corps, 1848–1918* (New York: Oxford University Press, 1992), p. 199.

2. See Andrej Mitrović, *Prodor na Balkan: Srbija u planovima Austro-Ugarske i Nemačke, 1908–1918* (Belgrade: Nolit, 1981).

3. Stojan Novaković, *Iz srpske istroije* (Novi Sad: Matica srpska, 1972), pp. 347–53, 362–66.

4. For example, in the writings of the Austro-Hungarian Chief of Staff Conrad von Hötzendorf or L. v. Südland (Ivo Pilar).

5. Milorad Ekmečić, *Srbjija između srednje Evrope i Evrope* (Belgrade: Politika, 1992), p. 112.

6. And indeed, by the 1930s most of the countries of Central and Southeastern Europe would be dominated by Germany.

7. Čedomir Popov, *Od Versaja do Danciga* (Belgrade: Nolit, 1976), pp. 496–507. Stevan K. Pavlowitch, *Yugoslavia* (London: Ernest Benn, 1971), pp. 92–93.

8. Audrey L. Helfant, "Yugoslav Reactions to German Unification" (unpublished article), p. 12.

9. In the nineteenth century some extreme but influential Croatian nationalists had argued that Croats were of Gothic origin, and as such superior (the term "master race" was even used) to the Serbs, who were merely Slavs.

10. Dorothea Grafin Razumovsky, *Chaos Jugoslawien* (Munich: Piper, 1992), p. 170.

11. Misha Glenny, *The Fall of Yugoslavia: The Third Balkan War* (London: Penguin Books, 1992), pp. 148–49.

12. Although the majority of Austrians today do not consider themselves Germans, in the period between the world wars the majority favored the Anschluss. Such sentiments were particularly strong during the economic crisis of 1929–33.

13. Especially in the conservative newspapers *Frankfurter Allgemeine Zeitung* and *Die Welt*. *Frankfurter Allgemeine Zeitung* recently criticized the French for their policy toward the Yugoslav disintegration with such bitterness that a commentator of *Le Figaro* wondered if there had ever really been German-French reconciliation. "Popustanje stega," *Vreme* (April 19, 1993).

14. Razumovsky, *Chaos Jugoslawien*, p. 40.

15. And not only in the media. See, for example, Michäla Wimmer, Stefan Braun, and Joachim Spiering, *Brennpunkt Jugoslawien—der Vielvölkerstaat in der Krise: Hintergrunde, Geschichte, Analysen* (Munich: Wilhelm Heyne, 1991).

16. Johann Georg Reissmüller, *Der Krieg vor unserer Haustür: Hintergrunde der kroatischen Tragödie* (Stuttgart: Deutsche Verlags-Anstalt, 1992), p. 58. The author is a leading conservative journalist and a co-publisher of the *Frankfurter Allgemeine Zeitung*. In his book one can find all the views of the increasingly influential German right both about the civil war in Yugoslavia and about the history of Yugoslavia. It is a veritable repository of German prejudices about Yugoslavia. For an attempt to give a balanced account of the Yugoslav disintegration, see Wolfgang Libal, *Das Ende Jugoslawiens: Chronik einer Selbstzerstörung* (Vienna: Europaverlag, 1991).

17. See Andrej Mitrović, "Srbi o Nemcima," *Knjizevne novine* 45:842 (June 1, 1992): 1, 5.

III

Reform in Postcommunist Societies: Transition or Regression?

Recession in Postcommunist Eastern Europe: Common Causes and Outcomes

Kazimierz Z. Poznanski

The political collapse of communism in 1989 came as a surprise to most observers of Eastern Europe, soon to be followed by another surprise—the collapse of the regional economy. The gross domestic product (GDP) was cut by about 48 percent in Albania, 36 percent in Bulgaria, and 33 percent in Romania during 1989–92. In Czechoslovakia and Slovenia, the decline was close to 22 percent from 1990 to 1992. The lowest rate of overall decline in 1990–92 was in Hungary and Poland, with about an 18 percent reduction, or back to the 1980 level. Even in 1993, the contraction in East European domestic product was far from over; for example, there was a 6 percent decline in Bulgaria.

The industrial sector cumulatively contracted by as much as 50 percent in Romania during 1989–92. From 1990–92, Albanian industry declined by a similar amount. In Bulgaria the decline was in excess of 45 percent in the same period. Even in the countries suffering the smallest downturn in industrial production, such as the Czech Republic, the cumulative rate of contraction was close to 39 percent during the period 1990–93. Poland went through about a 35 percent decline as well, with all of it concentrated between 1989 and mid-1991. While Hungary's losses during 1990–92 were less aggravated than Poland's, the fact that its recession extended through part of 1993 made its record slightly worse.

The unusual depth of the recession—often compared to the Great Depression of the 1930s—indicates that an extraordinary factor, or rather combination of factors, must be responsible (without necessarily implying that the mechanisms of these two occurrences are identical). While the recession has been uneven in its severity, it has nevertheless been a regionwide phenomenon, suggesting some similarity in the combination of forces responsible for the downturn in all the countries. Moreover, since other industrial countries have been spared such a deterioration during recent years, it would seem that the recession is of an internal nature rather than related to external shocks, such as the energy crisis that hit the region a decade earlier.

Many hypotheses have been advanced to explain the prolonged recession, and it is the purpose of this chapter to reexamine several of them. My exploratory discussion suggests that the recession may have been caused mainly by microeconomic supply-side factors: that is, by distorted incentives for state enterprises. Macroeconomic demand-side factors, while evidently present, have been less significant in causing the crisis, though it seems that deflationary measures, aimed at stabilization, might have been too harsh. That these monetary shocks have often only partly succeeded could be attributed largely to an inadequate microeconomic, supply-side adjustment by enterprises.

Furthermore, the dilution of property rights in the public sector, causing anxiety over returns on investment, might well have been one of the most significant supply-side factors behind the recent recession. Postcommunist governments inherited a greatly weakened property structure, where the party-state was only nominally in charge of the public assets. While ultimately necessary, both decontrol of enterprises and privatization of their assets have initially further undermined the property structure. This process occurred both where property changes were conducted largely by governments and where such changes took place without much governmental control.

The Economic Recession

Universal Recession

While a few East European countries reported a decline in GDP as early as 1988 or 1989, only in 1990 did the economic recession assume a truly regional dimension (Table 1A). Albania, after experiencing a strongly positive rate of growth in 1989, saw its GDP descend by 13.1 percent. Meanwhile, Poland's GDP fell by 11.6 percent, and Bulgaria's by 9.1 percent. Romania's fell by 8.2 percent, for the third year of contraction in a row. In Hungary, the negative rate was 3.3 percent, while Czechoslovakia registered a 1.8 percent loss. Most of the former Soviet republics also experienced declines, though generally small ones (with Uzbekistan and Turkmenistan escaping negative rates).

The bulk of the decline came from a reduction in industrial production, practically all within the dominant public sector (Table 1B). The sharpest decline in total industrial output was in Poland by 24.2 percent, while Romania, with a 19 percent reduction, was the second worst case. This decline was executed without proportional trimming of the work force, though entrants to the market—most of them young people—found few jobs available. The reduced hiring was responsible for a sudden rise in unemployment, as in Poland, where the rate of joblessness reached 6.1 percent. As a consequence of the relatively slow reduction in the existing work force, losses in productivity of labor were often reported as well.

In 1991, GDP contraction worsened in almost all these countries—the one important exception being Poland, where the rate of decline was much lower than in 1990 and the lowest among all East European countries. The deepest loss was experienced by Albania, with a 29.4 percent negative rate. Czechoslovakia reported a 14.3 percent decline, and Romania a loss of 13.7 percent. Hungary showed a 11.9 percent loss, and the negative rate for Bulgaria was 11.7 percent. This was also the year when the former republics of the Soviet Union experienced a further deterioration in national product. For example, there was a 10.0 percent reduction in Estonia, and a 14.3 percent loss in Russia.

The year 1991 also witnessed an acceleration in the decline of industrial production—the single exception again being Poland—with most countries' output falling in excess of 20 percent, while Albania suffered a dramatic 30.0 percent downturn. This time, large-scale losses in agricultural production took place as well (Table 1C). In Czechoslovakia, the agricultural sector experienced a 8.4 percent decline (after recording a 3.9 percent loss in 1990), while in Bulgaria the respective reduction was 6.4 percent. (Romania showed a 1.2 percent increase, however.) With total production universally falling, unemployment rates climbed, often reaching ranges which for the first time seemed truly alarming (e.g., 11.8 percent in Poland, and 11.5 percent in Bulgaria).

In 1992, only one independent country—Poland—demonstrated positive growth, around 1.5 percent. (For the record, East German production increased by 7 percent in 1992, due to enormous financial help from West Germany, which itself was thrown into stagnation under the burden of unification transfers.) Two other countries—Czechoslovakia and Hungary—showed some signs of recovery, but ended up with a further decline in their national product, as did the rest of Eastern Europe, though in all cases the output losses were less than in 1991. In contrast, the contraction accelerated in the former Soviet Union, with Russia reporting a 22 percent decline.

Industrial output continued to fall in 1992, except in Poland, where this process was reversed in midyear, the increase driven by the construction sector. By the end of 1992, Poland's monthly output was 4.2 percent above the respective figure for the last month of 1991. That this increase did not produce stronger overall growth in the national income was due mostly to a sharp decline in agriculture of 11.9 percent. Even sharper losses in agriculture were reported by Czechoslovakia (13.2 percent) and Hungary (22.7 percent) in 1992. Unemployment increased almost everywhere, even in recovering Poland, where it climbed to 13.6 percent by the end of 1992.

The regional crisis continued through 1993, though this time at least Albania joined Poland in turning its economy around. The Czech Republic registered another, rather small loss in national product, but Slovakia's GDP fell by 4.7 percent in that year. Other countries in the region continued to experience considerable output losses, with Bulgaria seeing its national product drop by an additional 6 percent. Russia suffered another year of very deep contraction, though not as extensive as that reported in 1992. While the crisis in Eastern Europe seemed to be bottoming out, that in the former Soviet Union probably had not yet reached its lowest point in 1993.

The decline in production has been paralleled by a sharp, mostly uninterrupted rise in unemployment, which reached levels as high as 25.0 percent in Albania, 16.4 percent in Bulgaria, 15.7 percent in Poland, and 12.1 percent in Hungary by the end of 1993 (Table 1E). A few countries avoided such drastic unemployment increases, one of them being the Czech Republic, where the unemployment rate was 0.7 percent in 1990, 4.1 percent in 1991, 2.6 percent in 1992, and then 3.5 percent in 1993. (However, in Slovakia the respective rates were: 1.6, 11.8, 10.4, and 14.4 percent.) Similarly, many of the former Soviet republics have kept their unemployment low, as in Russia, where the official rate of unemployment for 1993 was 1.1 percent (or 4 to 5 percent unofficially).

With these increases in unemployment have come some positive effects, however, including the reduction of overmanning in the state sector inherited from the communist past. Due to its disciplining effect, the emergence of an excess supply of labor has helped to keep inflation in check. High unemployment, by putting the brakes on wage demands, has allowed enterprises to raise financial funds available for production restructuring. In many enterprises, even those still under public ownership, trimming the work force—along with other rationalization measures—has already triggered recovery, while often allowing for wage increases as well.[1]

Inflationary Pressures

In 1989 certain countries started showing a rapid price acceleration, the most striking case being Poland (Table 1F). Already very high in 1988, at 60.2 percent, inflation intensified in 1989 to reach 244.1 percent. Other countries maintained relatively low rates in 1989, except for Hungary, with a rate of 17 percent. In 1990, inflation increased everywhere, including Czechoslovakia, where it climbed from 1.4 percent in 1989 to 10 percent in 1990. In Bulgaria the increase was from 6.2 to 19.3 percent, while Poland allowed its price index to more than double to 584.7 percent (though most of the increase occurred only early in that year).

This price acceleration in Poland in 1990 followed the state decision to further liberalize prices, another step in a decade-long process of progressive freeing of prices by the state.[2] By 1989, about 65 percent of prices in Poland were already outside of state control, including the most politically sensitive area—foodstuffs. Upward corrections in deregulated prices were combined with state decisions to raise administrative prices, sometimes by a multiple. Such increases in state-controlled prices were the primary reason behind inflation acceleration in Bulgaria and Czechoslovakia, both of which delayed their decision to free prices.

In 1991, Poland showed a greatly reduced rate of inflation, though still relatively high, while in all other countries price indices increased, sometimes quite drastically. In Bulgaria, for instance, the annual rate of inflation was at 254.3 percent, with monthly rates early in the year approaching hyperinflation but then slowing down. Romania's inflation reached 165.5 percent that year, though just one year earlier the respective rate was 4.2 percent. In Czechoslovakia, prices increased sharply during the initial few months of 1991, and then reached low monthly increases, producing an overall 57.9 percent annual rate of inflation.[3]

The rapid acceleration of inflation in Czechoslovakia can be largely attributed to price liberalization on a massive scale. Early in 1991, as high as 85 percent of prices were freed at one time; this followed the removal of food subsidies in mid-1990 as well as the devaluation of currency in 1990. Around the same time, Bulgaria, faced with rampant price increases, abolished almost all subsidies and removed practically all price controls. While during the last month before price liberalization the rate of inflation in Bulgaria was 13.6 percent, right after this reform the monthly rate increased to 122.9 percent. In Poland, the respective rates in 1990 were 17.1 versus 79.6 percent.

By 1992 all these countries, except Albania, Romania, and Slovenia, registered considerable progress in arresting inflation, although in Bulgaria the rate continued to be relatively high. In Romania—where liberalization of prices had proceeded in phases since late 1990, when the state freed many prices, though not for foodstuffs—inflation accelerated to 210.9 percent. Both Bulgaria and Romania, under pressure from their restless populations, had to restore price controls for some essential goods. Far more extreme inflation developed in most of the former Soviet republics, as in Russia, where the 1992 rate exceeded 1,400 percent—compared to 100 percent in 1991.

While considerable progress has been made in cooling inflation, thus wiping out welfare-detracting shortages, only the Czech Republic and Slovakia have moved it into safe ranges. However, low rates of inflation may be difficult to maintain, given the fact that price increases have been kept in check mostly by a very restrictive wage policy (Table 1G). Progressive taxes on wage raises (absent in Hungary, and abolished by Poland in 1992), combined with the undervaluation of currency, drove real wages to uneconomically low levels. This represented a threat to production restructuring, and once these measures are corrected, pressure on prices due to higher costs of production may increase.[4]

While the Czech Republic benefits from a balanced budget, most of the other countries have continued to be under pressure to finance their budgets through the inflationary method, tapping the credit market at the expense of the productive sector. This is the case in Hungary, whose budget has been in deficit for many years, with its 1992 imbalance amounting to 7.5 percent of the national product. After briefly balancing its budget in 1990, Poland watched the deficit reappear, to reach 6 percent in 1992, and about the same in 1993. While price liberalization has often been the primary source of the early inflation, in the later stages of transition, as in Poland, fiscal imbalances tend to contribute to inflation most.

Resolving budget imbalances may be difficult, as their sources are often of a structural nature. The initial surplus in Poland was not sustainable, despite drastically reduced spending executed at the risk of a political backlash. In certain countries, including Romania, easy spending has continued, including generous credit offered at negative interest rates to loss-making enterprises. Still, in most cases, the primary source of fiscal weakness has been the loss of tax revenues, in large part due to tax evasion and nonpayments.[5] In Czechoslovakia and Hungary, visible progress has been made in modernizing tax schemes and solidifying collection.

The External Sector

The post-1989 transition period has also been one of foreign trade difficulties, with many countries seeing their exports go down in real terms. In 1989 the value of total exports fell by 12 percent in Bulgaria, or by 2.3 percent in volume terms, while in Romania export value declined by 10 percent, or 10.8 percent in volume terms. Only in Hungary, Poland, and Yugoslavia did volumes not shrink, but their respective rates of increase were very low (Table 1H). The principal source of this poor export performance was the diminishing scope of trade within the CMEA (Council for Mutual Economic Assistance) regime, though in the case of Romania, substantial losses in exports to Western markets were a factor as well.

In 1990, exports deteriorated even more, except for Poland, which managed to increase its total sales abroad by 15.1 percent in volume terms. In Bulgaria, export volume fell by 23.4 percent, and in Romania by 41.5 percent. Elsewhere, the decline was relatively modest, as in Hungary, where export volume shrank by 4.3 percent. Again, the main source of the decline was a further, yet more drastic, "trade destruction" within the CMEA. In Bulgaria and Romania this was combined with diminishing sales to Western markets. Decline in both Czechoslovakia and Hungary was mitigated by strong expansion of exports to Western countries. Poland, meanwhile, managed to increase exports to both markets.

Total export contraction continued in 1991, this time with Poland registering a decline in volume as well, though a modest one. Bulgaria's exports fell by 30.1 percent and the Czech Republic registered an 8.4 percent decline in export volume, with all contraction taking place early in the year, and Hungary performed poorly as well. The major reason for this decline was the sharp reduction in regional trade, particularly with the Soviet Union, or more specifically Russia; this followed the official dissolution of the CMEA early in the year. In 1991, Russia's trade with the former CMEA declined by 43 percent, while its trade with Western countries fell by 16 percent.

In 1992, Hungary and Poland registered modest increases in total exports, even though their shipments to the former Soviet Union fell again. Export momentum came mostly from sales to Western countries, particularly high in the case of Poland. In Bulgaria export volumes showed a modest rise, much of it due to the bottoming out of "trade destruction" with the former Soviet Union, and its industry managed to begin a return to Western markets. For comparison, real exports from Russia outside of the former Soviet Union fell officially by 26 percent in 1992—but most likely by less unofficially, given large-scale unreported sales.

The Czech Republic continued its export expansion through 1993, while Romania experienced its first increase in export volume in 1992; but otherwise the picture for Eastern Europe was bleak. Hungary reported a 13.1 percent reduction in exports, Bulgaria suffered a 13.4 percent decline, and Slovakia and Poland also saw their exports contract. Apparently about two-thirds of the total decline in Hungary's exports was due to lower shipments in nonfood goods such as clothing, footwear, and textiles. In part, this reversal in exports was due to lower demand in the now economically depressed Western economies, a trend only partly mitigated by trading concessions.[6] In countries such as Hungary and Poland, this downturn was also caused by currency overvaluation; meanwhile, the Czech Republic kept its currency grossly undervalued.

A similar pattern of deterioration can be found in the balance of payments of individual countries. In 1990, only Hungary and Poland earned positive balances of trade, the most remarkable performance being demonstrated by the latter. After producing about $200 million in surplus during 1989, Poland reported a $2.2 billion surplus in 1990. Poland's current account deficit of $1.8 billion in 1989 was converted to a surplus of $700 million. In contrast, Romania generated a sizable trade deficit—in part related to state efforts to divert outputs to the bare domestic market—and ended 1990 with a current account deficit of $1.6 billion.

In 1991 most of the countries showed trade surpluses, among them Bulgaria, Czechoslovakia, and also Poland, which produced only a small surplus this time, about $100 million (or possibly a modest deficit, if customs data are utilized). In 1991 Hungary showed a trade surplus, though its value deteriorated by $1.3 billion.[7] This same year Hungary reported its first surplus on current account balance in two decades, the major sources of this improvement being tourism and deposits on private foreign-exchange accounts. Romania showed another trade deficit, and a deficit of $1.3 billion on its current account.

In 1992, the Czech Republic ran a trade deficit of $900 million and a surplus of $1.5 billion in invisible exports, so that its current account balance for the year was $600 million, up from a surplus of $300 million in 1991. Poland ended 1992 with a negative current account of $800 million, all due to the deficit of $1.8 billion accumulated in the second part of the year. This was largely due to the trade deficit that year, estimated at $2.7 billion (though calculations based on payment rather than customs data showed a trade surplus of $500 million). Hungary also allowed its trade balance to deteriorate in the second part of 1992, producing a deficit of $400 million, though it concluded the year with a positive current account.

In 1993, the only country with a sizable positive current account balance was the Czech Republic, while Hungary and Poland reported negative balances. Hungary incurred a trade deficit of $3.4 billion and a $1.5 billion current account deficit by mid-1993. In Poland, the trade deficit of the first half of 1993 led to the accumulation of a $2.8 billion current account deficit. With deficit accumulation continuing in the second half of the year, Poland produced a $3.3 billion deficit, forcing it to borrow abroad or deplete its reserves of foreign currency. It is these deficits that led the recent economic recoveries in both countries, even though earlier expectations were that exports would bring them out of their post-1990 recessions.

Demand-Side Hypotheses

Monetary Contraction

In the search for underlying causes of the regional recession, a good starting point is to examine the sharp deflationary measures implemented after 1989 (commonly called "shock therapy"), since they were among the first methods adopted by many postcommunist reformers, with one of the few exceptions being Hungary. In Poland, such measures were initiated, as mentioned above, in 1990. In 1991 similar steps were taken by Bulgaria and Czechoslovakia. In 1992, Russia also moved ahead with a program to remove excess money (overhang) from the economy. In almost all countries, the fight with monetary overhang was combined with one-time or stepwise price decontrol, thus requiring harsher monetary restrictions than if prices had temporarily remained fixed by the state.

Concern over inflation, either in the form of a monetary overhang combined with shortages of goods or an open price-spiral, was not new to these countries. In Poland, for example, the last two communist governments led by Messner and Rakowski—with the latter trying its own "shock therapy"[8]—clearly made final monetary stabilization their primary task. This preoccupation with inflation was consistent with the monetary conservatism of communist leaderships going back to the first postwar years.[9] It also reflected the paradigm developed later in the communist period which described the major deficiency of state-planned economies in terms of permanent shortages.[10]

These shock therapies—whether executed, as in the case of Czechoslovakia and Poland, or abandoned, as in Russia—were invariably followed by a sharp decline in production. In Poland, early in 1990, the one-time drop was followed by a flattened output for months. Eventually, there was a modest increase later in the year. When another shock was applied early in 1991, however, production began declining again. In Czechoslovakia in 1991, output decline was extended over a somewhat longer period, with a major loss coming one quarter after the application of multiple stabilization measures. Russia also registered a sharp dive in production after its aborted shock therapy, clearly intended to follow Poland's program of 1990.

Such a sharp decline surprised reformers, as well as their advisers, since (as documented in official macroeconomic projections) only a minor, short-lived contraction of production was expected.[11] The actual results were also inconsistent with what is commonly understood to be the usual economic impact of such stabilization programs. In the best-known, similarly conceived cases from Latin America, monetary shocks succeeded in extinguishing hyperinflation almost instantly (though not always permanently) with little output loss. In countries with chronic deflation, such measures usually helped to increase output immediately, though frequently these economies turned to recession again later.

One explanation of these surprising results is that, while properly designed, monetary shocks have not been executed properly. It is said that at least in the case of Poland (and perhaps also of Yugoslavia) excessive damage to production should be mainly blamed on the indecisiveness of the deflationary programs.[12] When Poland's economy started feeling the first serious pangs of monetary contraction in mid-1990, the government of Mazowiecki decided to ease restrictions.[13] With a brief return to softer financing of the state enterprises, the credibility of the reformers was compromised, so that another, relatively harsher dose of monetary restrictions was required.

Other economists are of the view that rather than being inconsequential, the deflationary measures were by and large excessive.[14] Brada and King argue that since there were no significant institutional reforms to affect supply-side incentives at the time of monetary shock in Czechoslovakia, Hungary, and Poland, only demand-side factors, such as major deflation and trade destruction, can be considered as a source of production losses in 1990.[15] If not for an excessive aggregate income reduction accomplished through temporary freezes or inflationary "taxation," there would have been a far less pronounced loss to production in these three countries.

This monetary overdose is often blamed on an overestimation of inherited imbalances, a point made by Brada with respect to communist

Czechoslovakia, which applied the most conservative monetarist policies.[16] Alexiev suggests that in the similarly conservative Soviet Union,
which allowed little open inflation, monetary (inflationary) overhang
might have been insignificant at the end of the communist rule.[17] Kolodko argues, in turn, that by the end of 1989, inflation in Poland was
rapidly subsiding and there was no need for a shock as harsh as that
applied in 1990.[18] Poland's reformers also tended to exaggerate the
remaining imbalances and thus the scope of needed deflationary
corrections.

The negative impact of monetary shocks is denied, however, by another group of economists, among them Berg and Sachs.[19] They argue
that, at least in the case of Poland, there is no evidence of a shock overdose. The real (i.e., corrected for price changes) decline in monetary
supply in Poland was far less than was typically implied. While real
wages, the main element of aggregate demand, fell by almost 35 percent in 1990, much of this decline was purely statistical, representing
"empty money." The real decline in consumer demand—one which
could possibly cause output to fall—was, the authors assert, only
4.8 percent (p. 141), and therefore could not be the primary source of
the production crisis.

The damaging effect of monetary shock is also negated on the
grounds that in countries such as Czechoslovakia and Poland, where
such measures were consequently applied, production losses did not ex-
ceed those observed in economies which avoided shocks or allowed
them to fade away.[20] One such country is Romania, where the production decline began in 1988, well before any effort to suppress the money
supply was entertained by the government. The 1991 monetary shock
was only partly executed, but production nevertheless fell drastically, so
that the combined production loss in shock-averse Romania proved far
worse than in shock-prone Czechoslovakia and Poland.

Inventory Adjustment

Another frequently identified demand factor behind the regional recession is downward inventory adjustment. The argument here is that the
communist economic system produced excess inventory of unsalable
finished (final) goods and above-rational stockpiles of materials (intermediate goods). Production rejected by customers was financed at no

real cost, while uncertainty over supplies caused state-enterprise managers to "hoard" materials. Any imposition of more rigorous financial discipline, as with shock therapy, might then be expected to cause an immediate decline in the demand for inventory, and thus a corresponding output loss.

What this argument implies is that production losses have been inevitable, due to distortions and waste left by the communist economy. This, in fact, is one of the rather numerous claims that the transition from a state-socialist economy will always be costly. Winiecki has even formulated a kind of law of "inevitable" output squeeze following any, even moderate, effort to put an end to permanent shortages.[21] This "law of motion" has been casually tested by Winiecki, who found that the amount of excess inventory in communist Poland comes very close to the actual size of production contraction that the country experienced in 1990–91.

An elaborate quantitative analysis, supporting the idea that perfectly rational inventory correction was by far the most important source of the 1990 output decline in Poland, has been provided by Berg and Sachs.[22] By this estimate, the consumption decline contributed 2.7 points to the loss of gross national product, while the decline in fixed investment contributed 1.9 points. By comparison, inventory correction contributed 6.2 percent to the total output decline estimated at minus 4.9 (less than the sum of negative changes—mostly due to the positive impact of hard-currency exports).

This argument raises theoretical questions, beginning with the claim that inventories under a command economy are a multiple of "rational" levels. If, unlike the authors, one began with the generally accepted premise that these economies were in a state of permanent shortage, one would wonder how excessive inventories were really possible. One would rather expect enterprises to be forced to work with an inadequate inventory, and periodically even halt production until supplies resurfaced. Evidence of breaks in production—followed by "spurts"—speaks to the relevance of this opposing argument, as well as tight bank control of inventories through limits on credit.

Even if there were some, or even many "unnecessary" inventories, and even if hardening of financial discipline wiped them out, it remains questionable that this kind of one-time shock could produce a recession as long as that in Eastern Europe. Rather this should have produced a

one-time adjustment to more restrictive credit, with only a limited impact on the rational expectations of suppliers affected by this adjustment. Even if inventory "corrections" of the size implied by Berg and
Sachs were really the primary cause of Poland's nearly three-year production decline, it is doubtful that the same factor could be the chief
cause of the six-year recession in Romania.

Moreover, to assess correctly the actual role of inventory reductions,
one would have to establish whether the registered decline in inventories wiped out only "excess" inventories. It could be that some, or even
most, of this shock-related decline was caused by production contraction. Such a decline in "usable" inventories could have also been related
to liquidity problems—to be expected in economies with a financial
system as primitive as these countries. If liquidity problems have really
troubled state-owned enterprises, then sales of "usable" inventories
could have been helpful in replenishing the cash holdings needed to
pay wages and other production costs.

Finally, one should be aware also of how difficult it is to collect reli-
able statistics on recent inventory changes in Poland or elsewhere in
Eastern Europe. There was never good reporting on inventory in the
communist past, so the base point is uncertain. Rostowski remarked
that recent price instability further obscures inventory analysis. For instance, depending on what prices stocks are calculated in, either a 2 to
3 percent increase or 30 percent drop is reported for Poland in 1990.
Schaffer notes that in 1990, inventories were not properly repriced in
Poland, thus helping state enterprises to generate large-scale profits.[23]

Trade Destruction

Looking beyond domestic components of aggregate demand, one may
ask whether certain external demand shocks may have caused the greatest damage to the economy. One possible source of such a shock could,
of course, be the collapse of the regional trading bloc, the CMEA. Already in desperate shape before 1990, as manifested in uncleared imbalances and a faltering volume of trade, the regime was formally dissolved
in 1991. This decision was accompanied by a sharp decline in demand
for products from bloc members. This trade destruction, to the degree
that the preexisting trade was rational, had to translate into a mutual
loss of welfare.

Most scholars view this demand shock as exogenous, that is, outside the direct control of the reformers in Eastern Europe, primarily because they ascribe blame for the collapse of the CMEA—both its timing and type of execution—to the Soviet Union. It is said that given its political and economic calculations, the Soviet Union unilaterally decided to abandon the bloc members. Alternatively, it is argued that the chaos that emerged at the end of Gorbachev's rule, involving state indecision, defaults on payments by enterprises, and so on, made trade with the Soviet Union impractical, so that the regime had to disintegrate for lack of interest.

While it is generally assumed that the CMEA collapse was, for the East European point of view, an uncontrollable development, this may not be completely so. It is true that the Soviet Union contributed to the demise of the trade bloc, when Gorbachev decided in mid-1990 to require hard-currency payments in intrabloc transactions. However, Eastern Europe also caused some damage to the regime—for example, in 1989, when Poland's government under Rakowski set an unfavorable cross-currency exchange rate for the ruble. In addition, Poland's decision in early 1990 to establish partial convertibility and permit unrestricted private entrance to foreign trade, however justified domestically, must be viewed as another such adverse measure.

Theoretically, it was possible for Eastern Europe to retain some form of the existing trading framework as a temporary solution, even if the Soviet Union had abandoned it. That they did not do so could again have been caused by the uncoordinated, often incompatible measures taken by reformers in individual East European countries. This explains why in addition to the decline in trade with the Soviet Union, intra-East European trade shrank as well. Intra-East European trade fell considerably in 1991, particularly between the more advanced northern countries and the less developed southern region. In 1993, following their formal separation, the Czech Republic and Slovakia watched their mutual trade decline by one-third.

Whatever the nature of this demand shock, its scope has been substantial, and thus one would expect the related negative output effect to be considerable as well. Rodrik calculated that given the loss of trade volume as well as changes in terms of trade, the estimated loss of output in Eastern Europe during 1990–91 could be as high as 7 to 8 percent of their national products.[24] In a separate estimate for Poland, Gomulka finds that in 1991 the output losses related to "trade destruction" within the CMEA were equivalent to 5 percent of the national product, with an additional loss of 1.5 percent reflecting the worsening of terms of trade with the former CMEA members.[25]

It is far from certain, however, that the CMEA-related loss of demand, while sizable, could have accounted for most of the production decline in the region. For example, in 1990, when Poland registered its sharpest single-year production decline, there was no parallel reduction in its trade with the Soviet Union.[26] In 1991 this trade took a major loss, so that it could have been responsible for some of the output contraction in that year. But at this point, Poland's exposure to trade with the Soviet Union was already low; in Hungary as well, ruble trade accounted for only 27.1 percent of the total volume in 1990.

It could be argued that sacrificing the regional trade regime was not such a high economic price to pay for speeding up the transition to the market, since much of the intraregional exchange of goods was presumably not economical. Given the precarious nature of pricing in the CMEA and the potential for political pressure by its single dominant member, the Soviet Union, the room for uneconomical trade was undoubtedly significant. Thus, the loss of trade volume could be considered as largely representing "creative destruction"[27] or the elimination of economic waste, making room for more efficient types of activities.

The idea of "creative destruction" in regional trade is consistent with the view that the recent recessions were largely due to decline in unneeded output.[28] But one should be wary of justifying trade or output losses—at least of the size found in Eastern Europe—on these grounds. This seems a theoretically dubious argument, because even if retaining bloc trade was not a first-order permanent solution, it could have easily been a second-best, temporary one. In other words, allowing slow adjustment in distorted segments of regional trade flows could have been economically preferable to their immediate elimination.

While one might expect promarket economic reforms in postcommunist Eastern Europe to result in some "trade destruction," one should be careful in interpreting the actual magnitude of the decline as reflecting the underlying scope of inefficient transactions allowed under the CMEA regime. Any trade, efficient or not, requires a fairly stable system of payments and contracts to facilitate it, and the CMEA was such a "public good." Without it, due to liquidity and confidence problems, both economical and noneconomical trade is likely to be adversely affected. Because the CMEA was not instantly replaced with an at least equally efficient payment/contract system, one might argue that both types of trade could have suffered.

Supply-Side Factors

Liquidity Crisis

Moving outside of the demand-side argumentation, it may be helpful to recognize that in order to function, markets require more than a correct price structure (i.e., undistorted signals of relative scarcities); they also need money to accommodate necessary resource allocation. For any deflationary shock to produce a positive output response to prices, money has to be provided by the financial system in sufficient quantity to allow for restructuring. Thus one should test whether the primary cause of the regionwide crisis might have been the possible overwithdrawal of credit, either due to credit restrictions that had been built into the "shock" or because the financial system, in particular banks, refused to supply credit to enterprises for production adjustment.

In fact, it has not been unusual for stabilization programs in developing countries outside of Eastern Europe, as in many inflation-ridden Latin American countries, to pursue a monetary contraction in combination with an unaccommodating credit policy. This has been done despite the fact that keeping credit lines open might help to reduce the negative impact of deflationary programs on output. Israel's heterodox stabilization program offers practical evidence that selective access to credit, in this case for export-oriented sectors, greatly contributes to reducing the costs of the price operation, as well as to the durability of lower inflation.[29]

Evidence from Eastern Europe suggests that indeed in most cases the amount of real credit has drastically declined following the monetary shocks. The credit squeeze has been very sharp in Czechoslovakia, where credit declined 26 percent in 1991,[30] and Poland, which witnessed an almost 40 percent reduction in real terms in 1990.[31] An extreme case would be that of Russia, where after a brief contraction of 60 to 75 percent, credit has been allowed to expand with no controls at all. Meanwhile, Hungary has been conducting a much more accommodating credit policy, with the interest rate not necessarily following each price increase.[32]

The credit supply decline has been caused by a number of factors, one being the decision by many reformers to use credit restrictions, such as credit ceilings and interest rate directives, as another anchor in monetary tightening. The fall in credit would be simply another manifestation of demand shock, if not for the fact that credit has also been restricted by banks, following their own even tighter policies. This has been reflected in a very high interest rate spread, due in part to a lack of response to refinancing rate reductions, as in Hungary, as well as the very high collaterals common in Poland. Increases in interenterprise credit, already widespread before shocks, have often somewhat mitigated shortages of bank credit.

East European industry has not only been largely left with an inadequate amount of credit but has also been poorly served by banks in allocating money. In particular, state banks have been notoriously unable to limit credit supplies to financially defunct state-owned enterprises.[33] Unpayable (bad) debts have been allowed to accumulate, with banks unwilling to execute their credit contracts and bankrupt the defunct enterprises to recover their loans. Collusion between banks and enterprises[34] has meant an extension of soft financing conditions, so that restructuring through "exit," allowing for rational redeployment of underutilized resources has been hampered.

The side effect of financing "bad" borrowers in the state sector has been a shortage of credit for the private sector. The private sector has suffered not only from the ongoing preference of banks to finance state-owned enterprises, but also from state pressure on commercialized banks to finance budget deficits. In Poland, less than 10 percent of total bank credit went to the private sector in 1990–91, and state bonds emerged as the major part of bank balance sheets. Accordingly, the process of restructuring through "entries" of private enterprises has been restricted as well.[35]

However, banks cannot be entirely blamed for the way they have acted, since they have found themselves in a situation for which they were ill-prepared. Their experience has been in executing money allocations decided through a budgetary process and with state "insurance," that is, a guaranteed bailout by the budget in case of defaults on loans to enterprises. They lack the skills needed to properly evaluate loan risks, and their recent "commercialization" has left them with inadequate protection against risk. To expect banks to engage in restructuring of their defunct customers would be even less realistic. Nor have they yet acquired the means or political clout to proceed with mass bankruptcies of their customers.

Even a well-established banking system could not properly manage intermediate capital allocation in the current environment, with its excessive "informational noise." The size of past debts of state-owned enterprises, for instance, provides very poor guidance for banks, for these often reflect a financial situation inherited from the communist period, with its passive money. High inflation, with multiple sources, complicates economic calculations of future cost-effectiveness of projects as well. Frequent, often unpredictable changes in state regulations on taxes, customs duties, and depreciation rates have further obscured calculations.

Organizational Routines

The above reference to banking leads me to a more general question of the adaptability of various types of economic agents, including organizations, to new conditions. In the neoclassical view, the answer is very simple: they can adapt in no time, since agents are assumed to be perfectly rational. Regardless of specific circumstances, economic agents display the same level of full rationality—the ability to recognize and implement both the best product mix and the best-practice techniques. Thus the real challenge for economic reformers is simply to get the prices right, so that complete and cost-free information is available and optimal choices can be made.

Within this neoclassical tradition, whenever agents fail to follow an optimum "trajectory"—meaning that the market fails—it is assumed that the state needs to intervene. With its insistence on achieving perfect, complete markets, the theory provides an ample excuse for state activism. It is also said that for any state intervention to succeed, this intervention must be credible. Individual agents will regress to previous habits if unpopular, or even just unfamiliar, measures taken by the state appear reversible at low cost to those affected. It follows from this argument that shock-therapy reforms have a greater chance for success than gradual ones.[36]

In the separate tradition of evolutionary economics, with its roots in the work of Schumpeter and Hayek,[37] individual agents are assumed to have limited adaptability while information is viewed as costly. If so, then the true challenge for reformers is not to set prices accurately but carefully to affect organizational behavior. It is not imperative to obtain a perfect or correct price structure immediately, but rather to make sure that all organizations steer prices in that direction. In fact, only by properly altering organizational behavior is there any assurance that prices will stay at their optimal levels for an extended period.

At variance with the neoclassical paradox of intervention in the name of perfect markets, the evolutionary approach presents the state as largely antithetical to the market. The latter theory perceives the state as the true source of "market failures" and not their only remedy. Thus monopoly rents are related to regulations blocking "entry," while, say, above-equilibrium wages (and unemployment) are caused by labor laws tilting bargaining power toward unions. Whenever state intervention is welcomed, the prescription is that action be taken cautiously, since it is not maximum credibility but rather the relative neutrality of an action which is critical.[38]

The root difference between the neoclassical and evolutionary views is in their understanding of what type of information is essential. While the former points to prices, the latter holds that the most relevant information is so-called tacit knowledge.[39] This type of organization-specific knowledge is acquired only through repetitive experience and is stored through "routines" (subconscious patterns of behavior). Such "routines" are the most essential organizational asset, for they allow organization members to respond "automatically" to variable price signals without overloading their limited computing capabilities.

Since, as Hayek argues, such organization-specific knowledge takes a long time to develop, it can be useful only if the environment around a respective organization remains relatively stable. "Routines" can be changed slowly in response to measured variations and, with a proper allowance of time, can even be fully transformed.[40] But if the amount of change faced by an organization is excessive, then "routines" are invalidated and the ability to process incoming signals is lost. A decline in efficiency, or even phasing out—in other words, bankruptcy—will then follow.

Working within the above paradigm, one might suggest that the crisis in Eastern Europe is a case of imposing too much change on state-owned enterprise. It could well be that rather than producing positive synergy, the simultaneous change of prices on all possible markets—for labor, capital, money, and foreign exchange—has depleted much of enterprises' ability to process information. This would explain not only the abruptness of the initial post-shock declines in production but also the durability of the East European recessions, since recovery can materialize only through the necessarily slow rebuilding of computing capabilities.[41]

But information overload is not the only means of disarming "routines"; adverse organizational changes might have the same effect. For instance, the loss of a segment of organization may reduce an organization's computing capability. Fragmentation of large enterprises has been widespread during the current transition. It has been a common practice to slice off "pieces" of state enterprises for privatization, as in Hungary.[42] Nor have these reorganizations necessarily been efficiency-optimizing, as blocks of "indivisible" state capital have often been sacrificed to facilitate small-scale acquisitions.

Incapacitation of "routines" may also be caused by erosion of organization "morale," such that cooperative behavior is replaced by indifference or sabotage, leading to efficiency loss. The threat of unemployment may stimulate efficiency, but if "rules" of terminating contracts are not spelled out, response to the threat may be negative. The same dysfunctional behavior may be caused by the presence of "rules" that reflect the politics of a given workplace rather than the economic imperative of labor productivity maximization. Largely unequipped to conduct orderly reductions and often highly politicized, state enterprises might have recently suffered a loss of "morale."

Property Vacuum

While the above behavioral hypothesis offers a broader view of plausible causes of the crisis than does one based on bank deficiencies, it still might be too narrow. Economies are built not only of organizations but of institutions that facilitate the credible commitment necessary for contracts.[43] The principal one is the institution of property rights—that is, the discretion over scarce resources recognized by law or custom. Property rights determine both the extent to which agents can internalize net benefits of their resource utilization and the level of costs of transacting or contracting.

Although the centrality of property rights was quickly gaining recognition during the final years of communist rule, there was no strong support for radical ownership reforms. The mono-party had no immediate plans for downsizing the state sector, except through pocket-size spin-offs to industrious members of the *nomenklatura*. The opposition did not object to state ownership either, but rather to the lack of genuine "social" control. Its preference was for a labor-management style like that of Yugoslavia. Both sides agreed on one point: these economies would benefit if the state sector was supplemented with a thriving private sector.[44]

The situation dramatically changed when postcommunist elites began formulating their plans for transition. The rapid transfer of state assets to private hands and the elimination of nonviable enterprises were declared a priority. Divestment of at least as much as half of the book value of existing state-owned enterprises within three years was adopted as a policy guideline in Hungary and Poland. Accordingly, preference was given to the least complicated forms of such transfer, such as give-away schemes that bypassed both the barrier of costly asset valuations and that of limited personal savings.[45]

In reality, few of the state assets have, as of 1993, gone into private hands, and even conversions of state enterprises into joint-stock companies have been limited, except in the Czech Republic, in Hungary, and Romania. Proponents of radical transfer find this situation the principal reason for the only partial success of monetary "shocks" and consider it a threat to the gains made by reform so far.[46] The opposite view holds that, while actual transfers of assets have been very slow, this is because such a complicated process could not take place much faster.[47] This means that policies built on the assumption of fast asset transfers could instead be blamed for contributing to the crisis.

Those economists who find the actual pace of divestment a failure place blame squarely on what they consider an ineffective political system. It is argued that give-away programs or other ideas suitable for transfer acceleration have been captured by political forces, where personal fortunes take precedence over concern for general wealth. Other economists disagree, saying that, however attractive they may be theoretically, programs such as the mass distribution of shares are not well enough tested for politicians readily to agree on them. This seems to be the case when radical "projects" are too vague to be credible, causing politicians to stall for time and to make repeated corrections.[48]

Supporters of rapid transfer argue that the slowness of privatization perpetuates old habits of the state-owned sector, so that new "games" are placed with old "tricks." This view implies that privatization programs do not affect state-sector enterprises until ownership transfer is complete, as if this were a world of policy making without "rational expectations" by policy makers. Those accepting the slow pace as an unavoidable reality argue that because of games of anticipation, strategies of state-owned enterprises might change before actual privatization takes place. Thus, depending on how privatization is executed, old "tricks" could be replaced with new ones even more threatening to economic efficiency.[49]

I have offered a hypothesis that radical privatization programs declared at the outset of transition, rather than being neutral, have undermined the property structure in the state sector.[50] A peculiar "property vacuum" has been created, since enterprises have been left without any firm deadlines or even clear-cut ideas on the exact form of privatization, while the state has abdicated its control functions. Thus, left in undefined legal condition and without close state supervision, centrally directed privatization programs have increased uncertainty over payoffs at the enterprise level. This uncertainty faced by enterprises appears to be directly responsible for output decline, as well as for stubbornly high rates of inflation.

This "property vacuum," seen basically as an unintended product of radical privatization, could have affected production levels in many negative ways. Faced with additional uncertainty, enterprises could have simply reduced their output. Moreover, it is possible that state enterprises, uncertain about the future, even found it advantageous to allow for decapitalization. Enterprises could not only have neglected investment for the sake of consumption—especially wages—because of the very short time horizon, but also engaged in asset stripping through sheer neglect.

High rates of inflation could also be attributed, in part, to increased uncertainty over the status of property, compounded by the ever-present threat of financial insolvency. The theory of "incomplete markets" posits that, when faced with higher uninsured risks, enterprises will attempt to insure themselves by charging higher prices. These price margins are added as a form of insurance premium whether the enterprise is a monopolist or not.[51] This particular explanation of inflation offers an alternative to arguments linking recent proinflationary tendencies to an ultramonopolistic industry structure.

Conclusions

The most common explanation of the regional recession, often based on Poland's case as the earliest "surprise," has been to attribute it to macroeconomic demand-side factors. Particular attention has been paid to the possible negative effects of macrostabilization (i.e., efforts to restore a state-budget balance and to remove inflationary overhangs). Another factor in this demand-type category identified as a possible source of recent recession is the inventory adjustment, or more broadly, the elimination of "unwanted" supplies. Finally, losses in the regional demand for exports, due to the collapse of CMEA, have been seen as an important, or even principal, cause of the output decline.

Given the amount of uncertainty over the actual role of demand shocks in driving the regional economy to recession, one might turn the search for causes to the supply side. It could be, for instance, that faced with a demand barrier—an equilibriated goods market—state-owned enterprises have worked out proper strategies, but for lack of credit have had no means to implement them. While it is true that banks, only recently converted from state-run to commercial institutions, have sharply restricted access to credit, there is also evidence that state-sector enterprises have been reluctant to borrow, except for wage payments.

Thus there could be a more fundamental supply-side factor at work than the credit shortage: the possible weakening of property rights and thus of incentives to economize. Since all postcommunist economies have launched large-scale denationalization of capital assets, this should logically have had some—initially mostly negative—impact on property rights. Indeed, there is evidence that these reforms, promising a turnover of assets to more efficient private use, have actually weakened incentives to employ resources effectively, though in many countries, production had already declined prior to passage of any major piece of privatization legislation.

Basic Macroeconomic Indicators, 1989–1993

(in percentage)

A. Gross Domestic Product

	1989	1990	1991	1992	1993
Albania[a]	11.7	− 13.1	− 29.4	− 6.0	11.0
Bulgaria	− 0.3	− 9.1	− 11.7	− 7.7	− 6.0
Czechoslovakia	1.4	− 1.8	− 14.3	− 7.0	—
Czech Republic	2.4	− 1.2	− 14.2	− 7.1	− 0.5
Slovak Republic	1.1	− 2.5	− 14.5	− 7.0	− 4.7
Hungary	0.4	− 3.3	− 11.9	− 5.0	− 2.0
Poland	0.2	− 11.6	− 7.6	1.5	4.0
Romania	− 5.8	− 8.2	− 13.7	− 15.4	1.0
Slovenia	− 0.5	− 4.7	− 9.3	− 6.0	1.0
Estonia[a]	—	− 8.1	− 10.0	− 14.4	− 2.0
Latvia[a]	—	2.7	− 8.3	− 33.8	− 19.9
Lithuania[a]	—	− 6.9	− 13.1	− 37.7	− 17.0
Russia[a]	—	− 4.0	− 14.3	− 22.0	− 13.0

[a]Net material product.

B. Gross Industrial Output

	1989	1990	1991	1992	1993
Albania	5.0	−7.5	−30.0	—	−1.0
Bulgaria	2.2	−17.2	−22.2	−16.2	−9.3
Czechoslovakia	0.8	−3.5	−24.7	−11.5	—
Czech Republic	1.7	−3.3	−24.4	−10.6	−7.1
Slovak Republic	−1.3	−4.0	−25.4	−12.9	−15.4
Hungary	−2.5	−4.5	−19.1	−9.8	3.8
Poland	−0.5	−24.2	−11.9	4.2	7.4
Romania	−2.1	−19.0	−18.7	−22.1	1.3
Slovenia	1.1	−10.5	−12.4	−13.2	−2.8
Estonia	0.7	−5.6	−9.0	−38.9	−26.6
Latvia	3.1	−0.2	0.6	−35.1	−34.6
Lithuania	4.2	−2.8	−4.9	−51.6	−46.0
Russia	1.4	0.1	−8.0	−18.0	−16.2

C. Gross Agricultural Output

	1989	1990	1991	1992	1993
Albania	10.7	−6.9	−24.0	—	15.0
Bulgaria	1.2	−6.0	−6.4	−12.5	−20.1
Czechoslovakia	1.7	−3.9	−8.4	−13.2	—
Czech Republic	2.3	−2.3	−8.9	−12.8	−0.8
Slovak Republic	0.6	−7.2	−7.4	−13.9	−12.5
Hungary	−1.3	−3.8	−5.0	−22.7	−25.0
Poland	1.5	−2.2	−2.0	−11.9	2.2
Romania	−5.0	−2.9	1.2	−13.2	12.2
Slovenia	0.3	1.7	−3.3	−10.0	−3.5
Estonia	7.6	−13.1	−20.7	−21.1	−16.8
Latvia	3.9	−3.5	−3.5	−13.8	−11.5
Lithuania	1.8	−9.0	−4.6	−23.6	−6.7
Russia	1.7	−3.6	−4.5	−9.0	−4.0

D. Gross Fixed Investment

	1989	1990	1991	1992	1993
Albania	10.9	−14.8	—	—	—
Bulgaria	−7.7	−18.5	−19.9	−1.5	−8.0
Czechoslovakia	1.6	6.1	−27.2	—	—
Czech Republic	1.7	6.5	−26.8	3.8	−10.5
Slovak Republic	1.4	5.2	−28.1	1.0	−2.4
Hungary	7.0	−7.1	−11.6	−6.4	—
Poland	−2.4	−10.6	−4.5	2.8	1.0
Romania	−1.6	−35.6	−26.0	−2.1	−0.8
Slovenia	−10.1	−9.8	−14.8	−14.5	11.0
Estonia	6.2	2.7	−12.0	−39.8	—
Latvia	4.2	−8.2	−36.3	−53.0	−37.0
Lithuania	−1.8	−10.3	−46.0	−34.3	−35.0
Russia	4.1	0.1	−15.5	−39.7	−15.0

E. Unemployment

	1989	1990	1991	1992	1993
Albania	—	9.8	9.4	26.7	25.0
Bulgaria	0.0	1.8	11.5	15.6	16.4
Czechoslovakia	0.0	1.0	—	—	—
Czech Republic	0.0	0.7	4.1	2.6	3.5
Slovak Republic	0.0	1.6	11.8	10.4	14.4
Hungary	0.3	1.7	7.4	12.3	12.1
Poland	0.1	6.1	11.8	13.6	15.7
Romania	0.0	1.3	3.1	8.2	10.1
Slovenia	—	5.3	10.1	13.3	15.4
Estonia	0.0	0.0	0.1	1.9	2.6
Latvia	0.0	0.0	—	2.1	5.8
Lithuania	0.0	0.0	0.3	1.0	1.6
Russia	0.0	0.0	0.1	0.8	1.1

F. Inflation (Consumer Price Index)

	1989	1990	1991	1992	1993
Albania	—	—	104.0	266.0	—
Bulgaria	6.2	19.3	254.3	79.4	72.9
Czechoslovakia	1.4	10.0	57.9	—	—
Czech Republic	—	—	56.7	11.1	20.8
Slovak Republic	—	—	61.2	10.2	23.1
Hungary	17.0	28.9	35.0	23.0	22.7
Poland	244.1	584.7	70.3	43.0	36.9
Romania	—	4.2	165.5	210.9	257.4
Slovenia	—	—	117.7	201.3	32.7
Estonia	—	—	283.0	968.6	87.6
Latvia	—	—	172.2	949.7	109.1
Lithuania	—	—	216.4	1,020.0	410.2
Russia	—	—	100.3	1,468.0	911.3

G. Real Wages

	1989	1990	1991	1992	1993
Albania	—	—	—	—	—
Bulgaria	3.0	6.9	− 39.4	19.2	− 10.4
Czechoslovakia	0.1	− 5.4	− 25.2	—	—
Czech Republic	—	—	—	10.1	8.6
Slovak Republic	—	—	—	—	—
Hungary	0.7	− 3.7	− 4.0	− 4.0	− 1.6
Poland	8.3	− 24.4	− 0.3	− 2.7	− 1.8
Romania	2.7	5.5	− 16.6	− 13.2	− 15.8
Slovenia	18.4	− 26.5	− 15.1	− 2.8	16.0
Estonia	—	6.8	− 43.1	− 30.8	5.0
Latvia	4.6	5.3	− 29.2	− 22.7	6.7
Lithuania	—	6.3	− 17.7	− 14.0	− 43.0
Russia	—	8.7	− 7.2	− 29.8	− 1.7

H. Export Volume

	1989	1990	1991	1992	1993
Albania	—	—	—	—	—
Bulgaria	−2.3	−23.4	−30.1	1.6	−13.4
Czechoslovakia	−2.0	−4.2	−4.9	7.2	—
Czech Republic	—	−3.0	−8.4	8.3	8.0
Slovak Republic	—	−8.3	19.5	6.3	—
Hungary	0.3	−4.3	−4.9	2.0	−13.1
Poland	0.2	15.1	−1.7	1.4	—
Romania	−10.8	−41.5	−4.8	8.0	0.3
Slovenia	—	—	—	—	8.0
Estonia	—	—	—	—	—
Latvia	—	—	—	—	—
Lithuania	—	—	—	—	—
Russia	—	—	—	—	−26.0

Sources: Economic Commission for Europe, *Economic Survey of Europe in 1993–1994* (Geneva: United Nations, 1994), and *Economic Survey of Europe in 1992–1993* (Geneva: United Nations, 1993).

NOTES

1. See B. Pinto et al., "Microeconomics of Transformation in Poland: A Survey of State Enterprise Responses," *WPS* (World Bank), no. 982 (September 1992).

2. K. Poznanski, "Poland's Transition to Capitalism: Shock and Therapy," in K. Poznanski, ed., *Stabilization and Privatization in Poland: The Economic Analysis of Shock Therapy* (Boston: Kluwer Academic Press, 1993), pp. 15–42.

3. See J. Svejnar, "Czech and Slovak Federal Republic: A Solid Foundation," in R. Portes, ed., *Economic Transformation in Central Europe: A Progress Report* (London: Centre for Economic Policy Research, 1993).

4. K. Crane, "Taking Stock of the 'Big Bang,'" in Poznanski, ed., *Stabilization and Privatization*.

5. See G. Kolodko et al., *Hyperinflation and Stabilization in Postsocialist Economies* (Boston: Kluwer Academic Press, 1992).

6. B. Kaminski, "Are Central European 'Associates' Getting Such a Bad Bargain from the European Communities?" International Trade Division, World Bank, 1993. Mimeo.

7. K. Mizsei, "Hungary: Gradualism Needs Strategy," in Portes, ed., *Economic Transformation*, p. 170.

8. B. Milanovic, "Poland's Quest for Economic Stabilization, 1988–1991: Interaction of Political Economy and Economics," in Poznanski, ed., *Stabilization and Privatization*, pp. 43–62.

9. See R. Portes, "Central Planning and Monetarism: Fellow Travelers?" in P. Desai, ed., *Marxism, Central Planning, and the Soviet Economy: Economic Essays in Honor of Alexander Erlich* (Cambridge, Mass.: MIT Press, 1983).

10. See P. Hare, "Economic Reform in Eastern Europe," *Journal of Economic Surveys* 1:1 (1987).

11. D. Rosati, "Recession and Recovery in the Transition to Market: The Case of Poland," *Working Papers* (Norwegian Institute of International Affairs, Oslo), no. 511 (April 1994), p. 3.

12. Crane, "Taking Stock," p. 82.

13. J. Rostowski, "Comments," in H. Siebert, ed., *The Transformation of Socialist Economies* (Tübingen: J.C.B. Mohr, 1992).

14. See D. Rosati, "Poland: Glass Half Full," in Portes, ed., *Economic Transformation*, pp. 211–73; or M. Nuti and R. Portes, "Introduction," in the same volume.

15. J. Brada and R. King, "Is There a J-curve in Economic Transition to Market Economy?" *Economics of Planning* 25:1 (March 1992): 37–54.

16. J. Brada, "The Economic Transition of Czechoslovakia from Plan to Market," *Journal of Economic Perspectives* 5:1 (Fall 1991).

17. Alex Alexiev, presentation made at the AAASS annual convention, Honolulu, December 23–25, 1992.

18. G. Kolodko, "From Output Collapse to Sustainable Growth in Transition Economies: The Fiscal Implications," *Working Papers* (Institute of Finance, Warsaw), no. 35.

19. A. Berg and J. Sachs, "Structural Adjustment and International Trade in Eastern Europe: The Case of Poland," *Economic Policy* 13 (1992).

20. M. Dabrowski, "Stabilization Program in Poland, 1990–1991," Batory Foundation, Warsaw, 1992. Mimeo.

21. J. Winiecki, "The Inevitability of a Fall in Output in the Early Stages of Transition to the Market: Theoretical Underpinnings," *Soviet Studies* 43:4 (1991).

22. Berg and Sachs, "Structural Adjustment," p. 146.

23. M. Schaffer, "The Enterprise Sector and Emergence of the Polish Fiscal Crisis, 1990–91," Center for Economic Performance, London School of Economics, August 1992.

24. D. Rodrik, "Foreign Trade in Eastern Europe's Transition: Early Results," *CEPR Discussion Paper,* no. 676 (June 1992).

25. S. Gomulka, "Poland: 'Glass Half Full,'" in Portes, ed., *Economic Transformation.*

26. Rosati, "Poland: Glass Half Full."

27. For more see S. Gomulka, "The Causes of Recession Following Stabilization," *Comparative Economic Studies* 15 (1991).

28. Berg and Sachs, "Structural Adjustment."

29. O. Blanchard et al., *Reform in Eastern Europe* (Cambridge: MIT Press, 1991), p. 9.

30. M. Hncir, "Money and Credit in Transition of the Czechoslovak Economy," in Siebert, ed., *Transformation of Socialist Economies.*

31. See Poznanski, "Poland's Transition to Capitalism."

32. For more details see F. Coricelli and G. Milesi-Feretti, "On the Credibility of 'Big Bang' Programs," *European Economic Review* 37 (1993).

33. See Rostowski, "Comments," p. 277.

34. See F. Coricelli and R. Rocha, "A Comparative Analysis of the Polish and Yugoslav Programs of 1990," in P. Marer and S. Zecchini, eds., *The Transition to a Market Economy* (Paris: OECD, 1991).

35. This point is elaborated in D. Begg and R. Portes, "Enterprise Debt and Financial Restructuring in Central and Eastern Europe," *European Economic Review* 37 (1993).

36. R. Dornbusch and S. Fischer, *Macroeconomics,* 5th ed. (New York: McGraw-Hill, 1990).

37. P. Schumpeter, *Capitalism, Socialism and Democracy* (New York: Harper and Row, 1942); F. von Hayek, "The Use of Knowledge in Society," *American Economic Review* 35 (1945); and *The Fatal Conceit: The Errors of Socialism* (Chicago: University of Chicago Press, 1988).

38. See Hayek, "The Use of Knowledge in Society."

39. Ibid.; M. Oakeshott, *Rationalism in Politics, and Other Essays* (New York: Basic Books, 1962).

40. For more discussion see P. Murrell, "The Evolutionary Approach to Economic Transition," in C. Clague and G. Rausser, eds., *The Emergence of Market Economies in Eastern Europe* (Cambridge, Mass.: Blackwell Publishers, 1992), and P. Murrell, "Evolutionary and Radical Approaches to Economic Reform," in Poznanski, ed., *Stabilization and Privatization,* pp. 215–31.

41. See W. Charemza, "East European Transformation: The Supply Side," in Poznanski, ed., *Stabilization and Privatization*, pp. 151–72.

42. For more detail see I. Grosfeld and P. Hare, "Privatization of Hungary, Poland and Czechoslovakia," *European Economy*, June 1991.

43. See D. North, "Institutions and Credible Commitment," *Journal of Institutional and Theoretical Economics* 149:1 (March 1993).

44. See Milanovic, "Poland's Quest."

45. See Gomulka, "The Causes of Recession Following Stabilization"; O. Blanchard and R. Layard, "How to Privatize," in Siebert, ed., *Transformation of Socialist Economies*.

46. J. Sachs, "The Economic Transformation of Eastern Europe," *Economics of Planning* 15:1 (March 1992).

47. K. Poznanski, "Market Alternative to State Activism in Rebuilding Capitalist Economy," *Economics of Planning* 15:1 (March 1992).

48. K. Poznanski, "Political Economy of Privatization in Eastern Europe," in B. Crawford, ed., *Market, State and Democracy* (Boulder: Westview, 1994).

49. Blanchard et al., *Reform in Eastern Europe*, p. 34.

50. Poznanski, "Market Alternative."

51. Charemza, "East European Transformation."

The Utopia of
Market Society in the
Post-Soviet Context

Stephen E. Hanson

Western analyses of the attempt to institutionalize a capitalist socioeconomic system in the former Soviet Union tend to fall into one of two camps. Advocates of "shock therapy"—the rapid adoption of policies promoting macroeconomic stabilization, price and wage liberalization, and privatization of state assets—point out the economic irrationality of continuing to subsidize old Stalinist industries and collective farms.[1] Opponents of shock therapy argue that a full-scale implementation of the market would cause disastrous levels of unemployment and poverty in the former Soviet republics.[2]

This policy debate over shock therapy has obscured more fundamental sociological questions about the effects of implementing capitalism in the post-Soviet environment. Indeed, there are a number of historical and institutional factors that make the "transition to a market economy" in the former USSR a far more complex phenomenon than is generally recognized by either supporters or detractors of the shock therapy approach.

To begin with, the geographical scale and cultural diversity of the region make implementing *any* unified and consistent economic policy extremely difficult. The Soviet Union occupied one-sixth of the earth's land surface; its territory included hundreds of different ethnic groups divided by arbitrary administrative boundaries inherited from the Stalin era. In short, the USSR can be seen as the world's last great multinational empire. Its collapse should logically be compared to the decline and fall of the Ottoman Empire, the Austro-Hungarian Empire, and even the Roman Empire, rather than to such radically different historical processes as the integration of Spain and Italy into postwar capitalist Europe.[3] In all these cases, the disintegration of imperial control led to decades of political instability, increases in ethnic conflict, and the intensification of border disputes, rather than to evolutionary institutional change. Thus, theoretically we should expect similar results from the collapse of the USSR.

Beyond this, the destruction of the Soviet Union marks the first time in history that an indigenous system of industrialization has fallen apart in peacetime—a fact almost entirely ignored by Western analysts. Accordingly, the predictable consequences of empire collapse outlined above will be complicated in the former USSR in unprecedented ways, as existing formal institutions for the production and distribution of goods cease to function. What happens when the "colonial outposts" that have to be abandoned in the wake of imperial decline include hundreds of industrial cities populated by millions of people? What happens when formerly colonized peoples still relying on the old imperial currency are forced to undergo the economic dislocations that result from macroeconomic stabilization in the imperial center? We have no overarching framework to make sense of these questions, let alone to provide possible answers. Instead, scholars have tended to see "Russia," "Ukraine," "Kazakhstan," and the other former Soviet republics as new states undergoing more or less successful transitions to "normal" West European patterns.

Once the historical particularities of the post-Soviet environment are grasped, several questions emerge. Why, in such conditions, did the idea of a "transition to a market economy" in the former Soviet Union become so universally accepted by Western policy makers and analysts? Why did the post-Soviet Russian government of Boris Yeltsin also initially embrace it so uncritically? Finally, might the shortcomings of the "shock therapy" program introduced in Russia after 1991—and the bitter political and social struggle surrounding its implementation—have been predicted?

In addressing these issues, I will take as my starting point Karl Polanyi's classic study of capitalist development in Western Europe from the eighteenth through twentieth centuries, *The Great Transformation*.[4] Polanyi's detailed analysis of the first historical attempt to institutionalize a full-fledged market society—that of nineteenth-century Britain—provides an ideal-typical model of liberal capitalism that can then be used to analyze the situation in the former Soviet bloc. In his reexamination of British economic policy during the Industrial Revolution, Polanyi highlights a critical point often lost in contemporary discussions of the post-Soviet economy: the idea of a society in which markets are the dominant principle of organization is less than two centuries old.

In order for a true "market society" to be created, Polanyi argues, all factors of production must be made available for purchase or sale on the market—most critically, land, labor, and money. But prior to the rise of capitalism in northwestern Europe in the 1700s, traditional restrictions on the sale of land, on the mobility of labor, and on the activities of money lenders greatly confined the scope of the market. Subordinating society entirely to the needs of the "self-regulating market" thus required nothing less than a sharp conceptual break with past human experience. Land had to be reinterpreted as "real estate"; a highly mobile working class had to be created out of a stationary peasantry; and banks had to be redesigned to encourage institutionalized forms of speculation on future economic growth. Indeed, Polanyi emphasizes, the first advocates of such a society appeared dangerously "Utopian" to many of their contemporaries—as, not surprisingly, does the advice of Western economists to many ordinary Russians today.

In this essay I will show how the program of "shock therapy" in Russia after the fall of the Soviet Union had its origins in the Utopian economic assumptions of the International Monetary Fund. These assumptions were enthusiastically embraced by Boris Yeltsin and his supporters in their search for an ideology to replace Marxism-Leninism; Yeltsin, however, did not understand that in the Russian context, implementing a market society would mean the destruction of much of the existing post-Soviet economy. The failure of shock therapy, in fact, was quite predictable given that under Soviet rule land, labor, and money were never commoditized.

By contrast, an informal process of commoditization of land, labor, and money had taken place to a much greater extent in the more marketized economies of Eastern Europe, making shock therapy there more feasible.[5] This distinction, however, was never taken into account by supporters of a quick "transition to the market" in Russia. Like the Benthamite supporters of a kind of shock therapy in England in the 1800s, economists affiliated with the International Monetary Fund and their supporters in Russia acted as if cultural and historical obstacles to market society could be safely ignored. By 1993 it was clear that at least in the case of post-Soviet Russia, the neo-Benthamites were in this respect mistaken.

This chapter is divided into three sections. The first summarizes Polanyi's argument about the nature of market society and of resistance to it in the European and global contexts. The second shows how the policy positions of the IMF, the Yeltsin government, and the anti-Yeltsin forces in the Russian Congress of People's Deputies from 1991 to 1993 can be understood in terms of Polanyi's interpretation of the Benthamites' struggle against Tory opposition to market society in England. In the third section I reassess the future of market reforms in post-Soviet Russia given the experience of the first two years since the collapse of communism.

The Utopia of Market Society and the Great Transformation

Although Polanyi's *Great Transformation* is universally recognized as a classic in the field of social science, his analysis of the liberal capitalist system has been strangely neglected by later scholars studying the effects of markets on peripheral societies. Polanyi's elegant literary style and detailed historical narrative may have served to obscure his underlying theoretical model of liberal capitalist institutions. In his work he first defines the "market system" in ideal-typical terms as an economy based on the formal commoditization of land, labor, and money—and shows how radically this ideal-type differs from the forms of economic organization generally found in human societies before the eighteenth century. Next he discusses how the imposition of the "self-regulating market" requires both a strong administrative state and continual concessions to social demands for protection from the full impact of the market system. Finally, he shows how the successful imposition of the self-regulating market in a core country places severe constraints on peripheral countries. I will deal with each of these points in turn.

Polanyi's model of the market economy takes as a starting point the uncontroversial idea that such a system makes production for gain the decisive motivation in economic life. More controversially, he then argues that throughout history prior to the rise of liberal capitalist England, the motivation to produce for gain was everywhere effectively subordinated to religious, political, or community concerns. Though almost all societies have had markets, restrictions on the scope and operation of these markets were such that no true "market society" could exist before the Industrial Revolution. Instead, Polanyi argues, economic life was overwhelmingly oriented toward norms of reciprocity, redistribution, and householding—all of which rely on the defense of personal status relations, rather than markets, as the key mechanism of institutional order.

Liberal capitalism, by contrast, is characterized precisely by the subordination of personal status relations to impersonal market forces. In order for the allocation of goods in the marketplace to take place efficiently, all protectionist measures in defense of local community interests must be removed. But this, in turn, requires that human and natural resources themselves be considered "commodities" that will find their efficient price in the market. In other words, not only consumer goods, but labor and land as well must be commoditized before a market system can function properly. Finally, in order to ensure that inefficient producers do not sustain their position in the market simply by borrowing or distributing goods to workers on a nonmarket basis, the medium of exchange itself must be allowed to find its market price without interference from political interests. The commoditization of money, Polanyi's third key element of the market system, thus ensures the subordination of all users of currency to impersonal market forces, since firms that are not "creditworthy" will be forced to shut down for lack of capital.

What is too quickly overlooked in classical economic theory, however, is that the process of commoditizing land, labor, and money is not a neutral one from a cultural perspective. Indeed, it amounts to a redefinition of human activity and of the natural environment in terms compatible with impersonal economic laws. In fact, Polanyi argues, a society that dogmatically enforced the commoditization of land, labor, and money in all spheres of social life could not exist for long:

To allow the market mechanism to be the sole director of the fate of human beings and their natural environment, indeed, even of the amount and use of purchasing power, would result in the demolition of society. For the alleged commodity "labor power" cannot be shoved about, used indiscriminately, or even left unused, without affecting also the human individual who happens to be the bearer of this peculiar commodity. In disposing of a man's labor power the system would, incidentally, dispose of the physical, psychological, and moral entity "man" attached to that tag. . . . Nature would be reduced to its elements, neighborhoods and landscapes defiled, rivers polluted, military safety jeopardized, the power to produce food and raw materials destroyed. Finally, the market administration of marketing power would periodically liquidate business enterprise, for shortages and surfeits of money would prove as disastrous to business as floods and droughts in a primitive society.[6]

Thus, the institutionalization of liberal capitalism in a precapitalist society can never be the result of a "natural" process; rather, the ideal of the "self-adjusting market implies[s] a stark Utopia"[7] which peripheral economies that have not yet commoditized land, labor, and money inevitably experience, at least initially, as extremely onerous.

The second part of Polanyi's analysis is concerned with the nature of political resistance to the imposition of market society. Such resistance has often been interpreted by free-market liberals as the product of a reactionary mentality devoted to reversing the "inevitable" movement of history toward global marketization. From the perspective outlined above, however, it is clear that opposition by conservatives and radicals alike to the commoditization of land, labor, and money in previously nonmarket societies is inevitable—and quite understandable. Indeed, as Polanyi describes in detail, the imposition of a "self-regulating market" in England itself was a politically contentious and drawn-out process. Even in the original core country of liberal capitalism, a concerted political movement on the part of committed Benthamite free-marketeers was ultimately necessary to ensure the complete commoditization of land, labor, and money.

Until 1834—almost a century after the beginning of the Industrial Revolution—no true labor market, in the modern sense, existed in England. Instead, under the so-called Speenhamland system, a minimum wage administered by the local parish was provided to all laborers in England regardless of their work status. This, in combination with the changing incentives of an industrializing economy, led to economic irrationalities that were predictable from the point of view of capitalist economic theory. Employers quickly learned that they could lower wages practically to zero, since wages under the subsistence level would be supplemented by the rates (local taxes). Workers, in turn, had no incentive to work hard for such low wages, and the general productivity of labor declined rapidly as a result. Finally, the increasing burden on local ratepayers meant that more and more independent economic actors were themselves forced to rely on state handouts for survival. Thus a dynamic process was set in motion that, had it continued indefinitely, might in principle have resulted in the pauperization of the entire English working population.

The failure of Speenhamland thus confronted the English elite with a stark choice: either abolish poor relief altogether, which would mean immense and unpredictable social dislocation, or abolish the emerging market society. Predictably, the elite split into two camps on this issue. The Tories, whose political power was based primarily on control over the local parishes in agricultural regions, opposed the abolition of Speenhamland on the grounds that without subsidies for the rural population, the traditional agricultural sector of English society would be destroyed. The Benthamites, who represented the emerging bourgeoisie, argued that this was precisely what economic laws demanded. England would *have* to destroy its existing agricultural system in the name of efficiency. The establishment of international "free trade" would allow for the purchase of cheaper agricultural goods from the continent, leaving England free to concentrate on extending its dominance in industrial manufacturing on a world scale.

After the passage of the Parliamentary Reform Bill of 1832, which eliminated the "rotten boroughs" where Tory influence was strongest, the Benthamites carried the day. Between 1834, when the Speenhamland system was finally abolished, and the 1860s, when a number of statutes regulating the impact of the market on particular social interests were passed, an uncompromising policy of labor commoditization took place. Despite the culturally unprecedented nature of such policies, the period saw a widespread insistence by economic liberals that the uprooting of long-standing communities in the interests of the "self-regulating market" was simply an inevitable consequence of economic laws.

Notwithstanding the professed antistatism of liberal ideology, getting society to obey these laws required a vast increase in the administrative power of the state. No longer required to regulate the economic life of the nation directly, state administration was now redirected toward the enforcement of severe penalties for "vagrancy," the establishment of an intentionally draconian system of workhouses, and the smashing of organized labor resistance to the market system.

By the end of the 1860s, traditional bases of opposition to the norms of market society had been crushed. Those who hoped to moderate the full consequences of commoditization of land, labor, and money, such as advocates of the welfare state and trade unionists, now accepted the entrenched market system. Those who still sought to eliminate the role of markets in culturally sensitive sectors were politically marginalized. Thus, within a few decades, the English population underwent an unprecedented, and ultimately successful, revolutionary experiment in changing human culture to fit the needs of a market economy.

The result, however painful the period may have been for members of uprooted communities, was to create the most powerful state in human history, in which no social obstacles prevented the efficient distribution of resources in all spheres of economic life. England's expanding economic power, and its ability to translate this power into global military dominance, meant that the consequences of the original commoditization of land, labor, and money in one country began to be felt throughout the world.

The third part of Polanyi's argument deals with the global dynamics of the market system from the mid-1800s through the Second World War. Having defined the market system as an economy decisively based on the commoditization of land, labor, and money, and having shown that attempts to introduce such as a system generated predictable opposition from elites wedded to local community interests and dislocated workers, Polanyi then extends the analysis to examine the effects of a *worldwide* market system on peripheral, noncommoditized economies. Here, in effect, Polanyi argues that the Tory-Benthamite split discussed in reference to the Speenhamland system arises once again—but on an international scale. Specifically, the defenders of international finance and free trade based in the core capitalist country, as well as their allies in peripheral states, now play the role of "Benthamites," while all those who resist the commoditization of land, labor, and money in order to defend premarket national cultures play the role of "Tories."

If the "Benthamites" win the political struggle over commoditization of the domestic economy in a peripheral regime, then the predictable social dislocation of traditional communities will occur, followed by the same rise in state economic power—assuming revolutionary violence does not intervene before the process of marketizing society is complete. If the "Tories" win, however, attempts to protect vulnerable sectors of the national population will be implemented. These measures will ultimately decrease the ability of the "Tory" state to acquire capital on the international market. Since propping up inefficient local economic communities inflates a national currency over time, those regimes which refuse to commoditize their domestic land, labor, and money supplies must inevitably pay the price of a decline in their international creditworthiness. This, in turn, will tend to further diminish the economic power of Tory states vis-à-vis Benthamite states—and make the threat posed by international markets to protected economic interests within Tory states even more severe.

According to Polanyi, it was precisely this situation that was exploited by fascist movements in East Central Europe in the late 1920s and early 1930s. In the economic environment of the Great Depression, "Tory" policies to maintain subsidies for traditional agricultural production and protected sectors of the working class could no longer be sustained. The only way for liberal capitalist elites in the region to keep their currencies on the gold standard—which all of them strove to do—was to pay the price of mass unemployment. Fascist demagogues thus sounded logical when they argued that the only way to protect "national" communities was to exit from the world market system altogether. Once fascist elites had actually come to power in Germany, Italy, and Spain and had reoriented their economies toward continuous military expansion, however, liberal market regimes were forced to defend themselves through nonmarket means as well. By the time the United States itself went off the gold standard in 1933, the global market system had been utterly destroyed, and wartime production methods began to dominate economies throughout the world.

Benthamites and Tories in the Post-Soviet Context

Polanyi concluded *The Great Transformation* by arguing that the Utopian form of market society institutionalized in England in the 1830s, and globally until 1933, had been destroyed for good by World War II. Polanyi was obviously wrong on this point. Beginning in 1945, the United States set up global financing and trading institutions, under the auspices of GATT and the Bretton Woods agreement, that closely paralleled those enforced by Britain in the period before the 1930s. Once again, the commoditization of land, labor, and money was held to be an unavoidable and "natural" evolutionary process. Those who resisted this process in the name of preserving community or national culture were held to be hopelessly reactionary. Finally, and perhaps most remarkably, from 1945 to 1971 the ability of national economies to peg their currencies to the gold standard again became the key symbol of their international creditworthiness.

The immediate effect of the relaunching of a global competitive market system was to produce a sustained period of economic growth from 1945 until the end of the Vietnam War. However, this economic boom to some extent masked the fact that wrenching problems of cultural dislocation were once again taking place in peripheral economies—a category that now included most of Africa, the Middle East, Asia, and Latin America. In response to the threat posed by marketization to local, inefficient forms of communal economic production, variants of the Speenhamland system were tried out throughout the Third World. Predictably, this led to many of the same economic irrationalities that had plagued England from 1791 to 1834. Western loans and aid helped disguise the problem in the short run, but by the 1970s and early 1980s, Third World "Tory" states found themselves hopelessly indebted due to their sustained subsidies to unprofitable industries and farms. As a result, promarket elites in the Third World were forced to take "Benthamite" austerity measures if they wished to remain creditworthy in international capital markets. The effect of these measures on the social cohesion of peripheral countries was predictably severe.

It is in this context that we must understand the ramifications of the collapse of the Soviet economy. In retrospect, the economic system set up by Stalin, despite its immense human cost, can be seen as an elaborate and temporarily successful strategy for industrializing society while resisting the commoditization of land, labor, and money. In each case, Stalin substituted the discipline of "revolutionary" commands, enforced by the party and the secret police, for the discipline of the self-regulating market. Rather than pursuing agricultural efficiency by converting land into private farms, Stalin created collective farms by reorganizing the old village commune into a sort of concentration-camp agricultural system. Rather than set up a true labor market, Stalin set wages according to a system of "revolutionary shock-work" that amounted to a giant administration of piece rates throughout the state economy. Managers then competed for needed surplus labor through informal offers of housing, vacation time, and other nonwage benefits. Finally, rather than allowing the value of the ruble itself to be set by the market, Stalin ruthlessly attacked anyone who dared to suggest that "interest rates" were needed in a socialist economy.[8] The ruble remained until the collapse of the Soviet Union essentially a barter coupon, not a currency.

After Stalin's death, the Communist Party leadership's decision to discontinue the use of terror as a primary means for enforcing norms of productivity meant that the economic distortions inherent in a non-marketized industrial economy would inevitably worsen. Khrushchev's ill-fated effort to rejuvenate the Stalinist system through campaigns, exhortations, and continual disruptions of the party and state bureaucracies could not counteract this trend. The choice, as in England in the 1830s, was either to end state support of inefficient working communities—and cause enormous social dislocation—or to reject, in fact if not in principle, the priority of economic growth. The party elite, after Khrushchev's ouster, chose the second option.

From 1964 through 1982, under the immobile leadership of Leonid Brezhnev, the Soviet economy thus in effect operated like a giant version of the Speenhamland system. As under Speenhamland, the guaranteed minimum wage for even unproductive workers reduced the incentive to work productively. Industrial managers found that it was in their interest to have as large a work force as possible, both to compensate for the worsening decline in the productivity of labor and because having a large number of workers increased the size of the wage fund allocated to a given enterprise under the planning system. Finally, as under Speenhamland, the distribution of nonwage benefits at the local level tended to increase the political power of local elites—in this case, regional party secretaries—even as the national economy grew at a slower and slower pace.

However, in contrast to the Speenhamland system, Brezhnev funded this noncommoditized industrial system primarily through foreign borrowing rather than local taxes. This, along with the adventitious increase in prices for Soviet oil during the OPEC crisis of the 1970s, allowed the party leadership to ignore the distortions and inefficiencies of the Soviet economy for a decade after they had effectively brought economic growth in the USSR to a halt in 1975.[9]

Remarkably, Gorbachev's *perestroika* campaign to revive Soviet socialism failed to address any of the critical causes of the decline of the Stalinist socioeconomic system. Insisting that tapping into the "human factor" through an attack on central bureaucracies would somehow unleash a surge of enthusiastic, high quality economic production in the USSR, Gorbachev refused to consider anything more than half-hearted moves in the direction of commoditizing land, labor, and capital. In short, Gorbachev remained to the end a committed "socialist"; he was only being sociologically accurate when he decried all attempts to portray *perestroika* as the "restoration of capitalism" in Russia.[10]

We are now in a position to see how the interaction between the IMF, Yeltsin, and the Congress of People's Deputies from the August coup of 1991 to the forced disbanding of the Congress in October 1993 can be analyzed in terms of the struggle between Benthamites and Tories described by Polanyi in *The Great Transformation*. Once Gorbachev's *perestroika* had brought about the disintegration of the Soviet system, the sole apparent model for economic development in the former Soviet republics was Western liberal capitalism. The stage was thus set for a classic battle between advocates of the "self-regulating market" and regional political elites who stood to lose their power base in the event of any successful commoditization of land, labor, and money in the former Soviet Union. What was being decided was the fate of a "Speenhamland system" that had encompassed hundreds of millions of people, created economic interdependence among hundreds of different ethnic groups, and produced tens of thousands of nuclear weapons.

The Benthamite position in this debate was clearly set out in the 1990 International Monetary Fund report, *The Economy of the USSR*.[11] Starting from the premise that "there is no example of a successful modern centrally planned economy" (pp. 1–2), the authors stressed the perils of gradualism, despite the complexity of the problem of transforming the Soviet system into a self-regulating market:

The authorities face an enormous task, involving reforms of the legal, financial and trade systems and also of vital sectors of the economy, especially agriculture, distribution, energy and manufacturing. These changes cannot be made in a matter of weeks. But the imperative is to make sufficient progress at the beginning so that reform is seen as an irreversible break with the past and the process gains an unstoppable momentum. The necessary economic reform cannot be implemented without an initial decline in output and employment, but delays in implementation would lead to an even larger and longer decline.

In fact, in a wholly noncommoditized economy such as that of the former Soviet Union, the full marketization of "vital sectors" such as agriculture, distribution, and manufacturing—that is, of all the basic components of the economic system—could not be made in a matter of years or even decades, let alone "weeks." But from the Benthamite perspective, the key was to smash all resistance to the workings of the invisible hand as soon as possible. Given the international free market system, the post-Soviet economy would have to break with Speenhamland sooner or later—so, the sooner, the better.

The experts of the IMF continued, therefore, by stressing the three most important elements of the "transformation of the Soviet economy": "macroeconomic stabilization, price reform in an environment of increased domestic and external competition, and ownership reform," (p. 16). But achieving these three goals would, the authors argued, require a bewildering variety of changes in the structure of the Soviet system. The key element underpinning all others, however, was to be the commoditization of money (p. 17):

Macroeconomic stabilization . . . requires that the budget deficit be reduced to a level that can be sustained without recourse to the inflationary creation of money. The reform effort also requires the imposition and maintenance of a tight credit policy and a rise in interest rates to control the potential inflationary consequences of price liberalization and to ensure the imposition of a hard budget constraint on enterprises, which will then be forced to respond to the market signals. Markets cannot begin to develop until prices are free to move in response to shifts in demand and supply, both domestic and external. The exchange rate, another key price, needs also to be moved to market clearing levels.

Remarkably, the entire passage quoted above contains no reference to the peculiarities of the Soviet system. It could be taken straight from any macroeconomics textbook describing sound monetary policy in a Western capitalist country. As in the original battle of the Benthamites against Speenhamland in the 1820s and 1830s, historical and cultural obstacles to the Utopia of market society were completely ignored.

But the history and culture of Russia in the post-Soviet context placed critical barriers in the way of the Benthamite economic strategy. England in the early 1800s had already undergone a centuries-long process of gradual commoditization of land, labor, and money; the Speenhamland system in this context represented only the last obstacle to the full flowering of the self-regulated market. The Russian Empire, by contrast, had only begun to introduce market reforms in the early twentieth century; all subsequent commoditization of land, labor, and money in the early Soviet period was brought to an end by Stalin's First Five-Year Plan. Thus the IMF recommendations on how to transform the former USSR ignored the fact that commoditization of money (i.e., the stabilization of the ruble) would have to be carried out in a context where commoditization of land and labor did not yet exist. But under these conditions, true "shock therapy" would have to result in the destruction of almost the entire post-Soviet economy.

To see why this is the case, it is necessary to return to our comparison of Brezhnevism with Speenhamland. In England, Polanyi argues, the abolition of Speenhamland caused enormous social dislocation as unproductive workers were kicked off the dole. At the same time, however, the creation of true labor markets allowed efficient industries to hire from an expanded pool of mobile workers.

But in the Soviet Union, *industry itself was in effect part of the Speenhamland type of system of poor relief.* Speenhamland distributed a minimum wage through the local parish; Brezhnevism guaranteed a minimal standard of living through subsidized factories administered at the regional level. Abolishing Speenhamland in the Soviet case thus would mean abolishing state-owned industry as well as Stalinist collective farms—but together, these accounted for over half of Soviet employment! Since most of the remaining jobs in the USSR were dependent on the party and state bureaucracies, there simply were no sectors of the economy left to fill in the gap in production left by the rapid dismantling of the noncommoditized Stalinist system.

Thus, commoditizing the ruble in the Soviet case would not simply involve the imposition of "hard budget constraints" on Soviet enterprises, as the authors of the IMF report suggested. Given the inefficiency of the entire state-owned sector of the economy in a global market context, a true marketization of the financial system in the "ruble zone" would inevitably mean forcing innumerable firms into bankruptcy. In practice, this would mean creating socially intolerable levels of unemployment within a matter of months.

Operating under the Utopian assumptions of the market society, however, the authors of the IMF report could not understand the extent of the disruption of cultural life that would result from a stabilization of the ruble in the post-Soviet context. Instead, the authors seemed to assume that the vast majority of Soviet production could eventually "adjust" to world market conditions after a process of enterprise privatization. There remained only the need for sufficient initial revenues to "help cover some of the costs associated with the economic reform—among them the costs of restructuring potentially viable enterprises, of cleaning up the balance sheets of banks, and beginning to catch up on the backlog of necessary infrastructure investments" (p. 26). But after decades of Speenhamland industry, the Soviet system contained few "viable" enterprises; it had no real banking system; and its infrastructure needed to be rebuilt almost entirely anew.

In this context, even the one departure from pure Benthamite liberalism in the IMF report, the call for a creation of a "social safety net," appears strikingly naive (p. 17):

The initial phase of the transition will involve considerable dislocation, and a shift to market prices will hurt those with low incomes. A social safety net, including an unemployment compensation program, will therefore be needed to protect the most vulnerable from short-term adverse consequences of the reform process; over the longer term a comprehensive system similar to that of other market economies will have to be developed. These safety nets will need to be designed in ways that are compatible with the requirements of the budget.

Exactly how a bankrupt state could protect the "most vulnerable" sectors of the population—that is, almost the entire post-Soviet working class and peasantry and much of the intelligentsia—in a way "compatible with the requirements of the budget" was left unclear.

The Utopian ideal of "shock therapy" marketization might well have remained confined to Western academic journals but for a remarkable historical coincidence. Just at the time Western economic experts were issuing their recommendations for the transformation of the Soviet economy, a new elite emerged in Russia around Boris Yeltsin that saw in the Benthamite program a Utopian answer to their own political problems. Yeltsin had been, until his ouster from the Politburo in 1987, a left-wing Leninist Utopian in the mold of Khrushchev; he was fired by Gorbachev for calling for an even more rapid dismantling of central institutions than that envisioned by *perestroika*. After suffering an apparent nervous breakdown in 1988, Yeltsin returned to politics in 1989 with a newfound confidence and a new political vision. This vision apparently dovetailed nicely with the recommendations of IMF economists. But in many respects, Yeltsin's program betrayed the Brezhnevite political training of its progenitor.

Yeltsin's vision, which he acted upon consistently from the time of his election to the Soviet Congress of People's Deputies in 1989 through the winter of 1993, relied on the incorrect assumption that a commitment to formal liberal capitalism could be combined with a popular defense of existing Russian culture and community. In other words, Yeltsin tried to act as a Benthamite in economic policy and a Tory in cultural policy. At first, this position pleased both Russian elites and Western economic advisers. In the long run, it would inevitably alienate both groups.

This tragically unworkable combination of free market economics with cultural populism was crystal clear in Yeltsin's speech to the Third Emergency Congress of the RSFSR People's Deputies in April 1991, a few months before the collapse of the USSR. Yeltsin's recommendations for remedying the disastrous Russian economic situation clearly echoed the recommendations of the IMF report and of the so-called "500-days plan" prepared by Yeltsin's advisers with IMF support in the fall of 1990:

First, the program sets out to make the ruble viable. Purchasing power will be stabilized through austerity measures and efforts to combat the budget deficit. People must know how grave the deficit problem is. Second, free-market structures must be put in place to organize supplies of materials. Third, we must finally make good on the commitment to the autonomy of producers. A regulative framework must be provided for privatization and denationalization. . . . Fourth, by April we must have a flexible policy for liberalization of prices. Transition to free prices must be made gradually and take account of the market situation but it must not stretch out too long. It is just as important to define an effective structural policy, prop up the export potential, give a leg up to key industries and develop a two-tier banking system and a system of finalized reserves. A land reform must be set in motion and agricultural production must be reshaped. We shall encourage foreign investment and pursue a realistic social policy.[12]

Like the IMF economists, and in somewhat more expansive detail, Yeltsin called for the creation of a social safety net to protect vulnerable members of the population. His understanding of the budget constraints confronting the Russian state in this area, however, was perhaps even less acute than that of the Western experts.

Finally, without seeing the contradiction between the self-regulating market and preservation of existing communal norms, Yeltsin concluded his address with a stirring call to revitalize Russian culture:

Esteemed deputies, Russia's renaissance will remain a remote prospect until culture gains more prominence in our lives. . . . Neglect of culture saps kindness, wisdom, tolerance, and competence. Cultural degradation affects interpersonal relations and people's attitude to their history and to the government. We must take speedy action to regain lost ground. The failure of politics from positions of strength suggests gigantic work to be done to achieve cultural revival.[13]

Successful adoption of free market reforms, Yeltsin argued, would somehow miraculously allow for indigenous Russian values to be realized more fully than ever before:

On its face it seems that one social system suffered a crushing defeat while the other gained the upper hand. There is no reason why we should feel defeated. We are returning to the international fold. The ideas of social justice and moral values originally came from Russia. Russia made a major contribution to global civilization. . . . Russia will finally occupy a rightful place in the international community, a place which will match its potential, its wealth of tradition and culture. Russia will remain a great country by virtue of its geographic position, resources, multiethnicity and most important of all, inexhaustible cultural potential and rich history.[14]

Unfortunately for Yeltsin's analysis, the norm of "social justice" operating in a self-regulating market economy would prove to have very little in common with any developed in Russia over the previous millennia.

The basic contradictions in Yeltsin's program were not immediately apparent to either Western or Russian political elites. As long as Gorbachev remained on the scene, arguing for the continuation of *both* the Soviet Union and fundamentally "socialist" economics, Yeltsin could plausibly counter him on both issues by positioning himself as a staunch advocate of Russian independence combined with market reform. At this stage, there appeared to be no need to make any ultimate choice between defending Russian culture and instituting market society.

Indeed, the alignment of Gorbachev's and Yeltsin's policy positions in the fall of 1991 greatly confused Western elites struggling to interpret the battle between the two men after the failed coup attempt. After all, neither Gorbachev nor Yeltsin seemed to be supporting the "logical" policy combination from the Benthamite perspective—preserving the Soviet Union while transforming it into a market society.[15] Ultimately, however, despite the reluctance of Western leaders to side with a man they considered too "Russian" compared with the "cosmopolitan" Gorbachev, the reality of Yeltsin's political ascendancy made it impossible for the West to prevent the division of the USSR into fifteen independent states. But even in this context, the insistence of Western policy makers and advisers on the rapid "marketization" of the Russian Republic, if not of the entire "ruble zone," continued unabated.

From the fall of 1991 until December 1992, Yeltsin continued to advocate the contradictory combination of Benthamite macroeconomic policy with Tory defense of local cultural communities outlined above. On the one hand, Yeltsin's prime minister, Yegor Gaidar, took straightforward Benthamite positions on every issue of macroeconomic importance. On the other hand, Yeltsin continued to try to placate the demands of his former supporters against Gorbachev in the Russian Parliament for protection of key industries and subsidies for agriculture. Officially, this policy was termed the "social partnership" approach to economic reform;[16] in practice, it amounted to a policy of giving in to all demands for higher wages from mobilized workers in inefficient industries—and thus of undermining the very stabilization policies being pursued by Yeltsin's economic team.

But such economically irrational policies make political sense when one remembers that practically every member of the Russian parliament—and indeed, of the entire former Soviet party and state bureaucracy still in place in most of the country—had a "Tory" interest in preserving Speenhamland industrialization and resisting the commoditization of land, labor, and money. The power of former party officials continued to depend, just as did the power of local parish elites in early nineteenth-century England, on their ability to distribute subsidized goods from state coffers. Marketization of the Russian economy would not only displace millions of people in "unproductive" economic sectors, it would destroy the power base of the vast majority of local politicians in the former Soviet context.

Unable to counter such potential opposition with any effective political machine of his own, and ideologically committed to a populist strategy of building legitimacy, Yeltsin in 1992 failed to make any serious effort to curtail the power of the antimarket legislature. The Congress, in fact, remained officially in control of the Central Bank, and thus effectively in control of macroeconomic policy. In such a situation, market reforms undertaken by Gaidar's government along the lines of the IMF program could only have the effect of raising prices without creating scope for competition by nonstate producers.[17] Meanwhile, continuing subsidies to inefficient firms throughout the country undermined Gaidar's attempts to keep the currency under some semblance of control.

By the time of the Seventh Congress of the Russian Congress of People's Deputies in December 1992, the mounting economic distress produced by this hybrid form of shock therapy had emboldened the anti-Yeltsin deputies. After a bitter debate, the Congress refused to reconfirm Gaidar as prime minister. His replacement, Viktor Chernomyrdin, showed himself initially to be completely unwilling to face the economic tradeoffs facing post-Soviet Russia if it continued to embrace market reforms, as the following exchange with a reporter during his first press conference shows:

Q: You have said that you want to stop the decline of production. Everyone would like to do that, perhaps, but this is not so simple. Either you give all the money to enterprises and generate hyperinflation in this way, or you will have a tight budget, and enterprises will go bankrupt. Which road will you choose?

Chernomyrdin: Can you suggest a third way? No? I am afraid that I will not be able to tell you anything now. . . . We will think about it.[18]

Although Chernomyrdin declared himself emphatically in favor of continued "reforms," it was clear that his view of the market had little to do with the sort of "market society" envisioned by the Benthamite representatives of the IMF.

During the first several months of 1993, Yeltsin continued his original strategy of combining calls for rapid macroeconomic stabilization with populist rhetoric about the defense of protected Russian communities. However, circumstances had made this strategy increasingly untenable. After the United States, Japan, and European powers pledged in May to provide $24 billion in aid to Yeltsin's government—conditional, of course, on the stabilization of the ruble—the pressure on Yeltsin to make a firm commitment to liberal capitalism increased. At the same time, the anti-Yeltsin and antimarket rhetoric of deputies to the Parliament became more and more strident, and popular support for Yeltsin's policies began to decline. Compromise between the Benthamite and Tory positions was becoming increasingly difficult.

For most of the spring and summer, Yeltsin stalled, claiming that there was nothing he could do to speed up the reform process as long as Parliament controlled the printing presses and blocked the implementation of laws on privatization and marketization. Instead, Yeltsin set in motion a complicated set of political maneuvers designed to marginalize the Congress of People's Deputies, replace the old Brezhnev constitution with a "Presidential" version, and elect a new Parliament, presumably more supportive of Yeltsin's policies. Meanwhile, however, the simultaneous inflation of the ruble and collapse of production continued to undermine political and social stability. By the fall, the patience of IMF and Western officials with Yeltsin's gradualist strategy had been exhausted.

More than any other single factor, it was the September announcement of the IMF that future installments of Western economic credits and aid to Russia would be postponed indefinitely pending real macroeconomic stabilization that spurred Yeltsin to decree the dissolution of the Congress of People's Deputies. After a bloody street battle between supporters of the Parliament and pro-Yeltsin troops on October 3, the president appeared to have consolidated control of the Russian government entirely in his own hands. Several anti-Western opposition parties were outlawed, press censorship was imposed, and a state of emergency was declared in the capital. Regional soviets that had sided with the Parliament were disbanded.

But in the autumn of 1993, it was still unclear what alternative economic policies Yeltsin might adopt. His reappointment of Gaidar as deputy prime minister seemed to signal a return to the strict liberal market policies favored by the International Monetary Fund. But the decision to leave the Central Bank in the hands of Gaidar's adversary Viktor Gerashchenko, even after the destruction of the Congress, indicated that the Yeltsin was not yet ready to cut off the supply of rubles to post-Soviet industries and collective farms.

Indeed, the disbanding of the Russian Parliament meant that Yeltsin, as the sole figure with power to change the course of economic policy in the country, could no longer blame his hesitation to introduce a full-fledged market economy on "opposition forces." Nor, having solicited Western support for so long, could he blame the IMF and the West for the social and cultural upheaval that would inevitably result from implementing the Utopia of market society. In short, the dilemmas of marketization in the post-Soviet environment remained as intractable as before. Meanwhile, social opposition to the entire project of Westernization in Russia was growing.

Conclusion

Applying the argument set out in Polanyi's *The Great Transformation,* the course of events in Russia from 1991 to 1993 begins to make sense. The ideological conception of a pure market society was initially embraced by post-Soviet elites precisely because it provided an alternative Utopia to the decayed vision of communism. But neither IMF economists nor Russian political elites realized, at first, that applying the principles of market society in the social environment created by the collapse of communism would be extremely problematic at best. In Polanyi's terms, the entire post-Stalinist economy can be seen as a giant "industrial Speenhamland system" unlike any other set of economic institutions in human history. If the Benthamites' struggle to introduce full commoditization of land, labor, and money in highly marketized England took several painful decades, then a similar process in the former USSR would seem to require centuries.

If the analysis presented here is correct, the idea that Russia (or the other former Soviet republics) might undergo a relatively smooth and consensual "transition to the market" must be discarded. Given the enormous obstacles to the implementation of a market society based on private landownership, labor mobility, and a capitalist currency system under post-Soviet conditions, the Russian economy was likely to develop in one of four directions.

The first possibility was that Yeltsin or his successors would adopt an authoritarian form of Benthamite rule, breaking communal and regional resistance to full commoditization of land, labor, and money by armed force. The level of coercion necessary for this, however, might be extremely high. For example, hundreds of subsidized industrial cities such as Stalin's steel-producing citadel Magnitogorsk would have to be shut down and their populations relocated. The privatization of land and closure of inefficient collective farms would displace an even greater number of people. Mass migrations of the unemployed to the West might occur.

The second possibility was that a military coup in Moscow would lead to the reimposition of a nonmarket, administrative-command economic system in Russia and perhaps some of the other former Soviet republics. However, like the imposition of authoritarian capitalism, this policy would require a very high degree of coercion to compel enterprises and collective farms to deliver their products to consumers in the absence of market incentives. It was unclear whether the former Soviet military, or the forces of the KGB and Interior ministries, still possessed enough organizational coherence to implement such economic policies consistently. In any case, if this approach was adopted, Western creditors would cut off further aid and credits to Russia.

The third possibility was that the Soviet empire would simply continue to disintegrate for the foreseeable future. In this case, the old Stalinist economy would gradually break up into smaller regional zones as large-scale coordination of economic activity ceased on the territory of the former USSR. Some regions—particularly those in the Russian Far East—might then be in a position to implement market reforms in collaboration with Western advisers and investors. Other regions would continue to depend on various ad hoc arrangements among local industrial and agricultural producers. But there would no longer be any possibility of transforming all of Russia into a single capitalist market.

Finally, there remained the fourth possibility emphasized by Polanyi himself in his analysis of the effects of the world capitalist system on peripheral societies: fascist movements both in Russia and elsewhere in the former Soviet Union might take power. One needed only consider the words of Yuri Vlasov in *Sovetskaya Rossiya,* describing the results of the first year of Yeltsin's reform effort, to see how such a movement might develop:

How can one talk of privatization and land reform? We are ruined, the liberalization of prices turned three-quarters of the people into paupers in a matter of weeks. People have no savings, no money—all has been lost in the struggle for survival, in the orgy of price rises. . . .

A host of profiteers and alien scum is reaching out for Russia. There is no choice: it's either them or us. We are becoming participants in the last, utterly shameful and tragic act—the collapse of a great country. . . . I cannot pass over in silence the mass betrayal in favor of the West—I never dared to think that we had so many traitors. Well, we will remember their names. . . . When the hour strikes, we will call them to account. . . .[19]

Yeltsin's disbanding of the Congress of People's Deputies in October 1993 temporarily eliminated the organizational basis of Russian fascism. However, the social forces that might strengthen fascist ideology in the region remained in place. Indeed, if Polanyi's argument is correct, the Utopian application of Benthamite economics to the Soviet system of Speenhamland industrialization might have inadvertently strengthened the fascist position.[20] In the noncommoditized social environment of post-Soviet Russia, rapid marketization in the post-Soviet context must inevitably be accompanied by massive unemployment and social dislocation, while slow marketization must lead to hyperinflation and the loss of foreign capital. As a result, calls for antimarket mobilization along ethnic lines could seem increasingly plausible to many Russians—especially if the collapse of Russian social order were conveniently blamed on the West, Jews, traders from the Caucasus, or other scapegoats.[21] The victory of fascism in Russia would inevitably provoke ethnic violence on a massive scale throughout the territory of the former Soviet Union. Given the presence of nuclear weapons in much of this territory, the consequences of such developments for world stability would be truly frightening.

NOTES

The author would like to thank Dia Lautenschlager, Eric Larsen, Willfried Spohn, and Jennifer S. Stevenson for research assistance, editorial revision, and useful commentary on earlier drafts of this essay.

1. While the initial advocacy of shock therapy concentrated on East European cases, most analysts who favored this approach made little distinction between the former Soviet Union and other postcommunist settings. See, for ex-

ample, Janos Kornai, *The Road to a Free Economy: Shifting from a Socialist System: The Example of Hungary* (New York: Norton, 1990); Jeffrey Sachs, "Building a Market Economy in Poland," *Scientific American* 266:3 (March 1992): 34–40; and "Privatization in Russia: Some Lessons from Eastern Europe," *American Economic Review* 82:2 (May 1992): 43–47.

2. Michael Ellman, "Shock Therapy in Russia: Failure or Partial Success?" *RFE/RL Research Report* 1:34 (August 1992): 48–61; David Kotz, "The Cure that Could Kill: Shock Therapy in Russia," *The Nation*, April 19, 1993, pp. 514–16; Richard Parker, "Delusions of 'Shock Therapy': Western Economists, East European Economies," *Dissent*, Winter 1993, pp. 72–80.

3. See, for an example of the latter approach, Giuseppe Di Palma, *To Craft Democracies: An Essay Concerning Democratic Transitions* (Berkeley: University of California Press, 1990).

4. Karl Polanyi, *The Great Transformation: The Political and Economic Origins of Our Time* (Boston: Beacon Press, 1944). For a rather different application of Polanyi's work to postcommunist affairs, see Maurice Glasman, "The Great Deformation: Polanyi, Poland and the Terrors of Planned Spontaneity," in Christopher G. A. Bryant and Edmund Mokrzycki, eds., *The New Great Transformation?: Change and Continuity in East-Central Europe* (New York: Routledge, 1994). This work appeared too late for me to incorporate it in this essay.

5. Whether shock therapy has had a beneficial effect on the more marketized economies of Eastern Europe is still a matter of debate. See, for example, Konstanty Gebert, "Where 'Shock' Too Often Rhymes With 'Crock': What's Really Going On with Poland's Economy," *Washington Post National Weekly Edition*, May 10–16, 1993; Parker, "Delusions"; and Kazimierz Poznanski, "Recession in Postcommunist Eastern Europe: Common Causes and Outcomes," in this volume.

6. Polanyi, *Great Transformation*, p. 73.

7. Ibid., p. 3.

8. Gregory Grossman, "Scarce Capital and Soviet Doctrine," *Quarterly Journal of Economics* 67 (August 1953): 334.

9. Alec Nove, *An Economic History of the USSR* (New York: Penguin Books, 1984), pp. 376–81.

10. Stephen E. Hanson, "Gorbachev: The Last True Leninist Believer?" in Daniel Chirot, ed., *The Crisis of Leninism and the Decline of the Left: The Revolutions of 1989* (Seattle: University of Washington Press, 1991), pp. 33–59.

11. *The Economy of the USSR: Summary and Recommendations*, the International Monetary Fund, the World Bank, the Organization for Economic Cooperation and Development, and the European Bank for Reconstruction and Development (Washington, D.C.: World Bank, 1990).

12. Boris Yeltsin, *Address to the Third Emergency Congress of RSFSR People's Deputies*, April 1, 1991, trans. by Federal Information Systems Corporation: Official Kremlin International News Broadcast, p. 6.

13. Ibid., p. 12.

14. Ibid.

15. It is remarkable in retrospect to see the offhand way in which the 1990

IMF report brushes aside the nationalities problem: "This study assumes that the republics will maintain an all-Union market, involving an absence of trade barriers between republics; a common currency and exchange rate, and therefore a common monetary policy; a common external tariff; and an agreed division of responsibilities for taxation and expenditures at different levels of government" (*The Economy of the USSR*, p. 16).

16. "Russian Government Seeks 'Social Partnership,'" Elizabeth Teague, *RFE/RL Research Report* 1:25 (June 19, 1992).

17. For a similar analysis, see Marshall I. Goldman, "The Chinese Model: The Solution to Russia's Economic Ills?" *Current History*, October 1993, pp. 320–24.

18. Official Kremlin International News Broadcast, "Press Conference by the Newly Elected Russian Premier, Viktor Chernomyrdin," December 16, 1992.

19. Yuri Vlasov, "Sinking with a Band Playing on the Upper Deck," *Sovetskaya Rossiya,* trans. by Russica Information Inc., November 14, 1992.

20. A similar point is made by Kotz, "The Cure that Could Kill."

21. The strong performance of Vladimir Zhirinovsky in the December elections to the new State Duma, which concluded as these lines were being written, appeared to validate this point.

Contributors

Ivan T. Berend is Professor of History at the University of California at Los Angeles. He has written many books on East European economic history, including *The Crisis Zone of Europe: An Interpretation of East-Central European History in the First Half of the Twentieth Century,* and (with Gyorgi Ranki) *The European Periphery and Industrialization, 1780-1914.*

Daniel Chirot is Professor of International Studies and Sociology at the University of Washington. His many works include *Social Change in the Twentieth Century, Social Change in the Modern Era,* and *Modern Tyrants: The Power and Prevalence of Evil in Our Age.*

Arista Maria Cirtautas is Assistant Professor of Government at Claremont-McKenna College. She has written several articles on East European politics and is completing a book on comparative conceptions of natural law in the American Revolution, the French Revolution, and the Polish Solidarity movement.

Aleksa Djilas is author of *The Contested Country: Yugoslav Unity and Communist Revolution, 1919–1953.* From 1987 to 1994 he was a Fellow at the Russian Research Center at Harvard University. He has since returned to Belgrade.

Liah Greenfeld is Associate Professor in the University Professors' Program and the Department of Sociology at Boston University. Her major works include *Different Worlds: A Sociological Study of Taste, Choice and Sources in Art* and *Nationalism: Five Roads to Modernity.*

Stephen E. Hanson is Associate Professor of Political Science at the University of Washington. He is the author of *Time and Revolution: Marxist Ideology and the Design of Soviet Institutions.*

Ewa Morawska is Professor of Sociology at the University of Pennsylvania. Her books include *For Bread with Butter: The Life-Worlds of East-Central Europeans in Johnstown, Pennsylvania, 1890–1940* and the forthcoming *Insecure Prosperity: Small-Town Jews in Industrial America, 1880–1940.*

Kazimierz Z. Poznanski is Associate Professor of International Studies at the University of Washington. He is the author of *Technology, Competition and the Soviet Bloc in the World Market* and has edited several volumes of essays on the postcommunist economic transition.

Willfried Spohn is Lecturer in Sociology at the University of Pennsylvania and Adjunct Professor of Sociology at the Free University of Berlin. He is the author of *Weltmarktkonkurrenz und Industrialisierung Deutschlands,* as well as recent articles on cultural pluralism in historical sociology (with Ewa Morawska) and religion and working-class formation in Europe.

Index